THE KINGFISHER
FOOTBALL
ENCYCLOPEDIA

Brazil and England contest their 2002 World Cup quarter-final in Japan's Shizuoka Stadium Ecopa. The 50,600-capacity arena hosts the bigger matches of two Japanese J-League sides, Jubilo Iwata and Shimizu S-Pulse.

THE KINGFISHER
FOOTBALL
ENCYCLOPEDIA

CLIVE GIFFORD

KINGFISHER

Kingfisher Publications Plc
New Penderel House,
283–288 High Holborn,
London WC1V 7HZ
www.kingfisherpub.com

First published by Kingfisher Publications Plc in 2006
10 9 8 7 6 5 4 3 2
2TR/0306/TWP/MAR(MAR)/150MA/C

Managing editor Russell Mclean
Editorial assistance Jennie Morris, Simon Mugford
Art editor Claire Legemah
Imaging and photo-manipulation Nick Harris
Illustrations Nick Harris, Mike Buckley,
   Malcolm Parchment
Consultant Anthony Hobbs
DTP manager Nicky Studdart
Senior production controller Lindsey Scott
Picture research manager Cee Weston-Baker
Picture researchers Russell Mclean, Clive Gifford
Indexer Sue Lightfoot

Note to readers: The website addresses listed in this
book are correct at the time of publishing. However,
due to the ever-changing nature of the internet, website
addresses and content can change. Websites can contain
links that are unsuitable for children. The publisher cannot
be held responsible for changes in website addresses or
content, or for information obtained through third-party
websites. We strongly advise that internet searches
should be supervised by an adult.

A CIP catalogue record for this book is available from
the British Library.

ISBN-13: 978 0 7534 1235 0
ISBN-10: 0 7534 1235 7

Printed in Singapore

CONTENTS

THE BEAUTIFUL GAME

Pelé described football as the 'beautiful game', and the emotion and loyalty football inspires in its fans means that this simple sport has much to live up to. But football delivers with ease – cramming dynamic action, breathtaking skills and heartstopping tension into 90 minutes of play. It is sport as drama, making heroes and villains out of its players, managers and officials. From its recognized beginnings in the 19th century to its global dominance today, football has provided great moments of excitement, celebration and despair; no other game has the same power to unite and divide.

RAPID GROWTH

In little over a century, football has boomed from a casual pursuit carried out by a small group of amateur gentlemen to a highly sophisticated, money-spinning sport that is played and watched by millions of people. As football has grown, dozens of changes have occurred. Some have involved the laws of the game – from the two-handed throw-in, introduced in 1883, to the backpass law for goalkeepers that was adopted 99 years later. Other changes – such as the arrival of promotion and relegation up and down a league – have shaped the competitions of which matches are a part.

Football's adaptability has been one of its strengths. Another great part of its appeal is that people of all ages and skill levels can play the game. At its most basic, football is a simple sport that can be enjoyed without expensive equipment and played almost anywhere – from a sandy beach to an office or hallway with a crumpled ball of paper.

The simplicity of football is a big selling point with new fans. The finer details of rules and tactics may pass them by at first, but the basics of the game and the skills of star players – their pace, ball control, passing, shooting and tackling – can be admired by almost anyone.

▲ Football arouses the emotions of players as well as fans. Here, Bayern Munich's Carsten Jancker (left) and Thomas Helmer are inconsolable after their team was beaten by Manchester United in the last minute of the 1999 Champions League final.

▲ Football is a sport that generates intensely strong bonds between supporters and their teams. This fan, facepainted in the national colours of Portugal, awaits the semi-final of the 2004 European Championships between Holland and Portugal.

▼ Barcelona's Ronaldinho (right) is one of the most famous footballers on the planet. Here, he holds off Michel Salgado of Real Madrid during a derby match between Spain's two biggest clubs in November 2004.

THE NUMBERS GAME

In its full version, football is a game in which two teams of 11 people play two halves of 45 minutes. Today, more than 50 million footballers around the world play in official competitions. Many millions more play the game on a regular basis – a survey by world football's governing body, the *Fédération Internationale de Football Association* (FIFA), estimates that figure to be more than 240 million. Top leagues, such as Serie A in Italy, the German Bundesliga and Spain's La Liga, attract millions of viewers globally. In 2003, games or highlights of the English Premier League were broadcast to more than 140 countries, attracting a television audience of 550 million. The final of the 2002 World Cup, between Brazil and Germany, was watched by a worldwide television audience of 1.1 billion – almost one sixth of the world's population.

▲ Football can be played practically anywhere, in almost any conditions. These South African schoolchildren are enjoying a casual but competitive game just days before their country won the right to host the 2010 World Cup.

▲ A mural of Brazil's Ronaldo brightens the wall of a building in Paris, France. Football's top players are global superstars at the centre of mini-industries. These generate money away from the players' work on the pitch, through personal appearances, endorsements, advertisements and merchandise.

THEN AND NOW

Going back in time 140 years, a modern football fan would be surprised to find no referees, corners or pitch markings at a game. Players wore coats and even top hats; they handled the ball in the air and wrestled with each other on the ground. Over time, football has evolved into the game that we know today.

► The referee's whistle was first blown at a football match in 1878. British firm Acme Whistles has sold an astonishing 160 million Acme Thunderer whistles, which have been heard at World Cups and in top leagues around the globe.

PITCHING UP

Unlike in most sports, the pitch in football can vary in size. Most are around 100m long and 65–70m wide. Back in the 1860s, a pitch could be as long as 180m. The first markings arrived in 1891, including a centre circle and a line running the width of the pitch, 10.98m in front of the goal line. A penalty could be taken from any point along that line. It was another 11 years before the pitch markings we know today were introduced. Since then, only two additions have been made – the penalty arc at the front of the penalty area (in 1937) and the corner quadrants (in 1938).

► Referee Ken Aston came up with the idea of red and yellow cards after a stormy World Cup game in 1966. Here, he sends off Italy's Georgio Ferrini in 1962.

▲ At the 2002 World Cup, held in Japan and South Korea, the grass at the Sapporo Dome was grown away from the stadium and then moved as an entire pitch into the arena on a cushion of air.

GOALS

To score a goal, a team has to propel the whole of the ball over the goal line, between two posts that are set 7.32m apart. On many occasions, controversy has raged over whether the ball crossed the line – from the 1966 World Cup final between England and West Germany to the Champions League semi-final in May 2005 between Chelsea and Liverpool.

Early goals consisted of just two posts. Following arguments over the height of a shot, a white tape was fitted to the posts, 2.44m above the ground. Wooden crossbars began to replace tape in the 1870s. Goal nets came later, invented by an engineer from Liverpool, John Alexander Brodie.

THE MEN (AND WOMEN) IN BLACK

Referees did not feature in early games of football because the sport's founders believed that gentlemen would never intentionally foul or cheat. Instead, each side had an umpire to whom they could appeal. By 1891, games were controlled by a referee in order to cut down on controversial decisions and long stoppages for debate, and the two umpires became linesmen. (Since 1996, linesmen have been known as assistants.) Despite often being described as the 'men in black', referees have played in all sorts of colours. Early referees tried to keep up with play dressed in the popular fashions of the time – trousers, a blazer and even a bow tie. They were first given a trial in January 1891, when Everton's Fred Geary became the first footballer to put the ball in the back of the net. Incidentally, that game was refereed by Sam Widdowson, who had invented shinpads 17 years earlier.

FACTFILE The Belgian referee at the 1930 World Cup final, Jean Langenus, wore a dinner jacket, golfing plus-four trousers and a red striped tie.

BOOTS AND BALLS

No game is complete without the football, 40 million of which are sold every year. It is the referee's job to check the match ball and spare balls for size (68–70cm), weight (410–450 grams) and correct air pressure. Modern footballs are made from leather or synthetic materials, with a waterproof outer coating. Brazilian club Santos pioneered the use of a white ball (instead of the traditional brown leather ball) for greater visibility during evening games. Early footballs were made from the inflated bladder of a pig or sheep, covered in a leather shell that was secured with a set of laces. Contrary to popular myth, footballs of the past were not heavier than today's, at least when they were dry. Without a waterproof covering, however, early balls soaked up moisture and gained weight.

Football boots were certainly heavier in the past. Originally, players used their heavy work boots, tying them up over the ankle. The boots often had reinforced toecaps, and players sometimes nailed metal or leather studs into the soles. Modern boots are lightweight and flexible, allowing a player to 'feel' the ball on his or her foot. Their soles come in a range of stud, dimple and blade patterns. Each design gives the right level of grip for a particular pitch condition.

> **FACTFILE**
> India withdrew from the 1950 World Cup when FIFA refused to allow their footballers to play in bare feet.

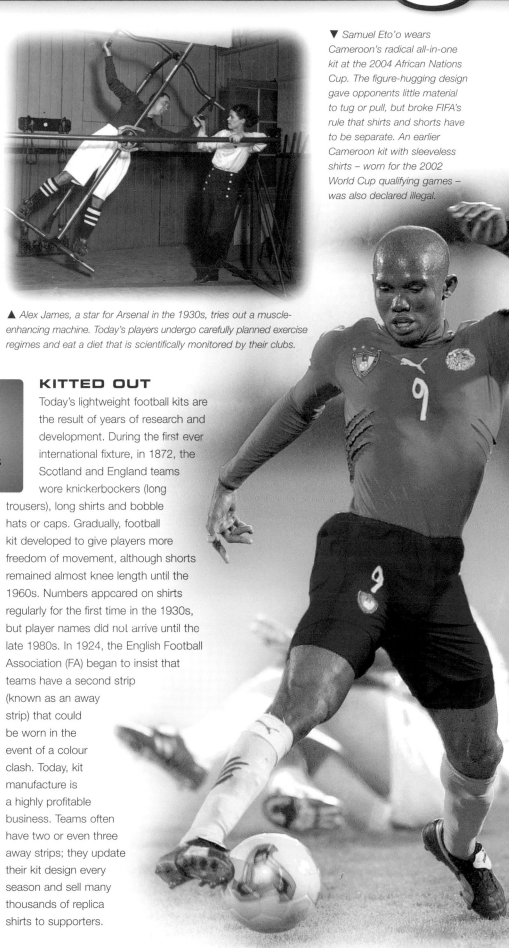

▼ *Samuel Eto'o wears Cameroon's radical all-in-one kit at the 2004 African Nations Cup. The figure-hugging design gave opponents little material to tug or pull, but broke FIFA's rule that shirts and shorts have to be separate. An earlier Cameroon kit with sleeveless shirts – worn for the 2002 World Cup qualifying games – was also declared illegal.*

▲ *Alex James, a star for Arsenal in the 1930s, tries out a muscle-enhancing machine. Today's players undergo carefully planned exercise regimes and eat a diet that is scientifically monitored by their clubs.*

KITTED OUT

Today's lightweight football kits are the result of years of research and development. During the first ever international fixture, in 1872, the Scotland and England teams wore knickerbockers (long trousers), long shirts and bobble hats or caps. Gradually, football kit developed to give players more freedom of movement, although shorts remained almost knee length until the 1960s. Numbers appeared on shirts regularly for the first time in the 1930s, but player names did not arrive until the late 1980s. In 1924, the English Football Association (FA) began to insist that teams have a second strip (known as an away strip) that could be worn in the event of a colour clash. Today, kit manufacture is a highly profitable business. Teams often have two or even three away strips; they update their kit design every season and sell many thousands of replica shirts to supporters.

▲ *Some modern boots have moulded dimples for playing on hard or artificial pitches; others have screw-in studs to give grip on wet or soft pitches.*

FOOTBALL'S ORIGINS

An alehouse in Victorian England seems an unlikely place to launch a sport that would become the world's biggest and most popular. Yet that is precisely what occurred in 1863 at the Freemason's Tavern in London, England. There, representatives of 12 clubs met to form the Football Association (FA) and draw up a single set of rules for the game.

HISTORY MYSTERY

No one knows where the first forerunner of football was played. The Ancient Greeks took part in a team ball game known as *episkyros* or *pheninda*, while the Romans played *harpastum*. Paintings dating back more than 2,000 years show men and women enjoying the Ancient Chinese game of *tsu chu*, in which players tried to propel a ball made of stuffed animal skin through bamboo goal posts up to 10m tall. During the Ch'in dynasty (255–206BCE), a form of *tsu chu* was used to help train soldiers.

In medieval Europe, games of mob football were so unruly and violent that the leaders of several countries, including Charles V in France and Oliver Cromwell in England, attempted to ban the sport. In contrast to mob football, the Italian game of *calcio* was first played in the 16th century by aristocrats and religious leaders, including three popes. Each team was made up of 27 players, and goals were scored by kicking or throwing the ball over a certain spot on the edge of the field.

GETTING ORGANIZED

By the late 18th and early 19th centuries, a kicking-and-rushing ball game was played in public schools and universities across Britain, but rules varied from place to place. In 1848, players at Cambridge University drew up football's first set of rules.

This attempt to bring order into the game had only limited success, and so in 1863 representatives of 12 clubs (including the Crusaders, No Names of Kilburn and Crystal Palace) met in London. They formed the FA, developed the laws of the game and, eight years later, set up the world's oldest surviving cup competition, the FA Cup. The first ever international, between England and Scotland, was played in 1872, and in 1888 the first football league was founded in England.

▼ *This illustration shows a friendly international game between England and Scotland in 1878. Between 1873 and 1888, Scotland lost just one out of 31 international matches.*

▼ *The Japanese game of* kemari *is at least 1,500 years old. Players had to stop the ball from touching the ground by juggling and passing it with their feet. This re-enactment was held to celebrate Japan's co-hosting of the 2002 World Cup.*

HIT THE NET

www.11v11.co.uk
The website of the Association of Football Statisticians has historic photos and features on football's early history.

www.womensoccer.com
An online magazine with news and features on international women's football.

www.innotts.co.uk/soccer/hist1.htm
Featuring articles on the history of the game, plus a timeline of football milestones.

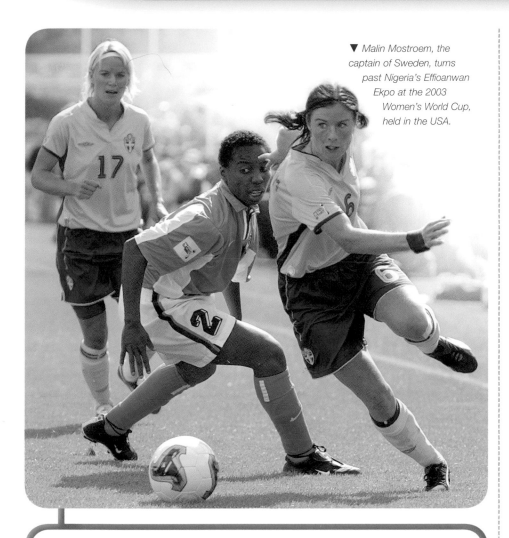

▼ Malin Mostroem, the captain of Sweden, turns past Nigeria's Effioanwan Ekpo at the 2003 Women's World Cup, held in the USA.

WHAT'S IN A NAME?

Around the world, many teams have taken their names from European clubs. Here are just a few:

ARSENAL LESOTHO
Lesotho Cup winners 1989, 1991

LIVERPOOL
Namibia, league champions 2002

BARCELONA
Ecuador, league champions 1995, 1997

EVERTON
Chile, league champions 1950, 1952, 1976

JUVENTUS
Belize, league champions 1999

MANCHESTER UNITED FC
Gibraltar, league champions 1999

AJAX CAPE TOWN
South Africa

QPR FC
Grenada, league champions 2002

THE WOMEN'S GAME

Women's football struggled from the beginning against male prejudice that it was 'unladylike' for females to play the game. Interest in women's football reached its first peak after World War I thanks to the exploits of the Dick, Kerr Ladies side (see page 81). The women's game was then stifled for almost half a century following the introduction of a ban on women playing at the grounds of FA member clubs. Between 1969 and 1972, bans were lifted in a number of countries and women's football slowly began to expand. The first European Championships for women were held in 1984, while an Olympic competition was launched in 1996. More than 60 nations entered the qualifying competition for the first Women's World Cup in 1991.

FOOTBALL EXPORTS

Football spread rapidly around the globe in the late 19th century. The game was exported first by British players and then by converts from other European nations, particularly to their colonies. Football was introduced to Russia in 1887 by two English mill owners, the Charnock brothers, while resident Englishmen founded Italy's oldest league club, Genoa, six years later.

In 1885, Canada defeated the USA 1-0 in the first international match to be played in the Americas. In Argentina, British and Italian residents encouraged the formation of South America's first club, Buenos Aires, in 1865. The first league in South America was set up 28 years later.

In 1904, FIFA was founded in Paris, with seven members: Belgium, Denmark, France, Holland, Spain (represented by Madrid FC), Sweden and Switzerland. Over time, FIFA became the dominant organization in world football. In 1930, it had 45 member nations; in 1960, that figure stood at 95. In May 2004, FIFA welcomed the Pacific island nation of New Caledonia as its 205th member.

▶ W. R. Moon of Corinthians, an English amateur team, poses for a photograph in his kit. Corinthians helped to spread football by touring the world. Their 1910 trip to South America inspired the formation of the famous Brazilian side Corinthians Paulista.

THE GLOBAL GAME

FIFA is in control of world football. At continental or regional level, the game is organized by six confederations. The traditional powerhouses of international football have been Europe and South America, home to the world's richest clubs and to the winners of every World Cup. But as other regions begin to exert more influence, the global game is changing.

▲ Steve Mokone was the first black South African to play professionally in Europe. From the 1950s, he starred for Coventry City, Dutch side Heracles, Spain's Valencia, Marseille in France and Italy's Torino. Mokone later played in Australia and Canada.

BALANCE OF POWER

Great advances have been made by the federations and national teams of regions outside Europe and South America. More and more national football teams have become truly competitive on the world stage, thanks to the emergence of dozens of high-quality footballers in Africa especially, but also in Asia, Oceania and North and Central America. Australia, for example, has reached just one World Cup, in 1974, but its national side has recently defeated France, Brazil and England. African sides have won two out of the last three Olympic Games and have performed well at the World Cup over the last two decades. There have also been strong showings by Japan, the USA, South Korea and Iran (all ranked within FIFA's top 25 sides in 2005) at recent international tournaments.

Today, FIFA is working hard to promote the game outside its traditional strongholds. African and Asian nations have been chosen to host many tournaments, including the World Cups of 2002 (South Korea and Japan), 2010 (South Africa) and the Women's World Cup of 2007 (China). Additionally, Africa and Asia now enjoy more automatic places at the World Cup than ever before.

> **FACTFILE** A European side has reached the final of all but two World Cups (1930 and 1950).

◄ Argentina's team lines up at the 2002 World Cup. Only two members of the 22-man squad, Ariel Ortega and Claudio Husain, played their club football in Argentina.

CONCACAF
Confederation of North, Central American and Caribbean Association Football
www.concacaf.com
Founded: 1961
Members: 35

Mexico and the USA – traditionally the strongest CONCACAF nations – have hosted three World Cups, while smaller nations such as Costa Rica have reached the tournament. CONCACAF teams have often been invited to play in South America's Copa America competition, and the federation actually includes two South American nations, Guyana and Surinam.

UEFA
Union of European Football Associations
www.uefa.com
Founded: 1954
Members: 52

As the most powerful confederation, UEFA was awarded 14 of the 32 places at the 2006 World Cup. It runs the two largest competitions after the World Cup – the European Championships and the Champions League. Thousands of foreign footballers play in Europe, but UEFA clubs may soon be forced to include a minimum number of home-grown players in their squads.

CONMEBOL
Confederación Sudamericana de Fútbol
www.conmebol.com
Founded: 1916
Members: 10

CONMEBOL teams have enjoyed great World Cup success, winning nine of the 17 tournaments. Brazil and Argentina are rarely out of the top five in FIFA's rankings, while Uruguay, Chile, Colombia and Paraguay frequently field strong teams. Domestically, leagues are suffering, with clubs in debt and top players heading to Europe. Nevertheless, Brazil enter the 2006 World Cup as favourites.

CAF
Confédération Africaine de Football
www.cafonline.com
Founded: 1957
Members: 52

Africa was not awarded an automatic World Cup place until 1970, but the rise of football in that continent means that the CAF will send five teams to the 2006 tournament. While national sides continue to improve, the domestic game struggles because of a lack of finance and the movement of its best players out of Africa. In 2001, for example, 979 African footballers were playing in Europe and 102 in Asia.

AFC
Asian Football Confederation
www.the-afc.com/english/intro.asp
Founded: 1954
Members: 44

Asian football is booming. The highly successful Asian Champions League was set up in 2002, and national leagues are increasingly well supported. Many foreign footballers play in Asia – more than 30 Brazilians are based in Japan, for example. All eyes are now turning to China. With a population of almost 1.3 billion, it has the world's largest pool of potential players and supporters.

OFC
Oceania Football Confederation
www.oceaniafootball.com
Founded: 1966
Members: 11

Football has struggled for support in Oceania. In the larger countries, it has to compete with more popular sports, while smaller nations suffer from a lack of finance, facilities and players. The OFC is campaigning strongly for an automatic World Cup place. Currently, the region's top side has to enter a play-off with the fifth-best team in South America. In the 2006 play-off, Australia beat Uruguay on penalties.

FACTFILE
Australia were the first OFC side to reach a World Cup, in 1974.

HAVE BOOTS, WILL TRAVEL

Football is flourishing all over the world, but Europe remains the most attractive destination for the world's top players. The globe's 20 richest clubs are all European, and this situation is unlikely to change for some time as a result of the huge sums of money that teams receive from television rights, advertising and qualifying for the

◄ Emmanuel Olisadebe was born in Nigeria, plays club football in Greece and represented Poland at the 2002 World Cup. Many other African-born footballers now play for a European country, including Djibril Cissé of France, Norway's John Carew and Belgium's Mbo Mpenza.

Champions League. This revenue enables European clubs to pluck the best talents from around the globe. At the 2002 World Cup, 75 per cent of the 351 footballers who took part played their club football in Europe. Just seven played in Africa, six in the USA, 36 in Central or South America and 38 in Asia or the Middle East.

In the past, South American club football held on to many of its stars. Every member of Brazil's 1970 World Cup-winning side played for a club in his home country. That state of affairs has changed, with hundreds of players moving to Europe in search of higher wages and the chance to play in the most prestigious competitions, from Serie A and La Liga to the Champions League.

HIT THE NET

www.worldsoccer.com
World Soccer magazine's website focuses on global soccer and its best players, teams and competitions.

www.footballasia.com/en
A website dedicated to football in Asia, with details of competitions, players and the continent's teams.

www.soccerstats.com
Get the latest football news and competition standings from around the world.

Alfredo di Stefano (in white) lashes Real Madrid's second goal past Eintracht Frankfurt keeper Egon Loy. Despite making a number of splendid saves, Loy conceded seven goals.

MADRID'S MAGNIFICENT SEVEN

Football's capacity to surprise, excite and above all entertain has rarely been better showcased than in the final of the fifth European Cup, in 1960. Real Madrid, winners of the first four competitions, met Eintracht Frankfurt in front of a record crowd of more than 130,000 at Scotland's Hampden Park. Eintracht took an early lead. Was Real's reign as the undoubted masters of Europe about to end? The answer was an emphatic no. Led by Hungarian genius Ferenc Puskas and Argentinian all-rounder Alfredo di Stefano, the Spanish side put on a dazzling display of attacking football. In an electrifying 45 minutes, Real went from 1-0 down to 6-1 up, courtesy of goals by both Puskas and di Stefano. But the enterprising German side were just as committed to attack. They fought back, scoring two goals and hitting the woodwork twice, while Real countered with their seventh and di Stefano's third goal to eventually triumph 7-3. No one who witnessed the game would ever forget the spectacle of Europe's finest club side playing at the peak of its skills.

BASIC SKILLS

In the words of former Liverpool manager Bill Shankly, 'Football is a simple game based on the giving and taking of passes, on controlling the ball and on making yourself available to receive a pass.' Shankly's words highlight the most fundamental skills in football.

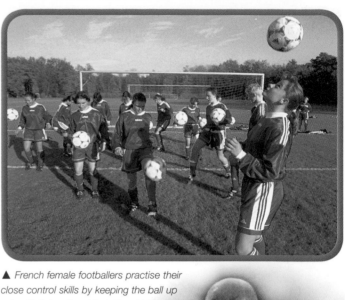

▲ French female footballers practise their close control skills by keeping the ball up using their head and feet. Good ball control only comes with hundreds of hours of practice.

BALL CONTROL

The world's top players, such as Zinedine Zidane and Ronaldinho, appear to control the ball effortlessly. Their easy command and movement of the ball masks thousands of hours of practice and training, often from a very early age. As children, many great footballers spent long hours playing games with a tennis ball, crumpled ball of paper or a battered piece of fruit.

Players can control the ball with any part of their body except for their hands and arms. Cushioning is a technique in which a player uses a part of the body to slow down a moving ball and then bring it under control with his or her feet. High balls can be cushioned using the chest, thigh or a gentle header to kill the ball's speed and bring it down. For a low, incoming ball, the foot is preferred – either the inside of the boot or its instep (where the laces are). A ball that is rolling across the pitch can be stopped with the sole of the foot – a technique known as trapping.

▶ David Beckham leans back to perform a chest cushion during a Real Madrid training session. A good chest cushion sees the ball drop at the feet of the player, who can then pass, run or shoot.

▲ Real Madrid's Zinedine Zidane brings the ball down during a Champions League match against Italian side Roma. He uses a sidefoot cushion to leave the ball at his feet.

◀ An instep cushion is used to control a ball arriving front-on. Here, the player meets the ball with the laces of his boot and instantly pulls back his foot, killing the pace of the ball.

SHIELDING AND OBSTRUCTION

When footballers have the ball at their feet, they are said to be in possession and have a number of options. These include: running with the ball; dribbling with the ball close to the feet; passing; shooting; and shielding the ball. Shielding or screening involves a player putting his or her body between the ball and an opponent to prevent the other player from gaining possession. This gives the shielding player crucial time to decide on the next move, which may be a pass backwards to a team-mate or a sharp turn and an attempt to play the ball round the opponent. Shielding players have to be careful not to hold, push or back in to the other player. They must also keep the ball close by and under control, otherwise the referee may award an indirect free kick for obstruction (in which a player unfairly blocks an opponent's path to the ball). An obstruction usually occurs when a player steps into the path of an opponent when the ball is several metres away.

◀ *Sergiy Nazarenko of Ukrainian side Dnipro Dnipropetrovsk shields the ball from FC Utrecht's Etienne Shew-Atjon during a 2004–05 UEFA Cup match.*

▶ *Pavel Nedved of Juventus hits a long instep drive pass during a Serie A match against Messina in 2004.*

PASS MASTERS

Passes can be made with a thrust of the chest or with a carefully directed header. Usually, however, they are made with one of three parts of the boot – the outside, the instep or the inside. The inside or sidefoot pass is the most common and accurate pass, allowing players to stroke the ball around with a high level of precision. Some players attempt as many as 60 or 70 passes in a game, most of which are sidefoot passes. At Euro 2004, Denmark's Thomas Gravesen averaged 81 attempted passes per game.

For longer passes, players tend to use the instep. This allows them to propel the ball with force. The instep can also be used for lofted drives that send the ball into the air as a cross or a clearance, as well as to stab down on the back of the ball. This makes the ball rise up at a steep angle, known as a chip. A pass's weight – the strength with which it is hit – is as important as accuracy for the pass to be successfully completed. At Euro 2004, strong passers such as France's Claude Makalele, Stilian Petrov of Bulgaria and Germany's Dietmar Hamann all completed 88 per cent or more of their passes.

◀ *Wigan's Jason Roberts (left) and QPR's Danny Shittu compete shoulder-to-shoulder for the ball.*

▲ *Arsenal striker Thierry Henry hits a perfect sidefoot pass, keeping his eye on the ball and letting his kicking leg follow through and point towards the target.*

MOVEMENT AND SPACE

Football is a dynamic, fast-moving sport. Throughout a game, pockets of space open and close all over the pitch. A player who has an awareness of where space exists, or where it will shortly open up, is a great asset to a team. Equally valuable is the ability to move into that space to receive a pass. The more space a player is in, the more time he or she usually has to receive the ball, control it and attack with it.

SPOTTING AND CREATING SPACE

The ball can zip around a pitch far more quickly than even the fastest of players. Good footballers make the ball do the work, moving it around with quick, accurate passes. Vision is the priceless ability to spot a pass, space or goalscoring opportunity that other players do not see, or before they do. Players with good vision look to move into space, timing their run to give a team-mate who has the ball a chance of making a pass that cannot be intercepted by an opponent. Once the ball has left the passer's control, he or she often moves into a position to receive a return pass. All players, not just midfielders and attackers, must be capable of passing well and moving into space to receive passes in return.

Players can create space for themselves or for team-mates through quick, agile movement and the use of feints or dummies,

► Germany's Michael Ballack advances upfield against Iceland in 2003. Keeping the ball under close control, he holds up his head in order to assess the options for a pass or run.

with which they attempt to fool a nearby opponent into thinking they are moving one way, before sprinting off in another direction. World-class players such as Zinedine Zidane, Michael Ballack, Pavel Nedved and Arjen Robben are particularly skilled at outwitting an opponent in this way to find space.

◄ A wall pass (also known as a one-two pass) is a classic way to cut out an opposition player. It involves two passes that must be hit quickly and accurately, with the first passer running on to collect the return ball.

FACTFILE
At Euro 2004, Portugal completed more passes than any other side – 2,504 in just six games.

▲ Dutch winger Arjen Robben (right) attempts to go round the outside of Portugal's Miguel in the semi-final of Euro 2004.

▲ Making space can be crucial to winning the ball at a throw-in. Here, one player makes a decoy run towards the thrower, dragging a defender with him and creating space in which a team-mate can collect the ball.

OFFSIDE

Teams have to stay aware of Law 11, the offside law, throughout a match. In 1847, under the rules of Eton College, being offside was known as 'sneaking'. A player was caught sneaking when there were three or fewer opposition players between him and the goal at the moment a team-mate passed the ball forwards. The rule has been tinkered with over the years. The most notable change came in 1925, when the number of players between the attacker and the goal was reduced from three to two. The result was a goal avalanche, as defences struggled to cope with the rule change and attackers took advantage. In the English leagues, for example, 1,673 more goals were scored in the 1925–26 season than under the old law in the previous year.

Today, a player is offside if, at the moment the ball is played, he or she is in the opposition half and is nearer the opponent's goal line than both the ball and the second-from-last opponent. That opponent can be an outfield player or the goalkeeper. Players cannot be offside in their own half or if they receive the ball directly from a goal kick, throw-in or corner.

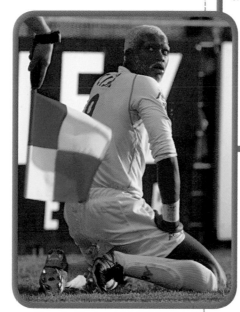

▲ Auxerre's Djibril Cissé (now at Liverpool) looks ruefully at the referee's assistant after being signalled offside in a 2004 French league match against Toulouse.

Being in an offside position is not an offence in itself. Referees must judge whether the player in an offside position is involved in active play at the moment the ball is struck. This controversial aspect of the law tests an official's judgement to the limit. Is a player who is offside but a long way from play, for example, involved or not? What if he or she is drawing defenders out as markers? If a referee does stop the game, an indirect free kick is awarded to the opposing team at the place where the player was judged offside.

▲ Here, the player at the top left of the picture is in an offside position when the ball is struck. The referee decides that he is not interfering with play, however, and awards the goal.

▲ You cannot be offside if you are behind the ball when it is played. This scorer receives the ball from a team-mate who is ahead of him, so he is onside and the goal is given.

HIT THE NET

www.soccerparent.com/49-camera-snapshot-sports.htm
A site featuring diagrams and animations that explain the key points of the offside law.

www.fifa.com/en/regulations/regulation/0,1584,3,00.html
View the latest laws of the game as approved by FIFA or download them in PDF format.

www.asktheref.com
A site for budding referees – learn more about the laws of the game and the jobs of football officials.

www.futsalplanet.com
A website dedicated to futsal, with tournament news and results as well as links to the laws of the game.

SMALL-SIDED GAMES

In many countries, children under the age of 11 play matches that feature six, seven or eight players per team. These small-sided games give young footballers an invaluable chance to see more of the ball and improve their control, passing and movement. Around the world, small-sided games are played by children, teenagers and adults of all skill levels on indoor or outdoor pitches at schools and leisure centres. Futsal is FIFA's official five-a-side game. A match lasts for 40 minutes (two halves of 20 minutes) and is played on a pitch the size of a basketball court, without surrounding boards or walls. Futsal was devised by a Uruguayan, Juan Carlos Ceriani, in 1930. The game flourished and developed throughout South America, with the first international competition – the South American Cup – taking place in 1965. The first futsal World Championship was held in 1989.

▲ Spain and Brazil battle it out in the final of the 2004 futsal World Championship, held in Taipei, Taiwan. Spain won the 40-match tournament, beating the Brazilians 5-4 in a penalty shootout after a 2-2 draw.

OFFICIALS

Frequently abused by players, managers and supporters, referees are football's guardians and the enforcers of its laws. Their job is to impose order on a match and prevent intimidation, injury and cheating.

THE REFEREE'S ROLE

Referees perform a surprisingly large number of tasks before and after a match. These include checking the goals, nets and balls and deciding whether the pitch and weather conditions are suitable for the game to go ahead. Afterwards, they write a report containing details of disciplinary actions and other important incidents. On the pitch, the referee runs the game. His or her duties range from adding on time because of injuries, other stoppages and time-wasting, to deciding whether the ball is in or out of play or has crossed the goal line. If a player commits a foul or breaks a law, referees must stop play and order a restart, such as a drop ball or a free kick. They can caution players and team officials, and even abandon a match if weather, crowd trouble or another factor makes the game unplayable. Referees have to follow the laws of the game, but they have a certain amount of freedom to interpret aspects of the rules as they wish. For example, if a player is fouled when his or her side is in a promising position, a referee may let the match continue, playing the advantage rule to keep the game flowing.

ASSISTANTS AND THE FOURTH OFFICIAL

A referee relies on his or her assistants as extra pairs of eyes. Referee's assistants indicate when the ball goes out of play and whether a goal kick, corner or throw-in should be awarded. They also use flag signals to point out that a substitution has been requested, a player is offside or whether an offence has taken place out of the view of the referee. A referee can consult with an assistant if he or she was closer to the action, but it is up to the referee to make the final decision. In some competitions, a fourth official carries out duties before and after a match and also performs touchline tasks. These include helping with substitutions and displaying the amount of time added on at the end of a game for stoppages.

▲ The fourth official checks the boot studs of Paraguayan substitute Nelson Vera in a World Youth Championship match against Uruguay.

> **FACTFILE** In 1998, English referee Martin Sylvester sent himself off after punching a player during a match in the Andover and District Sunday League.

▼ Managers and team officials can be cautioned or sent off if they use abusive language or do not behave responsibly. Here, Celtic manager Martin O'Neill is sent off during a 2002 UEFA Cup match against Celta Vigo.

▲ Referee Dermot Gallagher shows attention to detail by asking Manchester United's Cristiano Ronaldo to remove his jewellery before continuing play in a 2004 Premiership game against Everton.

◄ Early in a game, a good referee talks to players to calm them down or issues verbal warnings rather than yellow and red cards. Here, Nicole Petignat tries to soothe AIK Solna's Krister Nordin in the first UEFA Cup game to be refereed by a woman, in 2003.

TOP-FLIGHT PRESSURES

Thousands of amateur referees give up their weekends and evenings for free, purely to give something back to the game they adore. In contrast, officials in charge of major championship matches are minor celebrities who are paid significant sums. This is a reflection of the importance of their job. Top referees have their performances assessed, attend training seminars, undergo regular medical checks and are tested for fitness. A referee may run between 9.5 and 11.5km during a match (even further if extra time occurs) and often has to sprint to keep up with play. Referees work in a harsh, unforgiving climate, in which footage from multiple cameras and slow-motion television replays are broadcast over and over again, highlighting each poor decision. Managers, players and fans often prefer to attack the officials' handling of a game rather than admit that a better or more fortunate side beat their team. Occasionally, referees even have to deal with physical threats from enraged players or supporters.

▲ Italy's Angelo di Livio (centre) and Christian Vieri plead with referee Byron Moreno as he sends off team-mate Francesco Totti during extra time in a 2002 World Cup match against South Korea. Totti received his second yellow card for simulation.

CAUTION

A player is shown a yellow card if he or she:

- is guilty of unsporting behaviour, such as simulation;
- shows dissent by word or action;
- persistently breaks the rules, by making repeated foul tackles for example;
- delays the restart of play;
- fails to stand at the required distance at a corner kick or free kick;
- enters or leaves the field of play without the referee's permission.

A player is sent off if he or she receives two yellow cards or one red card. Red-card offences include a very dangerous tackle, spitting and stopping a goal with a deliberate handball.

SIMULATION

Looking out for contact in the penalty area during a fast-moving attack is especially difficult for an official. In the modern game, attackers appear to fall to the ground under the slightest pressure from an opponent. Referees have to judge if a foul was committed or whether the attacker was guilty of 'simulation'. Many people think that simulation is only about diving without contact in order to win a free kick or a penalty. It is actually defined as pretending to be fouled in any way to gain an advantage. In a game at the 2002 World Cup, Hakan Unsal of Turkey kicked the ball at Brazil's Rivaldo, hitting his leg. Unsal was penalized for foul play, but Rivaldo fell to the floor, pretending he had been hit in the face. Unsal was sent off, but video replays clearly showed Rivaldo's simulation. The Brazilian received a FIFA fine of £5,180 and widespread condemnation.

▲ Deportivo la Coruña's Juan Carlos Valeron goes flying after a lunging tackle by Gianluca Zambrotta of Juventus. The referee has to decide in a split second if a foul was committed and, if so, whether it is serious enough for a booking or a sending off.

RED-CARD RECORDS

FASTEST IN A TOP LEAGUE
Ten seconds – Giuseppe Lorenzo, Bologna v Parma, 1990

FASTEST IN THE WORLD CUP
55 seconds – José Batista, Uruguay v Scotland, 1986

MOST IN ONE MATCH
20 – Sportivo Ameliano v General Caballero (Paraguay), 1993

DEFENDING

Compared to strikers or creative midfielders, defenders are rarely praised as match-winners. Yet the foundation of every successful team is a composed, secure defence. Defending consists of a range of individual skills allied to good teamwork and understanding between players so that they defend as a unit. Defenders require strength and excellent heading and tackling skills, along with intense concentration, quick reactions and bravery. But, in truth, all players must defend if their side is to remain competitive in a match.

▲ Portugal's Nuno Gomes (left) and Russia's Alexei Bugaev challenge for the ball. Forceful tackles that target the ball, not the player, are a key part of defending.

▼ With Joseph Yobo (right) in support as defensive cover, Nigeria's Nwankwo Kanu challenges Freddie Ljungberg of Sweden for the ball during a match at the 2002 World Cup.

TRACKING AND TACKLING

The two keys to defending well are denying the opposition the chance to score and winning the ball back. As soon as an opponent gets the ball, defenders try to get between the ball and their goal and close down space. Defenders spend much of a game tracking opponents as they make runs and closing down the player with the ball to delay his or her progress. This is called jockeying. The aim is to slow down an attack until the defending side is in a stronger position. The defender tries to shepherd the attacker into a weaker position, such as near the sideline where there is little support. When a defender has cover from nearby team-mates, he or she may make a tackle. The defender should stay on his or her feet in order to gain possession.

▶ This attacker has spotted a weak pass by an opponent and reacts quickly to make an interception. Sometimes, attackers drop back to help their team defend.

FALLING FOUL OF THE LAW

Many of football's laws, such as obstruction (see page 17), apply to defenders. A defender who is jockeying must be careful not to commit a foul, such as pushing, holding or shirt-pulling. A poorly timed tackle may result in a foul being awarded for kicking or tripping. Tackles from behind are especially risky, often leading to a yellow or red card if the defender makes contact with the attacker. A professional foul is a deliberate foul made to deny an attacking side a clear goalscoring chance. Two of the most common types are using the hands or arms to stop a goalbound ball and bringing down an attacker with the ball when he or she has a clear path to goal. Both should result in a sending off.

▲ *Central defender John Terry shouts to Frank Lampard as Chelsea defend an attack by Portsmouth. With Petr Cech in goal and world-class defenders such as Ricardo Carvalho, Chelsea romped to the 2005 league title, losing just one game.*

DEFENSIVE FORTRESS

During periods of open play, defending teams mark opponents man-to-man or with a zonal system (see page 62). At corners and free kicks from a wide position, they tend to mark man-to-man. A team may also try to catch out attackers by playing an offside trap (see page 62). Communication between defenders is crucial to prevent attackers getting free and into space to score. Certain teams equipped with highly skilled defenders who work well together have been able to squeeze the life out of opposition attacks. The AC Milan side of 1992–93, for example, scored 26 goals and conceded only two during their entire nine-game Champions League campaign. In England, Chelsea hold the record for conceding the fewest goals in a season (2004–05) – just 15 goals in 38 matches.

▲ *Real Madrid's Ivan Helguera and David Beckham hurl themselves bravely into the path of the ball to block a fierce shot from Asier del Horno of Athletic Bilbao.*

CLEAN SHEETS

Goalkeepers and defenders are especially proud of a clean sheet – a game in which their side does not concede a goal. Clean sheets are usually credited to goalkeepers, but in truth they depend on a solid defence as well as midfielders and strikers who are willing to chase, harry, track and tackle. Italy has a reputation for producing some of the world's finest defenders. Between 1972 and the 1974 World Cup, the Italian defence helped keeper Dino Zoff to play 1,142 minutes – more than 12 matches – without conceding a goal. The run was finally ended by Haiti. Another Italian keeper, Walter Zenga, holds the record for clean sheets in the World Cup. He did not let in a goal for 517 minutes (almost six games) in 1990. The world record in professional football is held by Brazil's Geraldo Pereira de Matos Filho, better known as Mazaropi. Playing for Vasco da Gama in 1977–78, he did not concede a goal for over 20 games, a total of 1,816 minutes.

> **FACTFILE** In 1968, Peñarol of Uruguay went unbeaten through the league season. They conceded just five goals in 18 games.

▶ *Italian defender Paolo Maldini makes a defensive header above Sweden's Hakan Mild, clearing the ball high into the air and safely away from his penalty area.*

LONGEST UNBEATEN LEAGUE RUNS (IN GAMES)

108	ASEC Abidjan (Ivory Coast), 1989–94
104	Steaua Bucharest (Romania), 1986–89
85	Esperance (Tunisia), 1997–2001
62	Celtic (Scotland), 1915–17
60	Union Saint–Gilloise (Belgium), 1933–35
59	Boca Juniors (Argentina), 1924–27
	Pyunik Yerevan (Armenia), 2002–04
58	AC Milan (Italy), 1991–93
	Olympiakos (Greece), 1972–74
	Skonto Riga (Latvia), 1993–96
56	Benfica (Portugal), 1976–78
	Peñarol (Uruguay), 1966–69
55	Dalian Wanda (China), 1995–97
	Empire (Antigua), 1997–2000
	Shakhtar Donetsk (Ukraine), 2000–02

GOALKEEPING

Goalkeepers are a breed apart. They have a different role to their team-mates and even look a little different, as they must wear a shirt that distinguishes them from other players and officials. The crucial last line of defence, keepers can be forgotten when things are going well, but singled out for abuse when they make a mistake that leads to a goal. Goalkeepers can also be match-winners thanks to their saves and decisions, their agility and bravery.

▲ *Irish keeper Shay Given stretches to make a diving save during a Premier League match between Newcastle United and Manchester United.*

◀ *At the 2003 Women's World Cup, Norway's Bente Nordby clears a dangerous ball by punching it firmly away from goal.*

KEEPING CONTROL

Goalkeepers are allowed to control the ball with their hands and arms, but otherwise they must obey most of the same rules as outfield players. Until 1912, keepers could handle the ball anywhere in their own half, but now handling is restricted to their penalty area, with several key exceptions. Goalkeepers cannot handle the ball:

• after releasing it and without it touching another player;

• after receiving it directly from a throw-in;

• if it has been deliberately kicked to them by a team-mate.

If a goalkeeper handles the ball in any of these situations or if the referee judges that the keeper is time-wasting with the ball in hand (known as the six-second rule), an indirect free kick is awarded. This can be dangerously close to the goal. In the 1990s, a law was passed to reduce time-wasting and speed up play. It banned keepers from controlling a ball from a throw-in or backpass with their arms or hands.

In the past, goalkeepers could be barged into heavily, but today they are well protected by referees. Even so, they have to be brave to dive at an opponent's feet, risking injury. If keepers foul or bring down an attacker, they may give away a penalty and even be sent off if the referee decides that a professional foul has been committed.

▲ *The Czech Republic's Petr Cech gathers the ball cleanly at the feet of Andy van der Meyde of Holland.*

A KEEPER'S SKILLS

To achieve a clean sheet, goalkeepers need more than supreme agility and the talent to make diving saves. Top keepers train hard to improve their handling skills, learning to take the ball at different heights and from different angles. They must be able to stay alert for the entire game. Many minutes can go by before, suddenly, they are called into action. Keepers need good decision-making skills, too, as a cross or shot may call for them to choose whether to try to hold the ball in a save, punch it away or tip it over the bar or round a post. Goalkeepers are in a unique position to see opposition attacks developing, and they must communicate instructions to their team-mates. They line up walls at free kicks and command their goal area, urging defenders to pick up unmarked opponents. A defence and keeper that communicate well can be a formidable unit.

▶ *Czech keeper Jaromir Blazek instructs his defenders during Euro 2004. Clear, decisive communication between a keeper and his or her outfield team-mates can snuff out many opposition attacks.*

DEFENCE INTO ATTACK

With the ball in hand, keepers have several ways in which they can move the ball to a team-mate or up the pitch (known as distribution). They can roll it out on the floor, looking for options to kick the ball; they can kick it straight from their hand; or they can throw the ball. Keepers launch the ball from their hand into the opposition half by using their boot instep to strike it on the volley or half volley. Sometimes, keepers aim their kick for a tall winger or wide midfielder who is close to the sideline. This move is often rehearsed on the training ground. Keepers can bowl the ball out underarm, usually to a nearby team-mate, or they can use a more powerful sidearm or overarm motion for maximum distance. A third option, the javelin throw, is often the quickest way to get the ball moving. Fast, accurate distribution from the keeper can be vital in turning defence into a rapid breakaway attack.

HIT THE NET

www.goalkeepersaredifferent.com
A fabulous website that is dedicated solely to keepers and is packed with quirky facts.

http://finesoccer.com/keepers.htm
This newsletter contains advice, drills and tips from the world of goalkeeping.

www.jbgoalkeeping.com/intro.html
An impressive coaching website, with short online videos, covering all aspects of the keeper's game.

► Spain's Iker Casillas practises handling the ball while on the ground. Keepers work hard in training to improve their handling, flexibility and reactions.

▲ Germany's Oliver Kahn rolls the ball out underarm. In 2002, Kahn was FIFA's Goalkeeper of the World Cup. During the following league season with Bayern Munich, he set a Bundesliga record of 737 minutes without conceding a goal.

FACTFILE
The world's first black professional footballer was a goalkeeper. Born in the Gold Coast (now Ghana), Arthur Wharton turned out in 1889 for Rotherham United in the English league.

► In a one-on-one situation, many keepers come off their line to narrow the angle – reducing how much of the goal the attacker can see. They stay upright for as long as possible to increase the chance of the shot striking them.

GOALSCORING KEEPERS

In 1882, goalkeeper James McAulay was pressed into service as a centre-forward and scored in Scotland's 5-0 defeat of Wales. Since then, many keepers have scored goals for their club or country. Some goals have been scored from long goal kicks that have caught out a defence or by goalkeepers running into the opposition's penalty area in the dying seconds of a game. Others have come from spot kicks in a penalty shootout (see page 31). A well-taken penalty by Portuguese keeper Ricardo knocked England out of Euro 2004, for example. A few keepers, mainly in South America, have become legends for their goalscoring feats from regular penalties and free kicks. Paraguay's José Luis Chilavert has scored a staggering 62 goals. In 56 of the 58 matches in which he has scored, his team has either won or drawn. Chilavert's first goal came in 1989, in an intense World Cup qualifying match that Paraguay won 2-1 thanks to the goalkeeper's last-minute penalty.

ATTACKING

As soon as a team gains possession of the ball, with time and in space, its players' thoughts turn to attack. There are many ways in which a team can launch an attack, from a fast drive into space by a player who is sprinting forwards and pushing the ball ahead, to a slow, probing attack in which many players keep the ball securely in possession and look for an opening.

BEATING OFFSIDE TRAPS

Some teams play an offside trap (see page 62), in which defenders move up in a straight line to catch opponents offside. Beating an offside trap takes cunning, skill and awareness. A perfectly weighted through pass can unlock the trap if the ball is collected by a player who stays onside until the moment the ball moves ahead of him or her. A long diagonal pass that switches play forwards and across the pitch may also work. The receiver makes a run from a deep position, staying onside until the ball moves ahead, then collects the ball behind the defence. Individual brilliance – such as dribbling or playing a short 'push and go' pass – can also beat some offside traps.

▲ Ludovic Giuly of Barcelona threads an accurate through pass between Shakhtar Donetsk defenders Anatoliy Tymoshchuk and Mariusz Lewandowski in a 2004 Champions League game.

▲ Atlético Madrid's Hugo Leal tries to weave past a trio of Espanyol defenders during the final of Spain's Copa del Rey in 2000.

▲ A push and go pass can beat a lone defender or an offside trap. The attacker pushes the ball past the defender and then sprints to collect it.

TEAM ATTACKS

Many attacks rely on two or more team-mates working together to create a promising position. The wall pass (see page 18), for example, is a good way of propelling the ball past a defender with two quick movements. Attacking players also make decoy runs that draw defenders in one direction, creating space for another attacker to run into. Using the full width of the pitch can be vital to the success of an attack. Full-backs, wing-backs or wingers who are in space near the sideline may join an attack and make an overlapping run down the line. Receiving the ball, they may be able to head further forwards to put in a cross or cut infield and move towards goal. An overload is a situation in which the attacking side has more players in the attacking third of the pitch than the defending team. Classic ways of creating an overload are through a counter attack – in which one side's attack breaks down and the opposition launches a rapid, direct attack – and an accurate long pass that is received by an attacker who is supported by team-mates, with only an isolated defender to beat.

SET PIECES

Set pieces are often planned in training. They are attacking moves made from a restart such as a free kick, corner or throw-in. If a team has a player who can throw the ball a long way, it may treat a throw-in that is level with the penalty area as if it were a corner. Often, a target player just inside the penalty area will attempt to flick the throw into the goal area. Mostly, set pieces are planned from corners and attacking free kicks (see page 30). At a corner, a team's tallest players or its best headers of the ball move up, usually from defence, to join strikers and attacking midfielders in the penalty area. Corners are sometimes played short to catch the defending team off guard, but usually they are whipped into the goal area. The attacking side looks for a header or shot on goal or a flick-on to a team-mate.

Schollen
Ibrahimovic 4
Mendes da Silva 2
Ibrahimovic 2
Zonneveld
Mendes da Silva 3
Ibrahimovic 3
Mendes da Silva 1
Stam
Ibrahimovic 1

MATCH ACTION

Swedish international Zlatan Ibrahimovic moved from Ajax to Juventus for £10.81 million in late August 2004, but a week earlier he had given the Ajax fans a solo goal to savour. In a Dutch league game against NAC Breda, Ibrahimovic received a pass with his back to goal, defender David Mendes da Silva on his back and another Breda player, Mike Zonneveld, close by. Winning a tackle with Zonneveld, Ibrahimovic twisted past da Silva and headed goalwards. Weaving his way to the edge of the penalty area, Ibrahimovic's options looked limited with four defenders around him. Yet with supreme balance and a series of feints and turns, he avoided the lunging tackle of Ronnie Stam. At the very last moment, when a shot with his right foot looked likely, Ibrahimovic switched the ball to his left foot to slide a shot past goalkeeper Davy Schollen. Ajax won the game 6-2.

MATCH MAGICIANS

Some attacks are inspired by a piece of individual skill, trickery and brilliance. A player may be able to break free from a defence with a sudden change of pace and direction or a trick move such as the Cruyff turn or a dragback. Some players can simply outpace a defence, bursting through to score. Dribbling – jinking and moving with the ball under close control to beat defenders – is one of the most exciting sights on a football pitch. Stanley Matthews, Maradona and Garrincha were all electrifying dribblers, while today's dribbling superstars include Ronaldinho, Cristiano Ronaldo, Ryan Giggs and Arjen Robben. Weaving, high-speed dribblers can sometimes open up a game by themselves. They strike fear into defenders who know that one false move or a poorly timed challenge will allow the dribbler to go past or perhaps give away a free kick or penalty.

▼ *Michael Owen, playing for Real Madrid, attempts to twist and turn sharply past Dynamo Kiev defender Tiberiu Ghioane in the Champions League. Dummy movements, stepovers and sharp turns are all ways of wrongfooting a defender.*

▲ *An unexpected piece of brilliance can open up a defence or result in a goal. Here, Edmilson launches a spectacular overhead kick to score Brazil's third goal against Costa Rica in the 2002 World Cup. In a game full of attacking football by both sides, Brazil finished as 5-2 winners.*

GOALSCORING

Players who score goals regularly are the most valuable of all footballers. But scoring is not just reserved for the strikers in a side. A successful team needs its midfielders to contribute a number of goals each season, while tall defenders who are experts at heading often score five or six goals per year from set pieces. For out-and-out strikers, goals are what they play for and are judged on. As Argentinian striker Gabriel Batistuta once said, 'Goals are like bread. I need them to live.'

THE GOALSCORER'S ART

Pace, power, accuracy, confidence and a deadly eye for a chance are just some of the qualities required to be a top goalscorer. Some skills can be honed in training – close ball control or swerving a shot, for example. Other qualities, such as confidence and vision, are harder to master. Football has got quicker at the highest level and most strikers need great pace to break past increasingly mobile defenders or into space to receive the ball before anyone else. Strength to hold off a challenge can be an asset, too. Some strikers, however, rely more on wits, fast reactions and ball skills to dribble through a crowded penalty area. Others are taller, stronger players who can score with towering headers or blasted shots. Most crucially of all, strikers have to be able to spot a goal chance and take it well. They need to react instinctively, using their vision to time runs into a scoring position. Once on the ball, they rarely have long to shoot. In an instant, strikers have to weigh up their options, know where the goal, defenders and keeper are, and hit a shot with enough pace, bend or accuracy to beat the goalkeeper.

FACTFILE In 1998, Atlético Mineiro's Edmilson Ferreira celebrated a goal by eating a carrot in front of the fans of rival Brazilian team America MG. His actions caused crowd trouble and incensed America's players, one of whom was later sent off for a scything foul on Edmilson.

OWN GOALS

An own goal is technically any goal in which the last person to touch the ball before it crossed the line was a player on the defending team. In practice, however, an own goal is awarded not only when the ball has been deflected, but also when a defending player has made a genuine error or caused a major change in the course of the ball. The history of professional football is littered with outrageous own goals. Among the most common are long backpasses to keepers who fail to collect or kick the ball, skewed defensive clearances that are sliced into the net, and misdirected headers. Spare a thought for Leeds United's goalkeeper Gary Sprake, who, playing against Liverpool in 1967, went to throw the ball out, failed to release it and ended up hurling it into his own net.

◀ Manchester United's Wayne Rooney hits a volley to score against Liverpool in a 2005 Premiership match. His thunderous shot is ideal for striking at goal from outside the penalty area.

FACTFILE
The world record for own goals in one game is a staggering 149! In the last match of the 2002 Madagascan league season, against champions AS Adema, Stade Olympique l'Emryne repeatedly scored own goals from the kick-off in protest at a refereeing decision in their previous game.

▶ Croatia's Davor Suker wheels away in delight after scoring against France at the 1998 World Cup. Suker's six goals made him the top scorer of the tournament and helped take Croatia to third place in their first World Cup.

▲ *When a scoring chance arrives, strikers need deadly accuracy and an ice-cold temperament. Here, Ruud van Nistelrooy calmly dispatches the ball into the net despite the dive of Czech Republic goalkeeper Petr Cech.*

▶ *Goalscoring midfielders are highly prized. French legend Michel Platini (far left) regularly found the back of the net. Here, at the 1984 European Championships, he scores one of three goals in a 5-0 thrashing of Belgium.*

FACTFILE Nigerian international Celestine Babayaro scored on his debut for Chelsea in a 1997 pre-season match against Stevenage Borough. By celebrating with a somersault, however, Babayaro broke his leg.

▲ *Brazil's Mauro Silva (left), Leonardo (centre) and Bebeto pretend to rock babies at the 1994 World Cup. The celebration – during a 3-0 victory against Cameroon – was in honour of striker Bebeto's newborn son.*

GOALSCORING RECORDS

ALL-TIME LEADING GOALSCORERS
Artur Friedenreich (Brazil)
1,329 goals (1909–39)

Pelé (Brazil)
1,281 goals (1956–77)

Franz Binder (Germany)
1,006 goals (1930–50)

MOST INTERNATIONAL GOALS
104 – Ali Daei (Iran), 1993–May 2005

MOST GOALS IN ONE INTERNATIONAL MATCH
13 – Archie Thompson (Australia), 2001

FASTEST INTERNATIONAL GOAL
8 seconds – Davide Gualtieri (San Marino) against England, 1993

FASTEST INTERNATIONAL HAT-TRICK
Inside 3½ minutes – Willie Hall (England), 1938

MOST HAT-TRICKS IN CONSECUTIVE MATCHES
4 – Masahi Nakayama (Japan) for Jubilo Iwata, 1998

FASTEST GOAL
2.8 seconds – Ricardo Olivera (Argentina) for Rio Negro, 1998

FASTEST OWN GOAL
8 seconds – Pat Kruse (England), playing for Torquay United, 1977

GOAL CELEBRATIONS

As fans celebrate a goal, so do players. For many years, celebrations were no more flamboyant than a simple punch of the air and a hug from a nearby team-mate. That all changed in the 1980s and 1990s, partly thanks to the acrobatic backflips and handsprings of Mexican striker Hugo Sanchez. Since then, players have rocked imaginary babies, danced the conga and pulled off spectacular gymnastic moves. Nigerian international Julius Aghahowa, for example, is famous for performing six or seven backflips in a row. Referees can penalize teams for time-wasting through overlong celebrations, and the authorities often take action against players who stir up opposition fans with rude or provocative gestures.

FREE KICKS AND PENALTIES

Referees award a free kick when a player breaks one of the laws of the game. Common free-kick offences are mistimed tackles, shirt-pulling, obstruction and offside. There are two types of free kick – indirect, which cannot be scored from without a second player touching the ball, and direct, which can be scored from directly and is awarded for more serious fouls. If a direct free-kick offence is committed by the defending team inside its penalty area, the referee may award a penalty.

FREE KICKS

Both types of free kick are taken from where the foul or offence was committed, although a recent rule change means that in some competitions the referee can move a kick 9m closer to goal if the other team time-wastes or shows dissent. Opposition players must move at least 9m away from the ball, giving the team taking the kick valuable possession in space and with time. Some free kicks are taken quickly to get the ball moving in the middle of the field. Wide free kicks are often crossed with pace towards the goal area.

Attacking free kicks engage the two teams in a battle of wits. Players on the defending side mark attackers in the penalty area and usually form a defensive wall to block a direct shot. The free-kick taker may pass to a team-mate in space or try to hit a cross or shot past the wall. Some great free-kick takers, such as Brazil's Roberto Carlos, rely on awesome power to blast the ball; others, including David Beckham, are famous for the bend they put on the strike.

THE KICK OF DEATH

Originally nicknamed the 'kick of death', the penalty kick was introduced in 1891. It has created more drama and controversy than any other aspect of the game. The reason is simple. A penalty is an outstanding opportunity to score, as the taker is one-on-one with the goalkeeper and all the other players are outside the penalty area. In certain situations, the referee can order the kick to be retaken – if the taker misses but a defender entered the area before the kick, for example. Penalty takers must hit the ball forwards and cannot make contact with the ball again until it has touched another player. Some penalty takers favour accuracy over power, aiming the ball low into the corner of the goal; others blast the ball. For the keeper, trying to figure out where the ball will go is a guessing game.

◀ The Czech Republic's Marek Heinz curls a free kick into the penalty area, aiming for the head of a team-mate.

▲ Juventus keeper Gianluigi Buffon shows excellent reactions to save a penalty from AC Milan's Christian Brocchi during the Italian Super Cup in 2003.

▼ *Monaco's defensive wall jumps in an attempt to block a free kick from Rivaldo (playing for Greek side Olympiakos). A wall reduces the options for a free-kick taker, but highly skilled players can bend the ball round or up and over it.*

PENALTY SHOOTOUTS

Tense and nailbiting, a penalty shootout is guaranteed to bring fans to the edge of their seats. Professional football's first shootout took place in England in 1970. In the semi-final of the Watney Mann Invitational Cup, lowly Hull City held a full-strength Manchester United team to a 1-1 draw. In the shootout that followed, Manchester United's Denis Law became the first player to miss a shootout spot kick, but his side ended up 4-3 winners. The first shootout in a major tournament was in the 1972 Asian Nations Cup, when South Korea beat Thailand in the semi-final. Germany lost the first European Championships shootout to Czechoslovakia in 1976, but defeated France in the first World Cup shootout six years later.

▲ *Portuguese keeper Ricardo (left) looks nervous before his shootout penalty against England's David James. Ricardo's effort proved to be the winning spot kick, taking Portugal into the semi-final of Euro 2004.*

In a shootout, five players per side are chosen to take one penalty each, all at one end of the pitch. A shootout is not considered to be part of the actual match, meaning that a goal is not added to a player's season or career tally. Neither penalty takers nor team-mates are allowed to score from a rebound – each player has just one shot at glory. The keeper knows this and often does his or her best to intimidate a penalty taker. If the scores are level after each team has taken five penalties, the competition goes into sudden death. Teams take one penalty each until one side misses and the other scores. On the rare occasion that all the players on the pitch, including the goalkeeper, have taken a penalty and the scores are level, the cycle begins again in the same order. Does this ever happen? Occasionally and spectacularly. In 2005, in the Namibian Cup, 48 penalties were needed to separate KK Palace from Civics (see box below), with several players taking three penalties each.

FACTFILE Tied games at the knockout stage of a competition used to be settled by tossing a coin or drawing lots. In 1954, Spain and Turkey drew 2-2 in a play-off to decide who would qualify for the World Cup. A blindfolded Italian boy, Luigi Franco Gemma, drew lots to decide the winner. Spain were knocked out.

MOST PENALTIES IN A SHOOTOUT

PENS	SHOOTOUT SCORE	COMPETITION
48	KK Palace 17 Civics 16	Namibian Cup, 2005
44	Argentinos Juniors 20 Racing Club 19	Argentinian league, 1988
40	Obernai 15 ASCA Wittelsheim 15	French Cup, 1996
34	Gençlerbirligi SK 17 Galatasaray 16	Turkish Cup, 1996

▲ *Ahn Jung-Hwan keeps his nerve to place a penalty past Spain's Iker Casillas. South Korea won the penalty shootout 5-3 to book a place in the last four of the 2002 World Cup.*

SNAPSHOT

BAGGIO'S PENALTY MISS

'The difference between heaven and hell is one minute,' said Spanish international Josep Guardiola after an epic 4-3 win over Yugoslavia at Euro 2000. For Italy's Roberto Baggio, six years earlier, it took mere seconds. In the final of the 1994 World Cup, Italy and Brazil were locked in a 0-0 stalemate. Extra time ended and a nerve-shredding penalty shootout began. With Italy 3-2 down, Baggio stepped up to take his side's pressure-laden fifth penalty. He decided to drive the ball down the middle, as he knew that Taffarel, the Brazilian keeper, tended to dive to one side.

Taffarel did dive, but Baggio sent the ball sailing high over the bar to hand the World Cup to Brazil. Baggio later wrote, 'It was the worst moment of my career. I still dream about it. If I could erase a moment from my career, it would be that one.' What is often forgotten is that two Italians before Baggio, Daniele Massaro and the highly experienced Franco Baresi, missed their penalties. Even if Baggio had scored, Brazil would have had the chance to win with their fifth spot kick. That said, the photograph of a crushed Baggio remains the iconic image of the 1994 World Cup.

Roberto Baggio hangs his head in disbelief as Brazilian players celebrate victory in the final of the 1994 World Cup.

FOOTBALL LEGENDS

From France's Alain Giresse to Brazil's Zico, the game of football has been lit up by the talents of thousands of highly committed and skilful players, all of whom have enthralled spectators and inspired their teams to great achievements. Packed into this section are profiles of more than 75 of the finest players to have graced the game.

> **KEY**
> Country = international side
> Caps = international games
> Goals = international goals
> (to 18/05/2005)

GAO HONG
China, born 1967
Caps: over 100 Goals: 0

An instinctive shot-stopper, Gao Hong (see page 74) began playing football for her factory team before moving to the Guangdong club in southeast China. She became a member of the Chinese national side in 1989 and played in both the 1995 and 1999 World Cups. Gao was in goal for China's two Asian Games successes, in 1994 and 1998, and she also won a silver medal at the 1996 Olympics. At the end of her international career, she appeared in the WUSA league for the New York Power.

GOALKEEPERS

PETER SCHMEICHEL
Denmark, born 1963
Caps: 129 Goals: 1

After playing for Hvidøvre and then Brøndby, Schmeichel became one of the best keepers of the 1990s after Alex Ferguson took him to Manchester United in 1991 for the modest fee of £550,000. The high point of his international career came with winning the 1992 European Championships, while the silverware poured in at club level. The hugely committed Dane redefined one-on-one goalkeeping, standing menacingly tall and large or bravely sprawling at an attacker's feet. After winning a treble (English Premiership, FA Cup and Champions League) with Manchester United in 1999, he moved to Sporting Lisbon and helped the Portuguese side win its first league title in 17 years.

He made a surprise return to the English Premiership in 2001, with Aston Villa and then Manchester City, before injury forced him to retire.

◀ Peter Schmeichel makes a typically brave save for Manchester City in 2002.

> **FACTFILE** As an amateur, Peter Schmeichel played as a striker. He showed those skills in the 1995-96 UEFA Cup, when he came up for an attack and scored with a header against Russian side Rotor Volgograd.

▶ Andoni Zubizarreta was Spain's first-choice international keeper for more than a decade.

ANDONI ZUBIZARRETA
Spain, born 1961
Caps: 126 Goals: 0

While notching up a record 126 matches for his country, Zubizarreta played hundreds more games for four Spanish clubs: Alaves, Athletic Bilbao, Barcelona and Valencia. He won two league titles with Athletic Bilbao, as well as a European Cup, a Cup-Winners' Cup and a league title with Barcelona. He retired from international football in 1998, after captaining Spain in his fourth World Cup.

BEST GOALKEEPER AT THE WORLD CUP

Since the 1994 World Cup, FIFA has given the Lev Yashin Award to the best goalkeeper of the tournament.

YEAR	WINNER
1994	Michel Preud'homme (Belgium)
1998	Fabien Barthez (France)
2002	Oliver Kahn (Germany)

LEV YASHIN
Soviet Union, 1929–90
Caps: 75   Goals: 0

In South America, Yashin was called the Black Spider. In Europe he was the Black Panther; but everywhere he was regarded as the finest goalkeeper of his era and, possibly, of all time. Blessed with extraordinary anticipation and agility, Yashin made countless, seemingly impossible saves and stopped as many as 150 penalties during his career, which was spent entirely at Moscow Dynamo. In 1954, he made his debut for the national team. Yashin's bravery, vision and shot-stopping skills helped the Soviets to an Olympic title in 1956, the European Championships crown in 1960 and a semi-final place at the 1966 World Cup. With Moscow Dynamo, Yashin won six league titles and two Soviet Cups. In 1963, he became the first – and still the only – goalkeeper to win the coveted European Player of the Year award.

▲ *Lev Yashin makes a great save at the 1966 World Cup.*

FACTFILE Gordon Banks won FIFA's Goalkeeper of the Year award a record six times.

GORDON BANKS
England, born 1937
Caps: 73   Goals: 0

'Banks of England' was as secure a keeper as any nation could call upon in the 1960s. During his ten-year international career, he kept 35 clean sheets and was on the losing side just nine times. His professional career began at Chesterfield, before a £7,000 move took him to Leicester City. In 1962, Banks made his debut for England, with whom he won the 1966 World Cup. The following year, he moved to Stoke City, but a car crash in 1972 caused Banks to lose the sight in his right eye. The accident ended his career in Britain, although he did play in the USA for the Fort Lauderdale Strikers in 1977–78.

▲ *Gordon Banks in action for Stoke City in 1972. Throughout his career, Banks trained tirelessly on angles and repeat drills to improve his strength and agility.*

MATCH ACTION

Brazil and England played a tense yet thrilling match in the group stages of the 1970 World Cup, with Brazil winning 1-0. In the tenth minute, Jairzinho slipped a high cross into the English penalty area. Rising high, Pelé headed the ball down fiercely towards the far post, with Gordon Banks seemingly stranded. The ball bounced just short of the line and a goal seemed certain. Yet Banks showed electrifying reactions, scrambling across his line and clawing the ball almost vertically upwards and over the crossbar. Pelé was stunned and later called it 'the greatest save I ever saw'. Few who witnessed it would disagree.

Tommy Wright

Pelé

Alan Mullery

Tostao

Banks 2

Banks 1

PAT JENNINGS
Northern Ireland, born 1945
Caps: 119 Goals: 0

Calm, gentle and seemingly unflappable, Northern Ireland's Pat Jennings famously received no formal coaching before joining his local team, Newry Town. A short spell with Watford followed, before he moved to Tottenham Hotspur in 1964. There he won the FA Cup, two League Cups and the UEFA Cup. In the 1967 Charity Shield match against Manchester United, a kick from Jennings sailed over the head of the opposing keeper, Alex Stepney, to score a memorable goal. Jennings was sold to Tottenham's north London rivals Arsenal in 1977, where he played for eight seasons. He came out of retirement to play his 119th game for his country at the 1986 World Cup.

▶ Dino Zoff organizes Italy's defence during the 1982 World Cup. Voted Italian goalkeeper of the century, Zoff once remained unbeaten in goal for Juventus for ten games.

▲ Pat Jennings tips the ball over the bar during a World Cup qualifying game against England in 1985.

▲ Sepp Maier won four league titles, three European Cups and a Cup-Winners' Cup with Bayern Munich.

SEPP MAIER
West Germany, born 1944
Caps: 95 Goals: 0

Josef-Dieter 'Sepp' Maier played for local club TSV Haar before becoming an almost ever-present member of the dominant Bayern Munich side of the late 1960s and 1970s. At his acrobatic best in the 1974 World Cup (which West Germany won) and in the 1975 and 1976 European Cup finals, Maier seemed impossible to beat. He was awarded German Player of the Year three times, a rare achievement for a goalkeeper.

The 1978 World Cup was his last, as a car accident forced him to retire a year later. Since then he has coached goalkeepers, including Germany's Oliver Kahn.

DINO ZOFF
Italy, born 1942
Caps: 112 Goals: 0

A true goalkeeping legend, Dino Zoff was rejected as a 14-year-old by both Juventus and Internazionale for being too small. He finally signed for Udinese – where he let in five goals on his debut – before moving to Mantova and then Napoli. In 1972, Zoff was bought by Juventus, where he won six Italian league titles, two Italian Cups and a UEFA Cup. Only one club title, the European Cup, eluded him – although he did win runners-up medals in 1973 and 1983. Zoff's first international call-up came during the 1968 European Championships. He debuted in the quarter-finals and was part of the side that won the final. A model athlete with intense concentration, Zoff broke many goalkeeping records (see page 23) and in 1982, at the age of 40, he captained Italy to their first World Cup success in the modern era. The oldest player to win a World Cup, Zoff retired shortly afterwards and went on to coach Italy's Olympic team, Juventus and Lazio. He coached Italy to the final of Euro 2000, where they lost narrowly to France.

MOHAMMED AL DEAYEA
Saudi Arabia, born 1972
Caps: 173 Goals: 0

Mohammed al Deayea can lay claim to being the finest goalkeeper the Middle East has produced. An agile shot-stopper, he was part of the Saudi side that won the 1989 World Under-16 Youth Cup – an impressive feat for a country that had no national team until 1976. Al Deayea lived up to his early promise, starring for his country at three World Cups (1994–2002). He performed heroics in a penalty shootout to win the 1996 Asian Cup and has won the Gulf Cup twice. At club level, he has spent most of his career at Saudi Arabia's dominant Al-Hilal side.

DEFENDERS

MARCEL DESAILLY
France, born 1968
Caps: 116 Goals: 3

Marcel Desailly is world-famous as one of the French players who won the World Cup and European Championship crowns in 1998 and 2000. He was born in the African nation of Ghana and came to France as a young child. A skilful and commanding central defender, Desailly began his career with FC Nantes and then Olympique Marseille. In 1993, he won the Champions League with Marseille, before moving to AC Milan and winning the Champions League again the following year. After a series of outstanding performances at the 1998 World Cup, Desailly moved to Chelsea, where he proved a popular leader. In 2004, Desailly retired from international football and left Chelsea to join Qatar's Al-Ittihad club.

▲ Marcel Desailly hits a long pass during France's 1998 World Cup game against Denmark.

FACTFILE World Cup winner Marcel Desailly became the third player to be sent off in a World Cup final when he was dismissed against Brazil in 1998 after receiving two yellow cards.

▲ In 1978, Daniel Passarella captained Argentina to the World Cup trophy on home soil.

DANIEL PASSARELLA
Argentina, born 1953
Caps: 70 Goals: 22

Passarella was a gifted central defender who made surging runs into midfield to build attacks. He was exceptionally good in the air despite being of average height, and struck devastating free kicks. In 298 Argentinian league matches, he scored an astonishing 99 goals. Passarella had success with River Plate before a move to Europe in 1982, first to Fiorentina and then to Internazionale. In 1985–86, he scored 11 goals for Fiorentina, a record for a defender that lasted for 15 years. He won the 1978 World Cup, played in the 1982 tournament and was picked for 1986, but was sidelined through injury. After retiring, Passarella became a coach, managing Argentina at the 1998 World Cup.

ELIAS FIGUEROA
Chile, born 1946
Caps: 47 Goals: 2

This elegant and skilled defender played almost all of his football in the left-back position. Figueroa appeared in three World Cups – 1966, 1974 and 1982 – and in 1974 he was voted the best defender of the tournament. He won the South American Footballer of the Year award an unprecedented three times in a row (1974–76). At club level, Figueroa won league titles in three different countries – the Chilean league with Colo Colo twice, the Brazilian league with Internacional on three occasions and the Uruguayan league with Peñarol five times. He ended his career in the USA, playing for the Fort Lauderdale Strikers alongside Gerd Müller and Teofilio Cubillas, the great Peruvian striker.

RUNE BRATSETH
Norway, born 1961
Caps: 60 Goals: 4

Rune Bratseth began his football career with Rosenborg Trondheim, but did not turn professional until the age of 23. In 1986, he moved to Germany's Werder Bremen for just £65,000. Bremen had bought a bargain, as Bratseth became their defensive linchpin, using his great pace and skill to operate as a centre-back or a sweeper. Bratseth won two Bundesliga titles and a European Cup-Winners' Cup with Bremen, and was twice voted Germany's best foreign import. One of his proudest moments came in 1994, when he captained Norway to their first World Cup finals since 1938. After the tournament, he retired and went on to became director of coaching at Rosenborg.

◀ Rune Bratseth powers away from the Republic of Ireland's John Aldridge at the 1994 World Cup.

Bobby Moore, England's captain, celebrates with the 1966 World Cup.

BOBBY MOORE
England, 1941–93
Caps: 108 Goals: 2

England's finest ever defender, Moore appeared to lack the pace and the commanding physique to be a great central defender. However, he was blessed with a wonderful eye for the game and always appeared to be one step ahead of opposition attackers. His tackling was clean and surgical, and he was very rarely cautioned. One of football's truly outstanding captains, Moore led England in 90 games – a record shared with Billy Wright – including the 1966 World Cup triumph. He spent most of his career at West Ham, only joining Fulham (alongside George Best) at the age of 32, before finally moving to the USA to play for Seattle Sounders and San Antonio Thunder. His close friendship with Pelé was cemented in 1970, when the two men played out an epic struggle for supremacy in England's World Cup game against Brazil. Pelé called Moore the greatest defender he had played against.

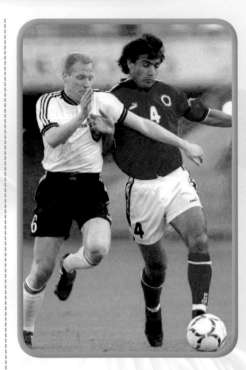

▲ *Matthias Sammer (left) was the first defender to win the European Player of the Year award since Franz Beckenbauer in 1976.*

MATTHIAS SAMMER
East Germany / Germany, born 1967 Caps: 74 Goals: 14

Matthias Sammer followed in the footsteps of his father, who played in midfield for East Germany and Dresden. As a midfielder, Sammer led East Germany to victory at the 1986 European Youth Championships. After Germany reunified in 1990, he moved into defence and was a commanding sweeper in the 1994 World Cup and two European Championships. A move to the Italian club Internazionale was short-lived and he returned to Germany to join Borussia Dortmund, with whom he won two Bundesliga titles and the 1997 Champions League. In 1996, he became the first player from the former East Germany to win the European Footballer of the Year award.

PAOLO MALDINI
Italy, born 1968
Caps: 125 Goals: 7

One of the very best defenders in world football, Paolo Maldini is, unusually, a one-club player. He made his first-team debut for AC Milan in 1985 and has played over 550 games for the Italian club, mostly at left-back, although he can also play as a central defender or as a sweeper. Maldini is able to read the game extremely well, tackle cleanly and move the ball forwards accurately. He debuted for Italy in 1988 and soon became a regular in the national side. He played in four World Cups and four European Championships, eventually retiring from international football after the 2002 World Cup. In 2003, Maldini lifted the Champions League trophy for AC Milan, and a year later he won his seventh Serie A league title.

◄ *Paolo Maldini, Italy's longest-serving defender, clears the ball out of his penalty area during the 1994 World Cup final against Brazil.*

MASAMI IHARA
Japan, born 1967
Caps: 123 Goals: 5

Ihara was one of the most recognizable stars of the Japanese league before his retirement in 2002, after 297 J-League games. A strong, skilled defender, excellent in the air and on the ground, Ihara played in central defence or as a sweeper. He began playing for Yokohama Marinos before the J-League was formed (in 1992) and enjoyed eight seasons with the club before joining Jubilo Iwata for one season and finishing his career with two years at Urawa Reds. By that time, Ihara had already become the first Japanese footballer to reach 100 caps, and he was a proud member of Japan's 1998 World Cup side, the first Japanese team to play in the World Cup finals.

▲ *Holland's Ruud Krol at the 1980 European Championships, which were held in Italy.*

FACTFILE
Ruud Krol held the record as the most-capped Dutch player for 21 years. His total was finally overtaken in 2000.

▶ *Franz Beckenbauer at the 1974 World Cup. Sixteen years later, he became the second man – after Brazil's Mario Zagalo – to have won the World Cup as both a player and a manager.*

RUUD KROL
Holland, born 1949
Caps: 83 Goals: 4

Krol was a vital part of the great Ajax and Holland 'total football' sides of the late 1960s and 1970s, comfortable playing in almost any defensive position. With Ajax he won six league titles and two European Cups (1972 and 1973). Krol was the last of the Ajax greats to move away, when in 1980 he played for Vancouver Whitecaps in Canada. He returned to Europe the following year to play for Napoli and later for Cannes in the French second division, where injury forced him to retire in 1987. He has since managed in a variety of countries, including Switzerland, Egypt and Belgium.

FRANZ BECKENBAUER
West Germany, born 1945
Caps: 103 Goals: 14

Der Kaiser made his debut for Bayern Munich in 1964 as an attacking inside-left. Just 27 games later, he was in the national side. At the 1966 World Cup, Beckenbauer played in midfield and scored four goals on the way to the final. By the 1970 tournament, he had moved into defence, where he revolutionized the ultra-defensive role of sweeper with his astonishing vision and silky skills on the ball. Time and again he would turn defence into attack, striding up the pitch to release team-mates or take a chance himself. With his stylish attacking play, it is sometimes forgotten that he was a masterful defender, always cool under pressure. In 1972, Beckenbauer won the European Championships with West Germany and was European Footballer of the Year. Two years later, he won the first of three consecutive European Cups with Bayern Munich and also captained his country to World Cup glory. In 1977, he made a surprise move to the USA, playing in a star-studded New York Cosmos team before returning to Germany in 1980 with Hamburg. He became West Germany's coach in 1984, leading the team to two World Cup finals and winning one.

HIT THE NET

www.planetworldcup.com/LEGENDS/wcstars.html
A selection of profiles of many great footballers, including Austria's Hans Krankl, Belgium's Jan Ceulemans and West Germany's Karl-Heinz Rummenigge.

www.rsssf.com/miscellaneous/century.html
A regularly updated list of footballers with 100 or more international caps. Clicking on a player's name reveals a list of all their international matches.

www.ifhof.com/hof/halloffame.asp
The website of the International Football Hall of Fame, with detailed biographies of 25 of the world's football legends.

▲ *Franco Baresi won three European Cups with AC Milan, including this triumph in 1989.*

FRANCO BARESI
Italy, born 1960
Caps: 81 Goals: 1

A tough, intelligent defender, Baresi made his first-team debut for AC Milan in 1978. He played 716 games for the club, winning six Serie A titles. Baresi had to wait until 1990 to break fully into the Italian national team, however. Although part of the 1982 World Cup squad, he was not picked to play and refused to appear for Italy while Enzo Bearzot remained manager. He played in both the 1990 and 1994 World Cups and superbly cancelled out the threat of Brazil's Romario and Bebeto in the 1994 final, which Italy lost only on penalties. Milan paid him the ultimate tribute on his retirement in 1997, dropping the number six shirt from their line-up.

HONG MYUNG-BO
South Korea, born 1969
Caps: 135 Goals: 9

An excellent passer of the ball, Hong played for Pohang Steelers in South Korea and for Bellmare Hiratsuke (now Shonan Bellmare) and Kashiwa Reysol in Japan. He is South Korea's most-capped player and a veteran of four World Cups. At the 2002 tournament, where South Korea reached the semi-finals on home soil, Hong was voted the third best player of the World Cup behind Oliver Kahn and Ronaldo. In November 2002, he became the first Korean to play in the American MLS when he signed for Los Angeles Galaxy.

LINDA MEDALEN
Norway, born 1965
Caps: 152 Goals: 64

Medalen started her career as a striker, making her debut for Norway in 1987 and going on to win the 1988 unofficial Women's World Cup and the 1993 European Championships. At the 1991 World Cup she was her side's top scorer, with six goals, as Norway finished runners-up. As Medalen's career progressed, she moved into defence, where her skill in the air and strong tackling helped Norway to win the 1995 World Cup, conceding just one goal in six games. Medalen played in the 1999 tournament, but a knee injury kept her out of the 2000 Olympics, which Norway won. At club level, she won five league championships and three cup competitions for the Norwegian side Asker SKK.

◄ *Linda Medalen holds off China's Ying Liu in the 1999 World Cup semi-final. The Norwegian retired a year later.*

JOHN CHARLES
Wales, 1931-2004
Caps: 38 Goals: 21

The gloriously talented Charles was equally skilled as a bustling, powerful centre-forward or as a hugely commanding central defender. In both positions, he was world class. Appearing in attack for Leeds United, he scored a record 42 goals in one season, while playing internationally as a central defender. In the Welsh side, Charles was joined by his brother, Mel, and team-mates Ivor and Len Allchurch – the first time that any national side had included two pairs of brothers. In 1957, the British transfer record was smashed as he moved to Juventus for £67,000. Charles became a genuine legend in Italy for his towering perrformances, generous behaviour towards fans and his sportsmanship. In a highly defence-minded league, he scored an astonishing 93 goals in 155 matches, helping Juve win three Serie A titles and two Italian Cups. He later moved back to Leeds, then on to Parma, Cardiff City and Hereford United, before retiring.

◄ *John Charles (right) battles for the ball at the 1958 World Cup. Charles' name is still revered by Juventus fans, who nicknamed him Il Buon Gigante – the Gentle Giant.*

MIDFIELDERS AND WINGERS

JAY JAY OKOCHA
Nigeria, born 1973
Caps: 70 Goals: 13

Okocha was playing in Nigeria for Enugu Rangers when he visited a footballing friend in Neunkirchen, Germany, and was asked to stay and play for the team. From Neunkirchen he moved first to Saarbrücken and then, in 1991, to Bundesliga side Eintracht Frankfurt. He was not yet 18. Okocha shone as an attacking midfielder for the German side before transferring to Fenerbahçe, where he scored 30 goals in two seasons and won the Turkish league. Internationally, Okocha was part of the emerging Nigerian side that won the African Nations Cup in 1994 and the Olympic title two years later. In 1998, he became the most expensive Nigerian player when he moved to Paris Saint Germain for an estimated fee of £14 million. In 2002, Okocha moved on a free transfer to Bolton Wanderers, where his match-winning displays made him a favourite with the fans.

◀ *Jay Jay Okocha stretches for the ball in Nigeria's 2004 African Nations Cup semi-final against Tunisia.*

STANLEY MATTHEWS
England, 1915-2000
Caps: 54 Goals: 11

The 'Wizard of the Dribble' made his first-team debut for Stoke City in 1932 and went on to amaze crowds with his sensational wing play, supreme control and ability to dribble through a defence at will. Matthews' dedication to fitness, years ahead of his time, ensured that his career was one of the longest in British football. He joined Blackpool in 1947 and inspired them to an incredible FA Cup triumph in 1953, in what is remembered as the 'Matthews final'. His England career ran from 1937 to 1954, although he only played in 54 of the 119 internationals the team contested, to the outrage of his many fans. He became the first winner of the European Footballer of the Year award in 1956, and in 1961 he returned to Stoke, for whom he played his last game in 1965, aged 50 years and five days. In the same year, he became the first ever serving footballer to be knighted.

▲ *Stanley Matthews (left) exhibits supreme poise, balance and skill on the ball as he takes on Scotland's George Young in 1948.*

FACTFILE Stanley Matthews was praised as one of the most modest and sporting players to ever grace the game. In his 33-year-long career, he never received a booking.

CARLOS VALDERRAMA
Colombia, born 1961
Caps: 110 Goals: 10

Famous for his flamboyant play and hairstyle, Carlos Valderrama was an exquisite passer of the ball in midfield, who would often link with the attack to devastating effect. He played for three Colombian teams – Union Magdalena, Millionarios and Deportiva Cali – before moving to France in 1988, where he won the league title with Montpellier. In 1996, he moved to the USA to play for Tampa Bay Mutiny and then Miami Fusion. Valderrama captained Colombia to three World Cup tournaments in a row (1990–98) and retired from international football after the 1998 tournament. Yet, even past his 40th birthday, Valderrama was still one of the biggest stars in the MLS.

▶ *Carlos Valderrama on the ball during Colombia's 1998 World Cup game against England.*

ALAIN GIRESSE
France, born 1952
Caps: 47 Goals: 6

At 1.63m tall and weighing around 60kg, Giresse was small for competitive football, but his tireless work in midfield caught the eye both at club level, for Bordeaux and Olympique Marseille, and with the French national team. Giresse appeared at two World Cups (1982 and 1986) and also won the 1984 European Championships. He played more than 500 matches for Bordeaux and scored the winning goal in the 1986 French Cup final against Marseille, whom he joined a few weeks later. Giresse went on to manage Paris Saint Germain and Toulouse, where his son Thibault Giresse now plays. In 2004, he was appointed head coach of the Georgian national team.

HRISTO STOICHKOV
Bulgaria, born 1966
Caps: 83 Goals: 37

As an attacking midfielder or a striker, the strong, stocky Stoichkov was surprisingly quick over a short distance and possessed unstoppable power, particularly in his left foot. He emerged as a skilful youngster at CSKA Sofia before moving to Barcelona. Unpredictable and prone to tempers, Stoichkov fell out with Barcelona manager Johan Cruyff when he was asked to play out wide. He later moved to Parma, Japanese side Kashiwa Reysol and the Chicago Fire in the MLS. He arrived at the 1994 World Cup as the star player in an underrated Bulgarian side that sensationally knocked out Germany before losing the semi-final to Italy. Stoichkov finished the tournament as joint top scorer. It was his finest hour as a player.

FACTFILE Stoichkov was banned for the 1985–86 season for his part in a riot involving players and supporters at the 1985 Bulgarian Cup final.

▲ Stoichkov during the Euro 96 match against Romania. The midfielder's goal won the game.

DAVID BECKHAM
England, born 1975
Caps: 80 Goals: 16

David Beckham is one of the most recognizable footballers on the planet. He began his career as a youth-team player at Manchester United, then had a short loan spell with Preston North End, before announcing his arrival in English football with a Premiership goal from inside his own half against Wimbledon. At the 1998 World Cup he was heavily criticized for kicking out at Argentina's Diego Simeone and receiving a red card in a thrilling game that saw England knocked out. But Beckham's excellence for club and country, particularly his trademark swerving free kicks, won back public support – notably when he ensured England's qualification for the 2002 World Cup by scoring with a last-gasp free kick against Greece. Having won a Champions League, Premiership and FA Cup treble with Manchester United in 1999, the midfielder joined Real Madrid in 2003 for a fee of £25 million.

◀ Real Madrid midfielder David Beckham whips a cross into the Real Mallorca penalty area.

WOLFGANG OVERATH
West Germany, born 1943
Caps: 81 Goals: 17

A midfield dynamo, good at defensive duties and strong in attack, Overath started with SV Siegburg as a junior before moving to Cologne at the age of 20. In his first season, he won the Bundesliga and received his first call-up to the national team. Overath played in three World Cups and shares with Franz Beckenbauer the record of being the only footballer to finish first, second and third in the tournament. He retired from international football after West Germany's triumph in 1974, but continued to play for Cologne until 1977, making over 750 appearances.

▲ Nakata shields the ball during a Serie A match.

HIDETOSHI NAKATA
Japan, born 1977
Caps: 62 Goals: 10

Nakata began his career playing for Japan's Bellmare Hiratsuke in 1995. He became the outstanding player in the J-League and was voted 1998 Asian Footballer of the Year. The same year, Nakata moved to Perugia, Italy, as the first Japanese footballer to play in Serie A. He was transferred to Roma in 2000, with whom he won the Serie A title, before making a series of moves within the Italian league – to Parma in 2001, then to Bologna and, in 2004, to Fiorentina. Nakata starred in Japan's World Cup campaigns of 1998 and 2002, and is a superstar in his home country.

MICHEL PLATINI
France, born 1955
Caps: 72   Goals: 41

A truly great attacking midfielder, Platini was the glittering jewel in a French side that suffered semi-final heartbreak at the 1982 World Cup. Two years later, he was top scorer at the European Championships, with nine goals, as France won the title. Forming a magnificent partnership with Alan Giresse and Jean Tigana, Platini exhibited immense skill and vision. At club level, Platini played for AS Joeuf, Nancy and Saint Etienne before turning down a transfer to Arsenal in favour of a move to Italian giants Juventus in 1982. He was Serie A's leading marksman three times and was crowned European Footballer of the Year three times in a row (1983–85) – a unique feat. Retiring in 1987, he went on to manage France and then led his country's bid to host the 1998 World Cup.

▲ Dragan Dzajic (left) and Willie Morgan wave to the crowd after Yugoslavia's 1-1 draw with Scotland at the 1974 World Cup.

GARRINCHA
Brazil,
1933-83
Caps: 50
Goals: 12

Manuel Francisco dos Santos was nicknamed Garrincha – meaning 'little bird' – at a young age. A small player at only 1.69m tall, a childhood illness had left his left leg bent inwards and his right leg 6cm shorter and bent outwards. Yet those who saw Garrincha play remember him as the greatest dribbler in the history of football. He also perfected the bending banana kick, which he used to great effect for his club side, Botafogo, scoring 232 goals in 581 matches. He also played in Colombia, Italy, and in France for Red Star Paris, but it was on the international stage that Garrincha became famous. He starred in the 1958

DRAGAN DZAJIC
Yugoslavia, born 1946
Caps: 85   Goals: 23

A left-winger for his entire career, Dragan Dzajic boasted lightning-fast acceleration and an eye for a delicate pass. He made over 580 appearances for Red Star Belgrade, scoring 287 goals, winning five Yugoslav league titles and four Yugoslav Cups. Dzalic also spent two seasons in France, where he scored 31 goals for Bastia. He was part of the Yugoslav side that entered the 1964 Olympics and reached the final of the 1968 European Championships, knocking out World Cup holders England along the way. Dzajic finished the tournament as top scorer. After retiring from football in 1979, he went on to become sports director of Red Star.

▼ England defender Ray Wilson fails to stop the mesmeric Garrincha as he surges down the wing in the 1962 World Cup quarter-final. Brazil won 3-1.

World Cup, which Brazil won, but went on to eclipse those performances at the 1962 competition. Voted player of the tournament, he was joint leading scorer as he struck two goals to knock out England in the quarter-final, and then two more to beat Chile in the semi-final. Sadly, his life away from football was troubled, and he died of alcohol poisoning at the age of 49.

▲ Platini skips a challenge during France's 4-1 win over Northern Ireland at the 1982 World Cup.

LUIS FIGO
Portugal, born 1972
Caps: 110 Goals: 31

Luis Figo's glittering career started on a high, as he was part of Portugal's 'golden generation' that won the European Under-16 competition in 1989 and the World Youth Cup in 1991. A darting wide midfielder, with exceptional dribbling and passing skills, Figo has twice been at the centre of transfer controversy. The first time was in 1995, when both Parma and Juventus claimed that he had signed contracts with them to leave his first club, Sporting Lisbon. In the end Figo moved to Barcelona, with whom he won the European Cup-Winners' Cup in 1997 and back-to-back Spanish league titles in 1998 and 1999. He then moved for a world-record fee to Barcelona's fiercest rivals, Real Madrid, where he won two league titles and the 2002 Champions League. Figo appeared at three European Championships, reaching the semi-finals in 2000 and the final four years later. In the summer of 2005, he came out of international retirement to help Portugal's bid to qualify for the 2006 World Cup.

> **FACTFILE** Luis Figo has played 14 matches in the European Championships, a record he shares with Zinedine Zidane, Lilian Thuram and Karel Poborsky.

▲ *Real Madrid's Luis Figo competes in the air with Wisla Krakow's Arkadiusz Glowacki during a Champions League qualifying match in 2004.*

ZINEDINE ZIDANE
France, born 1972
Caps: 93 Goals: 27

The son of Algerian immigrants, Zidane grew up in a poor area of Marseille with posters of his idol, Uruguayan striker Enzo Francescoli, adorning his bedroom wall. His first club was Cannes, followed by Bordeaux, where he won France's Young Player of the Year award in 1992. His international debut in 1994 was sensational – he scored both of France's goals in a 2-2 draw with the Czech Republic. In the 1995–96 season, Zidane played 57 matches – more than any other French player – and he appeared jaded as he underperformed at Euro 96. But a move to Juventus in the same year saw him regain his best form, as he helped the Serie A giants win two league titles. Zidane was a key part of the world-beating French side that captured a double of World Cup (1998) and European Championships (2000). Away from football Zidane is famously shy, yet he bursts into life on the pitch, where he uses superb vision, sharp acceleration and a delicate touch to break down crowded midfields and defences. Considered the best midfielder in the world, he won World Player of the Year titles in 1998, 2000 and 2003.

ENZO SCIFO
Belgium, born 1966
Caps: 84 Goals: 18

One of only a handful of players to have taken part in four World Cups, Vicenzo 'Enzo' Scifo (see page 87) was born to Italian parents and became a Belgian citizen at the age of 18. He was a teenage footballing prodigy, scoring a staggering 432 goals in just four seasons as a junior. After joining Anderlecht in 1980, his silky midfield skills helped the club to three Belgian league titles in a row (1985–87), while with the national side he reached the semi-finals of the 1986 World Cup. Scifo's moves to Internazionale and then Bordeaux were both failures, but his career was reignited at Auxerre. He went on to enjoy spells at Torino, in Italy, and Monaco, before rejoining Anderlecht towards the end of his career.

WORLD-RECORD TRANSFERS

PLAYER	FROM	TO	FEE	YEAR
Zinedine Zidane (France)	Juventus	Real Madrid	£45.62m	2001
Luis Figo (Portugal)	Barcelona	Real Madrid	£37m	2000
Hernan Crespo (Argentina)	Parma	Lazio	£35.5m	2000
Gianluigi Buffon (Italy)	Parma	Juventus	£32.6m	2001
Christian Vieri (Italy)	Lazio	Internazionale	£32m	1999
Rio Ferdinand (England)	Leeds United	Manchester United	£29.1m	2002
Gaizka Mendieta (Spain)	Valencia	Lazio	£29m	2001
Ronaldo (Brazil)	Internazionale	Real Madrid	£28.49m	2002
Juan Veron (Argentina)	Lazio	Manchester United	£28.1m	2001
Rui Costa (Portugal)	Fiorentina	AC Milan	£28m	2001

JOHAN NEESKENS
Holland, born 1951
Caps: 49 Goals: 17

After making his debut for Holland in 1970, the exceptionally talented Neeskens played international football for a decade. He starred in two World Cup campaigns, which both led to heartbreaking defeats in the final. In 1974, Neeskens scored a beautiful chip against Brazil and converted the first penalty to be awarded in a World Cup final, against West Germany. Neeskens won three Dutch league titles and three European Cups with Ajax, the European Cup-Winners' Cup with Barcelona, and spent six seasons in the USA before retiring in 1986.

▲ *Hagi pushes forwards at the 1994 World Cup.*

GHEORGHE HAGI
Romania, born 1965
Caps: 125 Goals: 34

Moody, unpredictable and outstandingly skilful, Hagi played for Steaua Bucharest from 1987, either in midfield or in a free role in attack. His superb ball skills and vision helped his club to three league titles in a row, as well as to the 1989 European Cup final. Hagi then played for Real Madrid, Brescia, Barcelona and Galatasaray, with whom he won the 2000 UEFA Cup. A linchpin of the Romanian team, Hagi scored a sublime goal from 35 metres out against Colombia at the 1994 World Cup, but he was sent off in his final international match, at Euro 2000.

▲ *Boniek scored all three goals in this 3-0 victory for Poland over Belgium at the 1982 World Cup.*

ZBIGNIEW BONIEK
Poland, born 1956
Caps: 80 Goals: 24

A hard-running attacking midfielder, Boniek won two league titles with Widzew Lodz and starred when the Polish side knocked Juventus out of the 1980 UEFA Cup. He joined the Italian club two years later and formed a deadly midfield partnership with Michel Platini. At Juventus, he won Italian league and cup titles, the European Cup-Winners' Cup and the 1985 European Cup (scoring the two winning goals). A member of three World Cup squads, Boniek scored four goals in 1982 as Poland came third. After joining Roma in 1985, he operated deeper and deeper in midfield and he played as a sweeper in the 1986 World Cup.

> **FACTFILE** Michael Laudrup is the only player to have appeared for Real Madrid in a 5-0 win over Barcelona and also for Barcelona when they have beaten Real 5-0.

▶ *Michael Laudrup challenges for the ball during Denmark's Euro 96 match with Portugal.*

SOCRATES
Brazil, born 1954
Caps: 60 Goals: 22

Named after the Ancient Greek scholar, Brazil's Socrates played as an amateur for Botafogo while studying to become a doctor. He turned professional with Corinthians in 1977. The tall, elegant midfielder became a firm favourite with the fans, scoring spectacular goals and threading superb passes around the pitch.

He captained two hugely talented Brazilian World Cup sides in 1982 and 1986, but neither team did its talent justice.

> **FACTFILE**
> In November 2004, at the age of 50, Socrates played for English non-league side Garforth Town in the Northern Counties League.

MICHAEL LAUDRUP
Denmark, born 1964
Caps: 104 Goals: 37

The peak of Michael Laudrup's international career came in the quarter-finals of the 1998 World Cup, where Denmark lost narrowly to Brazil 3-2 – despite his younger brother, Brian, scoring a goal. Laudrup was much in demand as an attacking midfielder, playing for Lazio and Juventus in Italy and winning five league titles in Spain with Barcelona and Real Madrid. Sadly, he missed out on Denmark's finest hour – their Euro 92 championship triumph, when he argued about tactics with the coach and was dropped.

▲ *Lothar Matthäus, Europe's most-capped player.*

LOTHAR MATTHÄUS
West Germany / Germany, born 1961 Caps: 150 Goals: 23

Matthäus began his career at Borussia Mönchengladbach before moving to Bayern Munich in 1984. A powerful midfielder with great stamina, Matthäus could play as a midfield anchor or be more creative, using his passing and vision to bring others into the game. He won six Bundesliga titles at Bayern Munich, plus the Serie A title with Internazionale. A veteran of five World Cups, Matthäus played a record 25 tournament games. He led West Germany to World Cup glory in 1990 and in the same year he was voted World Footballer of the Year. He retired from international football after Euro 2000.

MARIO COLUNA
Portugal, born 1935
Caps: 57 Goals: 8

Like Eusebio, Mario Coluna was born in Mozambique and played for Portugal. Coluna was often overshadowed by the great striker, but he was a superb footballer in his own right. His 17-year-career with Benfica began in 1954. He captained the side in the early 1960s and appeared in five European Cup finals (1961–63, 1965 and 1968). He also led Portugal to third place in the 1966 World Cup. Coluna moved to Olympique Lyonnais towards the end of his career and later became Mozambique's minister of sport.

SUN WEN
China, born 1973
Caps: 152 Goals: 106

A legend in women's football, Sun Wen won seven regional championships with Chinese side Shanghai TV, before moving to the USA in 2000 to play for Atlanta Beat. Playing in midfield or attack, she has become one of the world's leading international goalscorers, thanks to her strong shooting, vision and eye for a goal. Sun Wen won both the Golden Boot (top scorer) and the Golden Ball (top player) awards at the 1999 Women's World Cup, where China were narrowly beaten on penalties in the final by the USA. In 2000, she was named FIFA World Player of the Century alongside the USA's Michelle Akers. After China's surprise World Cup exit at the hands of Canada in 2003, she retired.

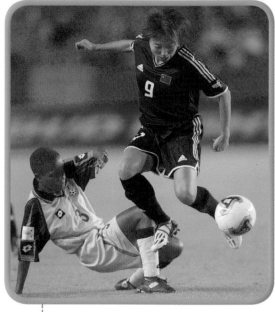

▲ *Sun Wen goes past Ghana's Mavis Danso at the 2003 World Cup. China won the game 1-0, courtesy of a goal from Sun.*

JAIRZINHO
Brazil, born 1944
Caps: 82 Goals: 34

Jair Ventura Filho, better known as Jairzinho, was an electrifying right-winger in a similar mould to his childhood hero, Garrincha. First capped for Brazil in 1964, he was moved to the left wing to accommodate Garrincha in the 1966 World Cup. At the 1970 tournament Jairzinho was moved back to his favoured right side, where he shone, scoring in each of the six rounds of the competition – a record to this day. At club level, Jairzinho spent most of his career at Brazil's Botafogo, also having short spells with Marseille in France, Portuguesa in Venezuela and the Brazilian side Cruzeiro, with whom he won the Copa America in 1976.

◀ *Jairzinho surges forwards during the third-place play-off at the 1974 World Cup. Brazil were defeated 1-0 by Poland.*

STRIKERS

JOHAN CRUYFF
Holland, born 1947
Caps: 48 Goals: 33

Cruyff was one of the game's finest ever players and a pivotal part of the Dutch 'total football' revolution. Blessed with great vision and remarkable ball skills, he is the only player to have a move named after him – the Cruyff turn. He won three European Cups in a row at Ajax, before following his old boss, Rinus Michels, to Barcelona in 1973 and helping them to win Spanish league and cup titles. Cruyff played as a centre-forward, but would drift around the pitch, creating confusion among defenders. His total of 33 goals for Holland would have been higher were it not for his refusal to play in the 1978 World Cup (see page 112). Cruyff later managed both Ajax and Barcelona to success in Europe.

► *Johan Cruyff was European Footballer of the Year three times.*

PAOLO ROSSI
Italy, born 1956
Caps: 48 Goals: 20

As a teenager, Paolo Rossi was released by Juventus due to a knee injury, but he went on to star for Italy at the 1978 World Cup. Juve tried to buy him back from Vicenza, but were outbid by Perugia, who paid a world-record fee of £3.5 million. A two-year ban for alleged match-fixing ended just before the 1982 World Cup, by which time Rossi was back at Juventus. After failing to score in the first four games of the tournament, the pressure was mounting. He responded with a fine hat-trick against Brazil, followed by two goals in the semi-final and one in the final to emerge as a World Cup winner and the tournament's leading scorer. Sadly, he was overcome by injuries and he retired in 1987, aged 30.

▼ *Puskas (left) fires in a shot in the 1954 World Cup final against West Germany. His goalscoring ratio at international level – almost one goal per game – was extraordinary.*

FACTFILE In his distinguished career, Puskas won five Spanish league titles, four Hungarian league titles, an Olympic gold medal (1952) and three European Cups.

FERENC PUSKAS
Hungary, born 1927
Caps: 84 (4 for Spain)
Goals: 83

A star for his club, Kispest (which became Honved), and his country, Puskas was short, stocky and an average header of the ball. But his sublime skills, vision and thunderbolt of a left-foot shot made him a devastating striker. After the Hungarian revolution in 1956, Puskas searched for a club in western Europe for more than a year. In his thirties and overweight, he was eventually signed by Real Madrid in 1958. He repaid Real's faith by heading the Spanish goalscoring table four times, netting four goals in the 1960 European Cup final and a hat-trick in the 1962 final. In 1966, he began a coaching career, which saw him take Greek side Panathinaikos to the 1971 European Cup final. In 1993, an emotional Puskas was welcomed home to act as caretaker manager of the national team.

FACTFILE George Best made 466 appearances for Manchester United between 1963 and 1974, scoring 178 goals. He was a substitute only once.

GEORGE BEST
Northern Ireland, 1946–2005
Caps: 37 Goals: 9

Best was just 17 when he made his first-team debut for Manchester United. He was the most gifted player to emerge from the British Isles, and its first superstar. A free spirit both on and off the pitch, Best's goalscoring exploits and his eye for an outrageous pass or move quickly made him a legend. He was also a fearless tackler and great dribbler, and was Manchester United's leading scorer five seasons in a row. Sadly, he was denied the biggest stage of all as Northern Ireland failed to qualify for the World Cup during his playing career. In 1974, Best sensationally retired from the game. He made a series of comebacks in England, the USA and, finally, Australia, where he appeared for the Brisbane Lions in 1983.

◄ *George Best was first capped for his country, Northern Ireland, at the tender age of 17.*

ROBERTO BAGGIO
Italy, born 1967
Caps: 57 Goals: 27

Blessed with great skill and vision, Roberto Baggio made his professional debut with Vicenza, in the Italian third division, at just 15 years of age. He broke into Serie A with Fiorentina in 1985, but when Baggio was transferred to Juventus in 1990, Fiorentina fans rioted for three days. The fee of £7.7 million made him the world's most expensive player at the time. Crowned World Footballer of the Year in 1993, Baggio scored spectacular goals for his country and the Italian clubs AC Milan, Bologna and Internazionale. In 2004, while playing for Brescia, he scored his 200th Serie A goal. He appeared in three World Cups and scored five of Italy's eight goals in the 1994 competition. However, Baggio will always be remembered for his costly penalty miss in the final of that tournament (see pages 32–33). The striker was given an emotional international send-off in 2004, when he played for Italy for the first time in five years, in a friendly against Spain.

► Baggio chases the ball in his final game for Italy.

DENNIS BERGKAMP
Holland, born 1969
Caps: 79 Goals: 37

Named after the Scottish striker Denis Law, Bergkamp was a product of the famous Ajax youth academy. He played in the Dutch league for the first time in 1986. The most technically gifted Dutch footballer since Johan Cruyff, Bergkamp often plays in the space between midfield and attack, where he uses his eye for an unexpected pass, plus world-class technique, to create as many goals as he scores. After a transfer to Italy failed to see him keep the form of his early career, Bergkamp moved to Arsenal for £7.5 million in 1995 and he has celebrated a decade with the London club, winning three Premier League titles along the way. In 1998, he was voted England's Footballer of the Year.

▲ Dennis Bergkamp brings the ball down moments before his sublime goal against Argentina at the 1998 World Cup.

FACTFILE Dennis Bergkamp's fear of flying has caused the striker to miss many international matches and European games for Arsenal.

Roa

Ayala 2

Bergkamp 1

Bergkamp 2

Ayala 1

MATCH ACTION

Dennis Bergkamp broke the deadlock in a tense 1998 World Cup quarter-final against Argentina with a sensational goal. On the stroke of 90 minutes, Frank de Boer hit a 50-metre pass into the penalty area. Controlling the ball with one delicate touch of his right boot, Bergkamp took a second touch to turn Argentinian defender Roberto Ayala, before shooting powerfully past keeper Carlos Roa. The goal saw Bergkamp become Holland's leading international scorer.

RAÚL
Spain, born 1977
Caps: 83 Goals: 41

Raúl González Blanco made his debut for the Real Madrid first team at 17 – their youngest ever player – and went on to score six times in his first 11 games. In the years that followed, Raúl became the biggest star in Spanish football and the country's all-time leading goalscorer. At club level, he has won two Spanish league championships and three Champions League titles with Real Madrid. Top scorer in the Spanish league twice, Raúl's goals in the 2003–04 Champions League campaign saw him become the first player to net more than 40 times in the competition.

GERD MÜLLER
West Germany, born 1945
Caps: 62 Goals: 68

The Bomber, as Gerd Müller was nicknamed, holds a series of goalscoring records. From 1963, he scored a club record 365 goals in 427 league matches for Bayern Munich. During 16 years with Bayern, he won four Bundesliga titles, four German Cups and three European Cups. For his country, Müller held one of the greatest international striking records, scoring more than a goal every game. His two strikes against the Soviet Union helped West Germany win the 1972 European Championships. Müller's tally of 14 goals from two World Cups remains a record, while his final international goal won West Germany the 1974 World Cup on home soil.

▼ *Gerd Müller shoots during West Germany's win over Morocco in the 1970 World Cup.*

▲ *Spain's Raúl was the top scorer during the qualifying rounds for Euro 2000, with ten goals from eight games. Here, he chases down the ball during Euro 2004.*

▲ *Fontaine is chaired off the pitch after scoring four goals in France's 6-3 defeat of West Germany in the third-place play-off at the 1958 World Cup.*

JUST FONTAINE
France, born 1933
Caps: 21 Goals: 30

Fontaine was born and brought up in Morocco before coming to France in 1953 to play for Nice. A relatively slight centre-forward with a real eye for goal, he scored 45 times in three seasons at Nice before moving to Stade de Reims, where he bagged 116 goals in just four years. Yet, going into the 1958 World Cup finals, Fontaine was third-choice striker behind Raymond Kopa and René Bliard. An injury to Bliard allowed Fontaine to start the first game, against Paraguay, in which he scored a hat-trick. He followed this up with a further ten goals in five games. His record of 13 goals at a single World Cup is unlikely to be beaten. In 1962, Fontaine retired after suffering the second double fracture of his right leg. The following year, he became the first president of the French footballers' union.

ZICO
Brazil, born 1953
Caps: 72 Goals: 52

The youngest and smallest of three football-mad brothers, Artur Antunes Coimbra (known as Zico) was given a special diet and training regime to build him up when he first arrived at the Brazilian club Flamengo. Sharp, quick-witted and with the ability to hit an explosive shot or take a deadly, curling free kick, Zico won four Brazilian league titles with Flamengo, as well as the Copa Libertadores and the World Club Cup (both in 1981). He scored a staggering 591 goals in his first 11 seasons with Flamengo and returned to the club in 1985 after a spell at the Italian Serie A side Udinese. Zico retired from international football after the 1986 World Cup finals, but went on to play in Japan for Kashima Antlers. In 2002, he became manager of the Japanese national team.

BOBBY CHARLTON
England, born 1937
Caps: 106 Goals: 49

Apart from a final season with Preston North End, Charlton was a one-club player with Manchester United, for whom he made his debut in 1956. Known around the globe for his trophy-winning exploits in both the World Cup and the European Cup, Charlton was one of the few survivors of the devastating Munich air crash, which claimed the lives of many of his Manchester United team-mates. As a player he showed great sportsmanship and dedication – in training, he even wore a slipper on his right foot to encourage him to pass and shoot with his weaker left foot. Operating as a deep-lying centre-forward with a phenomenal shot from either foot, Charlton remains the record goalscorer for both England and Manchester United, scoring 245 times and making 751 appearances in total for the club. He was knighted in 1994.

▼ Bobby Charlton's 1970 World Cup campaign was his fourth in a row as part of the England squad.

◀ Roger Milla challenges for the ball during Cameroon's second-round victory over Colombia at the 1990 World Cup

FACTFILE In 1990, Andriy Shevchenko played for the Kiev under-14 team in a youth tournament in Wales. Welsh striker Ian Rush was so impressed, he gave the young Ukrainian his football boots.

ROGER MILLA
Cameroon, born c.1952
Caps: 81 Goals: 42

Roger Milla's celebratory corner-flag dance remains the most memorable image of the 1990 World Cup, as his four goals helped Cameroon to become the first African side to reach the quarter-finals. In the same year, the veteran striker was voted the African Footballer of the Year. He had won the award before, way back in 1976, the year he moved from Cameroon's Tonnerre Yaoundé to play for Valenciennes in France. Milla went on to play for Monaco, Bastia and Saint Etienne, and won the African Nations Cup twice with Cameroon (1984 and 1988). At the age of 42, he came out of retirement for the 1994 World Cup to become the oldest ever player and scorer in the competition.

ANDRIY SHEVCHENKO
Ukraine, born 1976
Caps: 58 Goals: 26

Shevchenko scored just one goal in 16 games in his first season in the Dynamo Kiev first team. He later made amends with a succession of goalscoring feats to propel Kiev to five Ukrainian league titles and strong showings in the Champions League. A multi-million-pound transfer to AC Milan followed in 1999 for the striker who has a perfect blend of pace and power. On three occasions Shevchenko scored 24 goals per season in what is regarded as an ultra-tough league for attackers. In 2004, after another outstanding campaign with Milan, Shevchenko was voted European Footballer of the Year.

▲ Andriy Shevchenko shoots for Ukraine against England during a friendly international in 2000.

CAROLINA MORACE
Italy, born 1964
Caps: 153 Goals: 105

Italy's finest female player, Morace made her international and Women's Serie A debut at the age of just 14. She went on to win 12 league titles with eight different clubs, and scored more than 500 goals. A lethal finisher, Morace was twice a runner-up with Italy in the European Championships. After retiring in 1999, she became the first female coach of an Italian men's professional team, Viterbese in Serie C. She later became coach of the Italian women's national side.

▲ *Ruud Gullit shoots against England at Euro 88.*

RUUD GULLIT
Holland, born 1962
Caps: 66 Goals: 17

In 1978, the dreadlocked Gullit started out as a sweeper for Dutch side Haarlem. He possessed great attacking flair, stamina, a tough tackle and a sweet pass. He was the subject of feverish transfer activity, moving to Feyenoord, PSV Eindhoven and AC Milan, with whom he won European Cups in 1989 and 1990. After a season at Sampdoria he moved to Chelsea, and in 1996 he was appointed player-manager of the London club. By winning the 1997 FA Cup he became the first non-British manager to lift a major domestic trophy in England.

KENNY DALGLISH
Scotland, born 1951
Caps: 102 Goals: 30

The only player to have scored over 100 goals for both English and Scottish top-division clubs, Dalglish gave defenders nightmares. He became a legend at Celtic – where he won four league titles and four Scottish Cups – thanks to a quicksilver turn and an icy coolness in front of goal. In 1977, Liverpool signed Dalglish as a replacement for Kevin Keegan. He became Liverpool's player-manager in 1985, winning three league titles. He won a fourth in 1995 with Blackburn Rovers to become one of the few managers to win the English league with different clubs.

DIEGO MARADONA
Argentina, born 1960
Caps: 91 Goals: 34

Diego Armando Maradona was a phenomenal footballer. Stocky and with a low centre of gravity, he conjured mesmeric, weaving runs through the tightest defences, lightning turns that left opposition players kicking at thin air and sublime shots, chips and flicks. Maradona debuted aged 15 for Argentinos Juniors. Calls for his inclusion in the 1978 World Cup squad were ignored by Argentina's coach, Cesar Luis Menotti, but he would appear at the next four tournaments. His finest hour came in 1986, when Maradona was the player of the tournament as he skippered an unremarkable side to World Cup victory (see pages 56–57). Maradona captained Argentina at the 1990 World Cup, where he reached the final, but the following year he failed a drugs test and was banned for 15 months. A further failed test during the 1994 World Cup saw him sent home after playing the first two games. His international career was over. Since then Maradona has battled with drug addiction, but in 2000 he was the joint winner of FIFA's Footballer of the Century award with Pelé.

FACTFILE Diego Maradona's moves to Barcelona in 1982 (for £4.2 million) and then to Napoli in 1984 (for £6.9 million) were both world-record transfers. After nine years at Napoli and a spell at Sevilla, he returned to Argentina with Newell's Old Boys and Boca Juniors.

▼ *The magical Maradona brings the ball under control at the 1986 World Cup.*

▲ *As well as appearing for Real Madrid (pictured) and Spain, di Stefano also played seven unofficial games for Argentina and four for Colombia.*

ALFREDO DI STEFANO
Spain, born 1926
Caps: 31 Goals: 23

To many people, di Stefano was the complete player, years ahead of his time. His astonishing energy helped him play all over the pitch – defending, tackling, unselfishly distributing the ball and creating chances for others as well as for himself. Born in a poor suburb of Buenos Aires, he played for his father's old club, River Plate, in a relentless forward line known as *La Maquina* (the Machine). A move to Europe in 1953 saw him become part of the legendary Real Madrid side that dominated Europe in the 1950s and early 1960s. Di Stefano formed a deadly partnership with Ferenc Puskas, scoring in five European Cup finals in a row. Real Madrid player and coach Miguel Munoz explained: 'The greatness of di Stefano was that with him in your side, you had two players in every position.'

JÜRGEN KLINSMANN
**West Germany / Germany,
born 1964 Caps: 108 Goals: 47**

Sharp and athletic around the penalty area and an outstanding goal poacher, Klinsmann was German Footballer of the Year in his first spell at VfB Stuttgart. He then moved to Internazionale, where he won the 1989 Serie A title. He was part of West Germany's 1990 World Cup-winning side, scored five goals in the 1994 competition and captained the team at the 1998 tournament. Klinsmann enjoyed spells with Monaco and, in 1994, the first of two stints with Tottenham Hotspur. The British media and some supporters were suspicious of a player who had a reputation for diving to win free kicks and penalties. But in his first Premiership season, Klinsmann's performances and 29 goals won the support of many fans, and in 1995 he was voted England's Footballer of the Year. The striker made moves to Bayern Munich, Sampdoria and Tottenham Hotspur once more, before retiring in 1998. In 2004, he was appointed Germany's manager for the 2006 World Cup campaign.

▲ Jürgen Klinsmann surges forwards with the ball during Germany's Euro 96 qualifying campaign.

EUSEBIO
**Portugal, born 1942
Caps: 64 Goals: 41**

Eusebio da Silva Ferreira was the first African footballing superstar. Lethal in the air and equipped with a power-packed right-foot shot, he scored an incredible 727 goals in 715 professional games. Eusebio played his early football for Sporting Lourenço Marques in his home country of Mozambique – a Portuguese colony at the time. The striker was at the centre of one of the fiercest transfer disputes when he arrived in Portugal. He was virtually kidnapped by Benfica to keep him away from rivals Sporting Lisbon. Benfica's £7,500 purchase proved to be one of the buys of the century. Over a 15-year career with Benfica, Eusebio scored at an awe-inspiring ratio of more than a goal a game. He was the Portuguese league's top goalscorer seven times, twice the leading goalscorer in the whole of Europe and the 1966 World Cup's top scorer, with nine goals for Portugal.

LUIGI RIVA
**Italy, born 1944
Caps: 42 Goals: 35**

Luigi Riva started his career with Italy's Legnano, before moving in 1963 to second-division side Cagliari, where he spent the rest of his career. He helped the Sardinian team gain promotion to Serie A and then to win the 1970 league title. Riva was Serie A's leading scorer three times (1967, 1969 and 1970). He was part of the Italian side that won Euro 68 and was the national team's leading goalscorer at the 1970 World Cup. Riva then suffered a broken leg that kept him out of action for six months, but he returned in 1971 to score his 170th league goal. Two years later, he turned down what would have been the world's biggest transfer – for £1.5 million to Juventus. After playing in the 1974 World Cup, Riva announced his retirement.

FACTFILE Luigi Riva had such a fearsome shot that he once broke the arm of a spectator.

▲ Benfica's Eusebio (right) competes for the ball with Cesare Maldini of AC Milan during the 1963 European Cup final.

GEORGE WEAH
**Liberia, born 1966
Caps: 61 Goals: 22**

In 1988, the Monaco manager Arsène Wenger (now at Arsenal), shrewdly plucked the young, raw Weah from Cameroon side Tonnerre Yaoundé. Weah exploded onto the European scene, winning the French league with Monaco in 1991 and Paris Saint Germain in 1994, before moving to AC Milan. A truly devastating finisher, Weah scored many spectacular goals to help AC Milan win two Serie A titles. He was voted African Footballer of the Year four times, and also won European and World Player of the Year awards in 1995 and FIFA's Fair Play Award the following year. He had short spells at Chelsea, Manchester City and in the United Arab Emirates late in his career, before retiring in 2002. A UNICEF ambassador since 1997, Weah has invested much time and money helping to build schools and clinics in his war-torn home country, Liberia.

FACTFILE In 1996, George Weah paid for his team-mates' kit and expenses so that Liberia could enter the African Nations Cup.

RONALDO
Brazil, born 1976
Caps: 87 Goals: 56

Ronaldo Luis Nazario de Lima became seriously hot property as an 18-year-old by scoring 58 goals in just 60 games for Brazil's Cruzeiro. Still in his teens, Ronaldo moved to PSV Eindhoven and, later, to Barcelona, where his great close control and devastating bursts of pace helped him become Europe's top scorer in the 1996–97 season, with 34 goals. He was sold to Internazionale for more than £18 million and was their top scorer in his first season. However, he then endured four injury-ravaged years, playing only a quarter of Inter's games. After a disappointing performance in the 1998 World Cup final, many doubted his ability to perform at the highest level, but he bounced back to become the 2002 tournament's top scorer. In August 2002, Real Madrid paid £28.49 million for the Brazilian.

FACTFILE
Ronaldo's ex-wife, Milene Domingues, broke the world record for keeping a football off the ground in 1995. She kept the ball in the air for nine hours and six minutes, making 55,187 touches in the process.

▼ Ronaldo shows his pace against Italy. In 2002, he won his third FIFA World Player of the Year award.

MIA HAMM
USA,
born 1972
Caps: 276
Goals: 158

Born with a partial club foot that had to be corrected by plaster casts, Mia Hamm went on to become the world's most famous female footballer. She was the youngest ever player for the US women's team when she debuted against China at the age of 15, and the youngest member of the US side that won the 1991 World Cup. Hamm played in three more World Cups, as well as winning two Olympic gold medals and one silver. A phenomenal all-round player with an icy-cool finish, she is the leading scorer in the history of women's international football. Hamm was also a founding member of WUSA, playing for Washington Freedom when the league began in 2001.

HENRIK LARSSON
Sweden, born 1971
Caps: 82 Goals: 32

A terrific goalscoring predator, Larsson played for Högaborg and Helsingborg in Sweden before being signed by Feyenoord manager Wim Jansen in 1993. After four years with the Dutch side he was signed again by Jansen, who was by this time manager of Celtic. Larsson soon became the Scottish Premier League's most feared striker. He scored 28 or more goals in five of his seven seasons in Scotland, as Celtic dominated the league. Larsson retired from international football following the 2002 World Cup, but changed his mind to help Sweden qualify for the 2004 European Championships. He moved from Celtic to Barcelona shortly after the tournament.

◄ The legendary Mia Hamm playing for the USA at the Women's Gold Cup in 2002. In the final against Canada, her golden goal in extra time secured the trophy.

MARIO KEMPES
Argentina, born 1954
Caps: 43 Goals: 20

Kempes was a powerful centre-forward who bristled with goalscoring intent. Having played for Instituto Córdoba and Rosario Central in his home country, Kempes moved to Spanish side Valencia in 1976 and was twice the top scorer in La Liga. Winner of the Golden Boot and the player of the tournament at the 1978 World Cup, he was the only European-based player in the Argentinian side that won the title. His second goal in the final against Holland showed his flair, as he made a surging run past three defenders. Returning to Argentina in 1981, he played for River Plate and for the national side at the 1982 World Cup, before embarking on a coaching career.

◄ Barcelona's Henrik Larsson battles for the ball during a 2004 friendly against Japan's Kashima Antlers. Barcelona won 5-0.

PELÉ
Brazil, born 1940
Caps: 92 Goals: 77

Edson Arantes do Nascimento simply had it all. Considered the finest footballer of all time, Pelé was a masterful attacker with seemingly limitless skills, creativity and vision. He was magnificent in the air, lethal on the ground, could dribble, pass and take swerving free kicks, and saw passes and opportunities that other players could not. His father had been a striker for Fluminense, and at 11 years of age Pelé was spotted by a former Brazil player, Waldemar de Brito, who took him to Clube Atletico Bauru. Four years later, Pelé trialled at Santos, for whom he made his debut aged 15. He would play for the São Paulo side for the next 18 years. Pelé was only 17 when he appeared at the 1958 World Cup, scoring a hat-trick in the semi-final and two superb goals in the final as Brazil won their first World Cup. A pulled muscle cut short Pelé's involvement in the 1962 competition and he had to be content with winning the World Club Cup for Santos. Injured by brutal tackling in the 1966 World Cup, Pelé was outstanding at the 1970 tournament. He retired from international football in 1971 – in front of around 180,000 fans at the Maracana Stadium – and from

club football in 1974. In tribute, Santos removed the number ten shirt from their team line-up.

Pelé later came out of retirement to play in a star-studded line-up at New York Cosmos. He went on to become Brazil's minister of sport and a UN and UNICEF ambassador. He remains one of the most respected figures in world football and, in 1999, he was voted Athlete of the Century by the International Olympic Committee.

▲ *Pelé wheels away in delight after scoring at the 1970 World Cup.*

> **FACTFILE** Pelé's father once scored five headed goals in one game, a feat Pelé never managed. However, his header in the 1970 World Cup final was Brazil's 100th World Cup goal.

MATCH ACTION

Against Uruguay in the 1970 World Cup semi-final, Pelé came close to scoring what would have been one of the greatest goals ever seen. A through pass from Gerson saw Pelé and the Uruguayan keeper, Ladislao Mazurkiewicz, racing for the ball just outside the penalty area. Pelé made an outrageous dummy to the left, letting the ball run to the other side of the bewildered keeper. The striker sprinted to collect the ball and hit a first-time shot from a tight angle. The ball sped past Uruguayan defender Atilio Ancheta, only to flash mere centimetres wide of the left post.

▲ *Germany's Birgit Prinz uses her agility to skip the tackle of Norway's Lise Klaveness in 2003.*

BIRGIT PRINZ
Germany, born 1977
Caps: 134 Goals: 83

Germany's best female footballer, Prinz is a tall centre-forward, imposing in the air but equally strong on the ground. With FFC Frankfurt she won the Women's Bundesliga title, the German Cup and, in 2002, the first UEFA Women's Cup. She then moved to the USA to play for Carolina Courage, scoring 12 goals in 15 games to help win the WUSA league title. With Germany she has won the European Championships three times and in 2003 she scored seven goals to propel her team to World Cup glory, finishing as the top scorer in the tournament. In the same year, she became FIFA World Women's Footballer of the Year, a title she retained in 2004.

GABRIEL BATISTUTA
Argentina, born 1969
Caps: 77 Goals: 56

Batistuta played one season for each of his home country's three biggest clubs – Newell's Old Boys, River Plate and Boca Juniors – before moving to Italy in 1991, the year of his international debut. In nine seasons and 269 games at Fiorentina, the striker was rarely off-form, netting 168 goals. He even stayed with the club after relegation, helping them win promotion back into Serie A. In 2000, he joined Roma for the huge fee of £22 million. There Batistuta finally won the Serie A title in 2001. A winner of two Copa Americas, Batistuta scored five goals at the 1998 World Cup as Argentina made the quarter-finals. The 2003–04 season saw him make a lucrative move to Qatar, where he played for Al-Arabi.

MARCO VAN BASTEN
Holland, born 1964
Caps: 58 Goals: 24

One of the coolest finishers in world football was just 29 when an ankle injury in the 1993 European Cup final effectively ended his playing career – although he struggled on until 1995. Renowned for spectacular goals in crucial contests, van Basten was European Footballer of the Year three times (1988, 1989 and 1992) and in 1988 he hit the headlines as Holland won the European Championships. He scored a hat-trick against England in the quarter-final, the semi-final winner versus Germany and a breathtaking volley from the tightest of angles in the final against the Soviet Union. With Ajax he won three league titles, scoring 128 goals. He then moved to AC Milan, hitting 90 goals in 147 games and winning three Serie A titles and two European Cups.

▶ *Marco van Basten on the rampage in Holland's 3-1 win over England at Euro 88.*

<table>
<tr><td colspan="4">LEADING INTERNATIONAL GOALSCORERS (TO 18/05/2005)</td></tr>
</table>

PLAYER	COUNTRY	CAPS	GOALS
Ali Daei	Iran	137	104
Ferenc Puskas	Hungary	84	83
Pelé	Brazil	92	77
Sandor Kocsis	Hungary	68	75
Gerd Müller	West Germany	62	68
Kiatisuk Senamuang	Thailand	117	64
Hassam Hossan	Egypt	163	64
Imre Schlosser-Lakatos	Hungary	68	59
Gabriel Batistuta	Argentina	77	56
Ronaldo	Brazil	87	56
Kazuyoshi Miura	Japan	91	56
Stern John	Trinidad	77	56

▲ *Argentina's all-time top scorer, Batistuta began the 1994–95 season by netting in each of Fiorentina's first 11 games, a Serie A record.*

HUGO SANCHEZ
Mexico, born 1958
Caps: 57 Goals: 26

Mexico's most famous player, Sanchez spent the peak of his playing career in Spain, scoring over 230 goals for Atlético Madrid and Real Madrid. He formed a lethal partnership with Emilio Butragueno at Real as they won five league titles in a row. Sanchez was La Liga's top scorer in five different seasons and in 1990 he won the European Golden Boot for a record 38 goals in one season. Sadly, his commitments to European football and frequent bust-ups with Mexican football officials meant that he appeared in only a fraction of the international games played by his home country. He had a disappointing tournament at the 1986 World Cup on home soil, scoring just one goal.

FACTFILE Playing for Manchester City in 1974, Denis Law scored a cheeky backheeled goal but did not celebrate – because the goal relegated his former club, Manchester United.

▲ *Denis Law unleashes a shot during a 1974 World Cup game against Zaire.*

DENIS LAW
Scotland, born 1940
Caps: 55 Goals: 30

In 1962, Manchester United paid £115,000 – a world record at the time – to bring the former Huddersfield Town, Manchester City and Torino striker Denis Law to Old Trafford. The money was well spent, as the quick-witted Scot formed a magnificent forward line with Bobby Charlton and George Best, scoring 160 goals in 222 games for the club. Fast over the ground and brave in the air, Law won the 1964 European Footballer of the Year award, as well as league titles and the European Cup with Manchester United, before moving to Manchester City and then retiring in 1974.

MARADONA'S WORLD CUP

Diego Maradona, the Argentinian striker with magical balance and touch, ended the 1986 World Cup with his hands on the trophy and a highly impressive five goals and five assists. Yet these statistics do not tell the story of his true impact, for Mexico 86 was Maradona's tournament. He roused a relatively ordinary Argentinian side into recapturing football's biggest prize (the South Americans had won the trophy on home soil in 1978) and wiped out the memory of a disappointing tournament in 1982.

In a tense quarter-final against England, controversy raged over Maradona's infamous 'Hand of God' goal (see right), but his second and winning goal was pure genius. The Argentinian collected the ball in his own half, then dribbled, twisted and turned through the English defence to score what was later voted the goal of the century. He would score a goal of similar brilliance in the semi-final versus Belgium. At this point, at the age of just 25, Maradona was without doubt the greatest footballer on the planet.

▲ Maradona deliberately handles the ball past England goalkeeper Peter Shilton to score Argentina's first goal in a 2-1 victory.

Diego Maradona, clutching the World Cup after his team's epic 3-2 victory over West Germany in the 1986 final, is carried around the Azteca Stadium on the shoulders of ecstatic Argentinian supporters.

THE BRAIN GAME

Football is a sport that calls for pace, power, stamina and skill, but it also demands mental agility. Footballers with the ability to think one step ahead of the opposition are highly prized, and such skills can win a match for their team. The same applies to managers and coaches. In the run-up to a match, they have several key decisions to make. They must decide who to select, which formation to play, and choose the tactics they will use in their bid to outwit the opposition.

TEAM SELECTION

To a casual spectator, team selection appears simple – just pick the team's best 11 footballers and tell them to play. With large squads of players, the truth is far more complex. Teams need flair, skill, composure, aggression, sound defensive skills and goalscoring abilities – all in the right quantities. Some players, despite being footballing superstars, may not play well with each other or work with the rest of the team, while other, less heralded players may actually perform a more effective job in a particular game. The way the opposition plays can dictate which players are selected, as can the fitness and performances of individuals. Star players, who would normally be first on the team sheet, may not be picked if they are recovering from injury or suffering from a lack of confidence or form. Both young, talented players emerging from the reserve team and experienced veterans at the end of their careers will have strong cases for a place in the side. It all adds up

▲ In 2000–01, Liverpool's 28-man squad played 61 games. No player appeared in all the matches. In 1983–84, their league and European Cup-winning team (above) played 66 games with a squad of just 16. Bruce Grobbelaar, Alan Kennedy, Sammy Lee and Alan Hansen appeared in every game.

▼ West Germany manager Josef 'Sepp' Herberger (right) is chaired off the field as his team wins the 1954 World Cup. Early in the competition, he sent out a weakened side that lost to favourites Hungary. Having already beaten Turkey, Herberger's gamble meant that his side got an easier draw, meeting Turkey again in a play-off that the Germans won 7-2.

to a complex puzzle that managers must solve. As the legendary Ajax and Holland coach Rinus Michels said, 'It is an art in itself to compose a starting team, finding the balance between creative players and those with destructive powers, and between defence, construction and attack – never forgetting the quality of the opposition and the specific pressures of each match.'

PICKING AND PLAYING

Picking the right players for the game ahead can be a tricky task. Managers are often criticized by fans for dropping a favourite player or not playing them in their favoured position. But they have to hold their nerve and go with what they feel is their best team for a particular match. Cesar Luis Menotti, for example, was attacked by the Argentinian public and media for refusing to include the teenage prodigy Maradona in his 1978 World Cup squad, fielding veteran striker Mario Kempes instead. But Menotti proved himself to be a strong-willed and clever coach, who surprised opponents with an exciting, attacking game, and his team went on to win the tournament by beating Holland in the final.

With large squads, coaches at the top sides often rotate and rest key players. In games against supposedly weaker opposition, they might field an understrength side. While resting your best players and giving youngsters first-team experience can bring benefits, it is a risky tactic. Liverpool manager Rafael Benitez discovered this in 2005, when his understrength side was knocked out of the FA Cup by Burnley.

FACTFILE FIFA changed its rules on substitutions in international friendlies in 2004, limiting a side to six subs. The move was prompted, in part, by the mass substitutions of England coach Sven-Goran Eriksson. In 2003, he made 11 substitutions during a game that Australia won 3-1.

SUBSTITUTIONS

Although they were allowed in some friendly matches, substitutes were not a feature of competitive games until the 1960s. Before this time, the lack of subs resulted in all sorts of heroics, from outfield players going in goal to footballers playing on in spite of a serious injury. One of the most famous examples is that of Manchester City's German goalkeeper

Bert Trautmann, who continued playing in the 1956 FA Cup final even though he had broken his neck. Today's managers have the chance to alter their team selection and tactics by making up to three substitutions in most competitions (more in friendly games). The timing and choice of substitutes can be crucial. They can bolster a winning side's momentum, help a defence to hold on to a lead or turn a losing team's fortunes around. In the 2002 World Cup, Philippe Troussier's second-half substitute, Hirosha Miroshima, took just three minutes to score the opening goal for Japan against Tunisia. Troussier's second sub, Daisuke Ichikawa, provided the cross for Japan's second goal.

◀ *Danish striker Jon Dahl Tomasson is often used as a substitute by AC Milan. During the 2002–03 Champions League (which Milan won), he came off the bench in the quarter-final against Ajax to score the injury-time winner.*

▲ *After leading South Korea to the semi-finals of the 2002 World Cup, Dutchman Guus Hiddink – a firm believer in attacking tactics – was made an honorary citizen of South Korea.*

▼ *With Manchester United losing 1-0 to Bayern Munich in the 1999 Champions League final, Alex Ferguson brought on Norwegian striker Ole Gunnar Solskjaer in the 81st minute. After another substitute, Teddy Sheringham, had equalized, Solskjaer scored this memorable winner in injury time.*

FORMATIONS

The way in which a team lines up on the pitch is known as its formation. The first football international, in 1872, saw two sides field heavily attacking formations. Scotland began playing in a 2-2-6 formation, with two backs, two half-backs (similar to midfielders) and six attackers. England went even further, playing 1-1-8 (eight forwards), but crowded goalmouths saw the game end 0-0.

EVOLVING TACTICS

Although England's eight forwards quickly became a thing of the past, attacker-heavy formations such as 2-3-5 persisted for over half a century. A change to the offside law in 1925 (see page 19) reduced the number of players needed between an attacker and the goal from three to two. It gave attackers more scoring chances and forced a rapid rethink for managers. None was quicker than Arsenal's Herbert Chapman, who, two days after a 7-0 loss to Newcastle, debuted his W-M formation (so named for the shapes the two groups of five players made). The change resulted in a 4-0 win

over West Ham. The W-M formation was effectively 3-2-2-3 and was adopted by many sides. Other teams played the *metodo* formation, devised by World Cup-winning Italian coach Vittorio Pozzo. It was also based on 2-3-5, but was effectively 2-3-2-3, with two of the forwards pulled back to link between midfield and attack and to defend against breaks by the opposition.

FOUR AT THE BACK

The arrival of four defenders at the back sounds like a negative formation, but it was first unveiled by the marvellous attacking Brazil side that won the 1958 World Cup. The Brazilian formation was actually 4-2-4, with two wingers up front feeding two central strikers. By the next World Cup, Brazil and many other sides were opting for a slightly less attacking 4-3-3 with an extra player to stop the midfield from being overrun. This formation can work with a single winger who switches flanks at will or it can feature two genuine wingers feeding a single striker. England won the 1966 World Cup playing 4-4-2 with no out-and-out wingers, but they had midfielders with the energy and stamina to add width to an

attack, as well as tucking in to defend when necessary. This formation is still widely used today. In the late 1980s and 1990s, AC Milan and Italy coach Arrigo Sacchi had success playing a modified 4-4-2 with the line of four defenders high up the pitch. In this 'pressing game', the defence tried to catch the opposition offside while the midfield closed down space. Juventus were one of several Italian clubs to copy this formation; playing it, they won Serie A and several European competitions.

◄ *Italy manager Arrigo Sacchi issues instructions to his players during a training session at the 1996 European Championships.*

▲ *The Serbia and Montenegro international Sinisa Mihajlovic (left) enjoyed six glorious seasons at Lazio as a powerful sweeper, strong in defence but with an eye for goal, especially from set pieces.*

SWEEPING UP

At many clubs around the world, and in Italian football especially, a different system is used at the back, with a sweeper (also known as a 'libero' or 'free man') in the centre of defence. Sweepers tend to play behind the main line of defenders, literally sweeping up loose balls and acting as a last line of defence if an opposition attack breaks through. In some formations, a sweeper can be ultra-negative. This was seen as the case with the *catenaccio* system, invented by Padova coach Nereo Rocco in the early 1950s and popularized by Helenio Herrera's Internazionale side of the 1960s. Effectively

◄ *Manchester City wing-back Shaun Wright-Phillips (now at Chelsea) powers past WBA's Paul Robinson. Wing-backs play on the flanks. They act as full-backs in defence, and also make attacking runs upfield.*

▲ Barcelona coach Ronald Koeman (left) and Ajax manager Frank Rijkaard shake hands before a game. As midfielders or defenders, the pair played in central defence in the Holland side that won Euro 88 by playing total football.

a 1-4-3-2 or 1-4-4-1 system, *catenaccio* aimed to stifle attacks with large numbers of defenders, relying on counter attacks by a few forwards. Italy has produced a long line of world-class sweepers including Giovanni Facchetti, Gaetano Scirea and Franco Baresi. But it took a German, Franz Beckenbauer, to show a different side to the

▲ A team often alters its formation after a sending-off. This side has lost its left midfielder (shown by the red arrow) and switches from a 3-2-3-2 system with wing-backs to a 4-3-1-1 formation with a flat back four, three in midfield and split strikers up front.

sweeper's art. Beckenbauer linked play going forward and would often surge ahead of his defence, creating an extra player in

attack and opening up the game. Since Beckenbauer's time, footballers such as Ronald Koeman, Lothar Matthäus and Switzerland's Ciriaco Sforza have mastered the position, while Traianos Dellas successfully operated as a sweeper in Greece's winning team at the 2004 European Championships.

TOTAL FOOTBALL

'Total football' was never quite formation-free football, but it did involve players switching positions and roles within the team with amazing frequency. Under Rinus Michels, defenders would crop up in attack, strikers in midfield and midfielders just about everywhere. It proved a hard system to defend against, but few sides could boast the quality of player to make it work, as it relied on excellent ball skills and very high energy levels. Today, players switch positions with remarkable ease and regularity, so much so that one might wonder why total football caused such a stir. Formations in the past were more rigid, however, with full-backs staying in their half and strikers staying upfield throughout the game. While this gave a team a shape and structure, it could also make it easier for opponents to mark dangerous players and defend.

FORMATIONS

A formation is the way in which a team lines up for a match. This is usually shown in terms of the numbers of outfield players from the defence forwards. In reality, football is a dynamic game and players move around the pitch. Sometimes, they are drawn out of position by an opposition attack. At other times, players choose to move out of position. For example, a central striker may drift out wide or drop back to find space.

3-2-2-3 formation

3-5-2 formation

4-4-2 formation

4-2-4 formation

TACTICS

Teams may kick off a game in one of several common formations, but there can be great variation in how they play within that formation and in the tactics they use. For example, a team that lines up as a 4-4-2 side may choose to play defensively, with midfielders tucking in, or aggressively, with one or more midfielders joining the strikers in attack.

TAILORING TACTICS

Managers start a game with what they feel are the best tactics for the players available and the opposition they face. They watch how a match unfolds closely, knowing they can change tactics at any time to exploit an opponent's weakness or to fix problems in their own team's play. Most top footballers can play in several positions. A manager may switch formations using the same players or bring on a substitute with different attributes and skills. In the 2004–05 Champions League epic between Chelsea and Barcelona, Chelsea manager José Mourinho started with one striker up front and the other tucked in behind to harass Barcelona's playmaker, Xavi. This tactic led directly to Chelsea's first goal. Later in the game, Mourinho removed the second striker in favour of a central defender to close out the game, which Chelsea won 4-2.

TACTICS IN DEFENCE

Teams have several choices about how they defend. Some managers prefer defenders to patrol areas of space that overlap, a system known as zonal marking. This tactic is

often used by Argentinian clubs and many national sides. It requires good communication between defenders. Alternatively, each defender marks an individual player, tracking their opponent's attacking runs throughout the game. Greece used this system, known as man-marking, to good effect at Euro 2004. They man-marked both French strikers, David Trezeguet and Thierry Henry, for example, a tactic that contributed to their 1-0 victory. When an opposing team features a dangerous playmaker positioned behind the strikers, a side may nominate a midfield player to man-mark him or her.

▲ *Michael Essien of Lyon is put under pressure by Celtic's Stilian Petrov during a 2003–04 Champions League game. Dynamic midfielders such as Essien are in great demand, as they can play the role of midfield anchor, breaking up opposition attacks and launching attacks of their own. He now plays for Chelsea.*

▶ *The offside trap is a defensive tactic in which the back three or four players move upfield in a straight line to catch an opponent offside. It can be very effective, but may be beaten by a player dribbling through the line or by a well-timed through pass combined with an attacking run.*

MATCH ACTION

A goal down and under pressure from a Danish attack down their right wing, Senegal scored a superb counter-attacking goal at the 2002 World Cup. Senegal's Henri Camara made a firm tackle on Martin Jorgensen and played a quick pass down the wing to El Hadji Diouf. Diouf, closely marked by Jan Heintze, spotted Salif Diao's run and backheeled the ball into his path. Diao hit a perfect pass to Khalilou Fadiga, who was sprinting into the centre circle. As Diao continued his run, Fadiga took the ball into the Danish half before playing a perfectly timed through pass. Racing between two defenders, Diao latched onto the ball and coolly dispatched it into the corner of the goal.

LONG OR SHORT

All teams seek to pass and move the ball into the attacking third of the pitch, where goalscoring chances can be fashioned. The way in which they get the ball there can vary greatly. For many decades, British teams favoured a direct style with few passes. Managers believed that hitting long balls towards tall target strikers in the opponent's penalty area created more goal chances, often through a defensive mistake. In continental Europe and elsewhere, a shorter, passing-and-moving game was often preferred, with sides keeping possession for relatively long periods as they looked for an opening in the opposition defence. Another tactic, originally favoured by many Central and South American teams, is to rely on pinpoint passing and skilful dribbling to get into the opposition penalty area. Some teams play a counter-attacking game, defending in large numbers and soaking up pressure. When they retrieve the ball, they move it rapidly out of defence with a long pass or by running with the ball. Fast, accurate counter attacking can catch the opposition off guard and outnumbered, but requires players with good pace and awareness. Many coaches mix up their passing and movement tactics – if their team is behind with only minutes to go, for example, they may switch to a direct style, pushing extra players up into the opposition penalty area to look for headers and knock-downs.

◀ *Portugal's Cristiano Ronaldo practises free kicks at a training camp ahead of Euro 2004. He is watched by team-mates Deco Souza (left) and Rui Costa (right), as well as coach Luiz Felipe Scolari.*

HIT THE NET

www.thecoachingcorner.com/soccer/index.html
A thorough grounding in the laws of the game and the key tactics.

www.pags.org/coaches/articles/43768.html
A short article on the key ways in which a player or team can attack without falling foul of the offside trap.

http://sportsvl.com/soccer/general/training.html
Links to football sites, many covering training, tactics and formations.

Fadiga 2

Diao 2

FACTFILE With half an hour to go in a 1957 English league game, Charlton Athletic were down to ten men and losing 5–1 to Huddersfield Town. But an astonishing comeback, featuring four goals from Johnny Summers, saw them triumph 7–6.

▶ *Bayer Leverkusen defender Boris Zivkovic (left) challenges Ruud van Nistelrooy of Manchester United. The Croatian-born Zivkovic often plays as a man-marker, sticking close to the opposition team's most threatening attacker.*

THE MANAGER'S ROLE

A successful team needs more than great tactics. It needs to be prepared, instructed and inspired to produce a great performance. Motivating players, directing them and giving them the confidence to perform is all part of a manager's job. Crucially, managers can determine the tone, style and attitude of their side through the players they buy and send out onto the pitch, as well as through their work on the training ground.

THE TEAM BEHIND THE TEAM

Behind the footballers at a major club or national side is a large team of staff. At the helm is the manager and his assistant coaches, some of whom may specialize in training goalkeepers or strikers, or may specifically work with younger players and youth teams. A top club will also include a fitness coach, a dietician and one or more physiotherapists and medical staff to help with players' preparation and recovery

▲ José Mourinho (second left), became Chelsea manager in 2004. Here, he unveils his coaching team. Assistant manager Steve Clarke (second right) was the only survivor from the coaching set-up of former manager Claudio Ranieri.

from injury. Videos of games that interest the management are studied in detail, while scouts are employed to check out and report on forthcoming opposition sides and to watch potential transfer targets in action. Many clubs and national teams also arrange visits from temporary personnel such as sports psychologists, balance and co-ordination specialists, as well as inspirational figures from other sports.

INS AND OUTS

With football clubs becoming increasingly big businesses, a manager's ability to deal profitably and successfully in the transfer market is essential. Some managers are highly prized for their ability to buy players cheaply and sell them for profit or to put together a team on a limited budget that can seriously challenge for honours. European Cup-winning manager Brian Clough was famous for working wonders with bargain buys. Scottish legend Archie Gemmill cost Clough's Derby side £66,000, while striker Gary Birtles was bought by Clough at Nottingham Forest for £2,000 in 1978 and sold to Manchester United two years later for £1.25 million. Many modern managers and clubs also have an eye for a bargain. Porto brought relatively unknown striker Mario Jardel from Gremio in Brazil in the 1996–97 season. The South American scored a staggering 130 goals

▶ Italian club Lecce paid just over £11,000 for young Bulgarian striker Valeri Bojinov (left) in 2002. It proved good business – three years later, they sold him to Fiorentina for more than £9 million.

> **FACTFILE** Irishman Tony Cascarino was sold in 1982 by Crockenhill FC to Gillingham for a new club strip and some corrugated iron to patch up the ground. The total cost was said to be £180.

in 125 appearances for the Portuguese side. Arsenal manager Arsène Wenger bought Nicolas Anelka in 1997 for £500,000; two years later, he was sold to Real Madrid for £23.5 million. Other managers are rated for their ability to bring promising youngsters through from their youth set-ups or to attract good players on loan from other clubs to help strengthen their side.

UNDER PRESSURE

Few people in sport are under as much pressure as the manager of a major club or national side. Managers stand or fall by their results. In the past, some managers stayed at clubs for season after season. Miguel Munoz, for example, managed Real Madrid for 417 games during the 1960s. At the top level today, few coaches stay in charge of the best teams for more than a handful of seasons.

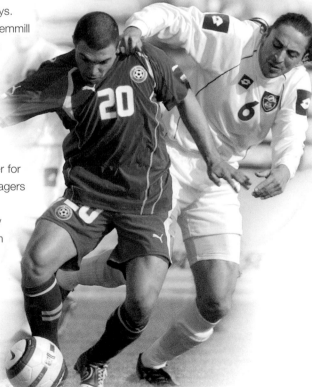

In the English league, there were more than 450 managerial changes between 2000 and the end of 2004. As of March 2005, the longest-serving managers in Italy and Germany had been in their posts for less than three seasons. Even recent success does not guarantee a long stay. Bobby Robson had taken Sporting Lisbon to the top of the Portuguese league when a shock loss to Casino Salzburg in the UEFA Cup saw him sacked in December 1993. Real Madrid's Vicente del Bosque had delivered two Spanish league titles, two Champions League trophies and other cups to the Spanish giants in just four years, but was dismissed in June 2003. In such an unforgiving climate, Alex Ferguson's record of more than 1,000 games in charge of Manchester United is quite remarkable.

▲ Ronaldo celebrates with the European Cup-Winners' Cup alongside Barcelona manager Bobby Robson. Robson has had a highly successful career as a manager since 1967.

◄ Bora Milutinovic has led five different countries to successive World Cups – a unique achievement in football management.

MANAGERIAL MIGRATIONS

Like modern players, top managers often move abroad to further their coaching careers. England are one of the few top national teams to have a foreign coach (Sven-Goran Eriksson), but many countries below the highest tier rely on the experience of foreign managerial talent. In the past, British coaches were influential abroad. Willy Garbutt helped shape Genoa into a powerful side, while Fred Pentland coached Athletic Bilbao to Spanish league success in 1930 and 1931. Jimmy Hogan, who used pass-and-move tactics years ahead of his time, worked with Austrian coaching legend Hugo Miesl to set up the Vienna School of attractive football. This created the Austrian *Wunderteam* that remained unbeaten in 14 internationals and narrowly missed out on glory at the 1934 World Cup and 1936 Olympics. Today, managers and coaches swap countries and continents frequently. Argentina's Hector Cuper managed Internazionale, Brazilian legend Zico has coached in Japan and Italian manager Cesare Maldini assisted Paraguay at the 2002 World Cup. Few globetrotting managers can compete with the Serbian Bora Milutinovic, however. He has taken five countries to World Cups (Mexico in 1986, Costa Rica in 1990, the USA in 1994, Nigeria in 1998 and China in 2002).

▼ Most national team bosses have had managerial experience at club level. Jürgen Klinsmann (right), Germany's coach at the 2006 World Cup, is an exception. He had never coached a major club side before his appointment in 2004.

▲ Globetrotting Frenchman Philippe Troussier has successfully coached Nigeria, South Africa and Japan, as well as managing club sides in Europe.

GREAT MANAGERS

There have been dozens of truly great managers and coaches in football. Some have been masters at discovering new talents and putting together successful teams on tight budgets; others are football visionaries who have helped to improve the skills and play of the world's biggest stars. Below are profiles of eight of the finest managers in the history of football.

HERBERT CHAPMAN
1878-1934

Only four teams have won the English league three seasons in a row, and Chapman created two of them. After arriving at Huddersfield Town in 1921, he won the league in 1924 and 1925. By the time Huddersfield made it three in a row, Chapman had left for Arsenal. They were in 20th place when he took over, but finished the season second, behind his former side. Arsenal went on to win a hat-trick of league titles, the first two under Chapman. The Englishman took tactics very seriously, and his W-M formation (see page 60) was taken up by many sides. He pioneered large-scale youth coaching, undersoil heating, top-class medical facilities and professional training regimes. Some of his proposals, such as numbered shirts and playing regular evening games under floodlights, were only adopted long after his death.

GIOVANNI TRAPATTONI
Born 1939

Trapattoni's managerial career got off to a flying start, winning the 1973 European Cup-Winners' Cup as caretaker manager of AC Milan, for whom he had played as a fearsome centre-back. After moving to Milan's great rivals Juventus, he enjoyed an unmatched run of success, winning six Serie A league titles, two UEFA Cups and, in 1985, a European Cup. The backbone of his side contained many of the players who won the 1982 World Cup, from keeper Dino Zoff to striker Paolo Rossi. Trapattoni won a further Serie A title with Internazionale in 1989 before moving to Bayern Munich in the 1990s, where he became the first foreign manager to win the Bundesliga. His teams were based on strong defences, usually with three central defenders linked to exciting attackers who were often bought from abroad. He was finally given a chance to coach the Italian national side at 63 years of age, but the team fell short at both the 2002 World Cup and Euro 2004, after which Trapattoni joined Benfica as head coach.

▲ Trapattoni argues with the officials during Italy's match against Bulgaria at Euro 2004.

◀ Herbert Chapman (right) watches an Arsenal match in 1932 alongside trainer Tom Whittaker (left) and star player Alex James.

BELA GUTTMANN
1900-81

The only manager to have won the top club trophy in both South America and Europe, Guttmann is a coaching legend. He was a gifted amateur player for MTK Budapest and appeared at the 1924 Olympics for Hungary. After retiring in 1935, he embarked on a 40-year-long coaching career that took him to Switzerland, Uruguay, Greece, Portugal, Brazil, Romania, Italy and Austria. He won national league titles in five different countries, including the 1955 Serie A title with AC Milan; he won the European Cup twice as coach of Benfica and also lifted the Copa Libertadores with Peñarol. He was a great influence on Gusztav Sebes, the coach of the magical Hungarian sides of the 1950s, and his forward-thinking 4-2-4 formation and styles of play are believed to have inspired Brazil to become the great attacking force of the late 1950s onwards.

JOCK STEIN
1922-85

Jock Stein began his coaching career as assistant manager at Celtic. In 1960, he moved to Dunfermline and beat his old club in the following season to win the Scottish Cup. In 1962, Dunfermline caused a major upset, knocking out top Spanish side Valencia from the Inter-Cities Fairs Cup. Stein moved on to Hibernian for a season before being appointed as the boss of Celtic. He quickly built one of British soccer's finest and most entertaining sides. Under Stein, Celtic won 11 Scottish league titles and, in 1967, overturned the mighty Internazionale to become the first British team to lift the European Cup. The 'Big Man' left Celtic in 1977 for an ill-fated spell at Leeds United, but later became Scotland's coach, guiding them to the 1982 and 1986 World Cup tournaments.

FACTFILE In the 1970s, two managerial legends, Jock Stein and Brian Clough, both had spells at Leeds United that lasted just 44 days.

ALEX FERGUSON
Born 1941

As European football's longest-serving top-flight manager, Sir Alex Ferguson has taken Manchester United to a record eight Premiership titles and the 1999 Champions League crown. A ruthless and highly driven player, Ferguson carried those attributes into his managerial career, first with East Stirling and then at St Mirren and Aberdeen. On limited resources at Aberdeen, he broke the monopoly of Celtic and Rangers to win three Scottish league titles; in 1983, his team defeated Real Madrid to lift the European Cup-Winners' Cup. Ferguson also served as assistant Scotland manager under Jock Stein, taking over in 1985 when Stein died. At Manchester United, Ferguson developed young talents such as David Beckham, Ryan Giggs and Paul Scholes, and proved to be a masterful player of mind games with rival managers. His transfer dealings have not always been successful, but he has made some excellent purchases, including Eric Cantona for £1.2 million and Peter Schmeichel for £550,000.

> **FACTFILE** Alex Ferguson has only been sacked once, in 1978, when Scottish club St Mirren fired him for a range of offences that included 'unpardonable swearing at a lady'.

RINUS MICHELS
1928-2005

The man behind 'total football', which revolutionized both Ajax and the Dutch national team, Marinus 'Rinus' Michels had been a centre-forward as a player, winning five caps for Holland in the 1950s. As coach of Ajax in the mid-1960s, he gave 17-year-old Johan Cruyff his debut. Michels later managed Cruyff at Spanish giants Barcelona and in the Dutch team that finished runners-up at the 1974 World Cup. Michels returned to Ajax in 1975 and became coach of German side Cologne five years later. He rejoined the Dutch national side in 1984 and, with a star-studded team, won the 1988 European Championships – Holland's first major trophy. Michels' achievements were acknowledged in 1989, when he was named FIFA's Coach of the Century.

VALERY LOBANOVSKY
1939-2002

A gifted mathematician, Valery Lobanovsky viewed football as a science, and was one of the first managers to analyze the performances of teams and players. His management style was strict, yet it enabled creative talents such as Oleg Blokhin and Andriy Shevchenko to flourish. After four years in charge of Dnipro Dnipropetrovsk, he was appointed coach of Dynamo Kiev, guiding them to five Soviet league titles between 1974 and 1981 and two European Cup-Winners' Cup victories (1975 and 1986). He also coached the Soviet Union in three spells, reaching the 1988 European Championships final, only to be defeated by Rinus Michel's Dutch team. After spells with the United Arab Emirates and Kuwait, he returned to Kiev in 1996, taking them to five Ukrainian league titles in a row (1997–2001) and reaching the semi-finals of the Champions League in 1999.

▶ Rinus Michels with Johan Cruyff during their time at Barcelona.

HELENIO HERRERA
1917-97

The well-travelled Argentinian Helenio Herrera was a tough manager who liked to control almost every aspect of a club. At Spain's Atlético Madrid, he won back-to-back league titles. After spells with Malaga, Valladolid and Sevilla, he joined Barcelona. Under his management, they won two Spanish titles and two Inter-Cities Fairs Cups. Internazionale liked what they saw and headhunted him in 1960. Herrera's reign and his use of *catenaccio* tactics (see page 60) coincided with Inter's most glorious era, in which they won three Serie A titles, two European Cups and two World Club Cups. Herrera was also in charge of the Italian national team during qualification for the 1962 World Cup, but by the time the tournament began, he was manager of Spain.

◀ In November 2004, Alex Ferguson celebrated his 1,000th game in charge of Manchester United by beating Lyon in the Champions League.

▶ Helenio Herrera poses with two footballs in 1971, while coach of Italian side Roma.

Lothar Emmerich of West Germany fires a shot past England's George Cohen (far left) and Martin Peters during the epic 1966 World Cup final at Wembley.

THE WINGLESS WONDERS

The tactics of England manager Alf Ramsey caused much debate at the 1966 World Cup. His midfield had no wingers, but did include a striker, Bobby Charlton, and the tough-tackling defender Nobby Stiles. The English defence was in top form and the Wingless Wonders, as Ramsey's team was nicknamed, cruised to the final against West Germany. It was, therefore, a shock when England fell behind to a Helmut Haller strike in the 12th minute. Stirred into action, England went 2-1 up with goals from Geoff Hurst and Martin Peters, only for Wolfgang Weber to equalize in the dying seconds of the game. In a World Cup first, the final went into extra time and two events passed into football folklore. First was the controversial goal awarded to Geoff Hurst in the 101st minute – even today, it is unclear if the ball crossed the line. Then came Hurst's third goal, which left no one in any doubt. His thumping shot into the roof of the net secured England an historic 4-2 win and made him the only player to score a hat-trick in the final of the World Cup.

GREAT SIDES

What makes a great team? Great footballers, managed brilliantly, playing with spirit and supported by passionate crowds, often triumph. Yet, assembling a team of superstars does not guarantee success. Sometimes, unheralded players gel together to win against the odds. In the last decade, Nigeria, Cameroon, Japan and South Korea have lit up world football by triumphing over more powerful nations. Similar upsets occur at club level – provincial side Toluca's rise to win the Mexican league, for example. This chapter looks at some of the world's great national and club sides over the years. The key word is 'some'; there are dozens of other successful teams, from Argentina's Independiente – the most frequent winner of the Copa Libertadores – to Olympiakos, who in 2003 won their seventh Greek league title in a row. The focus in this section is on sides that at one point in their history were especially exciting, revolutionary or dominant in the football competitions in which they played.

NATIONAL SIDES

▶ Hungarian goalkeeper Gyula Grosics gathers the ball under pressure from England's Stan Mortensen. Hungary's 6-3 win condemned England to their first home defeat to a team from the continent.

HUNGARY
Founded: 1901

The Hungarian national team of the 1950s was quite exceptional and one of the few sides at club or international level to change the way football is played. Organized at the back by the dependable Jozsef Bozsik, Hungary brimmed with attacking talent thanks to Zoltan Czibor, Sandor Kocsis, Nandor Hidegkuti and Ferenc Puskas. At a time when almost every side played the W-M formation (see page 60), coach Gusztav Sebes devised a simple but devastating alternative. Hidegkuti was the team's centre-forward, but he played very deep, allowing Puskas, Kocsis and other team-mates to raid forwards into space. Opposition teams simply did not know how to play against a side that swept all before it, winning the 1952 Olympics and scoring 220 goals in 51 matches during the first half of the decade. In 1953, the team earned its nickname – the Magnificent Magyars – by beating a stunned England 6-3 at Wembley. That memorable win was followed by a 7-1 destruction of the English team in Budapest. From June 1950 to November 1955, Hungary's international record read: played 50, won 42, drew seven, lost one. The defeat was heartbreaking, however, as it came in the final of the 1954 World Cup. After taking a 2-0 lead against a West German side they had thrashed 8-3 in the group stages, Hungary – fielding an unfit Puskas – lost 3-2. That single defeat should not detract from one of the finest teams ever to grace the international stage.

> **FACTFILE** The team was still at its peak when the Soviet Union invaded Hungary in 1956. Many of its star players were on tour with their club, Honved, and chose not to return home. Puskas signed for Real Madrid, while Kocsis and Czibor joined Real's great rivals, Barcelona.

WEST GERMANY
Founded: 1900

West Germany staged a major shock when they courageously toppled the favourites, Hungary, to win the 1954 World Cup thanks to two goals from Helmut Rahn. Their side of the mid-1960s finished runners-up at the 1966 tournament and third in 1970. Manager Helmut Schön then rebuilt the team shrewdly, keeping the superb

Sepp Maier in goal and moving Franz Beckenbauer from midfield into defence, where he played alongside Hans-Georg Schwarzenbeck and one of the best full-backs of the 1970s, Paul Breitner. Schön incorporated the talented Günter Netzer into midfield and often played a 4-3-3 formation, with Uli Hoeness in attack alongside goal machine Gerd Müller. West Germany's players had an incredibly strong team spirit because they came almost exclusively from just two clubs – Bayern Munich and Borussia Mönchengladbach. Their self-belief was evident as they powered to the 1972 European Championships title and then went a step further, winning the 1974 World Cup on home soil. By this time, the talented but outspoken Netzer had been replaced by Wolfgang Overath, while midfielder Rainer Bonhof had also played his way into the side. A defeat to Czechoslovakia in the 1976 European Championships final signalled the end of a remarkable period in which West Germany had become the first team to hold the European and World crowns at the same time.

◄ *West German defender Berti Vogts holds the World Cup aloft in 1974, with Hans-Georg Schwarzenbeck (number four) and Rainer Bonhof (16) to his left.*

USA (WOMEN)
First international match: 1985

Women's international football came of age during the 1990s, with the arrival of World Cup and Olympic competitions. The decade's most successful nation was undoubtedly the USA. With a team built around a core of footballers who have played together throughout the 1990s and into the 21st century, the USA won two out of a possible three Olympic titles (1996 and 2004) and two out of four Women's World Cups (1991 and 1999). Their record in World Cup matches is remarkable, with 20 wins, two draws and just two defeats. Four players appeared for the American team in all four World Cups: Joy Fawcett, Julie Foudy, Mia Hamm and Kristine Lilly. Hamm was considered the world's finest female striker, while in 2000 Lilly became the first footballer of either sex to pass 200 international caps. For a number of the US women's team, 2004 proved a successful swansong, with victory over Brazil to win Olympic gold.

► *American winger Kristine Lilly leaps over a tackle from Australia's Thea Slatyer at the 2004 Olympics. The USA remained unbeaten throughout the tournament.*

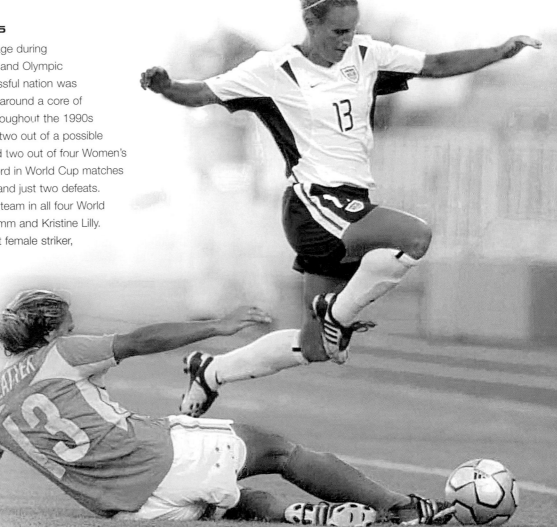

FRANCE
Founded: 1919

France has a long and illustrious football pedigree. It has produced several superb sides, particularly in the late 1950s – the era of Raymond Kopa and Just Fontaine – and in the early 1980s, with an attractive team led by Michel Platini. But it was the side of the late 1990s that finally translated great promise into World Cup success (see pages 92–93). As World Champions, France entered Euro 2000 with the majority of their key players still at their peak, including flamboyant keeper Fabien Barthez and strong, skilled defenders in Marcel Desailly, Lilian Thuram and Bixente Lizarazu. In midfield, a blend of flair and dynamism was headed by the world's best attacking midfielder, Zinedine Zidane. Up front, young livewires such as Sylvain Wiltord and Thierry Henry were intent on making their mark. Five players scored two or more goals in their six-match Euro 2000 campaign, which ended with France beating Italy 2-1 to become the second team (after West Germany in 1974) to hold European and World titles at the same time.

▲ France celebrate their Euro 2000 triumph after a golden goal from David Trezeguet (centre, with Fabien Barthez's hand on his head) sealed victory.

SOUTH KOREA
Founded: 1928

At the 2002 World Cup, co-hosts South Korea were given little chance of success by many people. In truth, the country boasted an improving side and had qualified for the previous three World Cups. Under the guidance of Guus Hiddink – a former Real Madrid and Holland coach – the South Koreans beat Poland 2-0 to record their country's first win at the World Cup finals. After a 1-1 draw with the USA, South Korea dumped a strong Portugal side out of the tournament courtesy of Park Ji-Sung's goal. An extraordinary second-round game versus Italy saw South Korea miss a penalty, then go behind, only to equalize two minutes before the final whistle. Urged on by an entire nation, the hardworking side defended resolutely and attacked with energy, skill and surprise. A golden goal three minutes before the end of extra time knocked Italy out of the tournament and sent the country into raptures. The drama was not over, however. A tense quarter-final against Spain ended in a thrilling penalty shootout, with keeper Lee Woon-Jae pulling off a magnificent save from Joaquin before captain Hong Myung-Bo slotted home the winning penalty. A narrow 1-0 defeat to Germany in the semi-final did not dampen the co-host nation's enthusiasm, and attendances at club level rocketed in the following seasons.

> **FACTFILE** Ahn Jung-Hwan struck the goal that knocked Italy out of the World Cup. Ahn played for Italian side Perugia, whose president was so enraged that he terminated the South Korean midfielder's contract.

HIT THE NET

www.fifa.com/en/organisation/na/index.html
A list of the 205 national associations affiliated to FIFA, together with the dates of their formation, kit colours and links to the websites of most of these associations.

www.kenaston.org/World_Cup/World_Cup_Videos.htm
This website contains short mpeg videos of a number of great World Cup goals, by players such as Pelé, Carlos Alberto (see pages 76–77), Michael Owen and Zinedine Zidane.

www.womensoccer.com/refs/usabios.shtml
A site containing biographies and achievement records of more than 35 members of the US women's team from the late 1980s to the present day.

▲ South Korea's Lee Chun-Soo (number 14), Choi Jin-Cheul (4), Hwang Sun-Hong (18) and Park Ji-Sung (21) celebrate their team's penalty shootout victory over Spain in the quarter-finals of the 2002 World Cup.

NIGERIA
Founded: 1945

In 1985, Nigeria's youngsters captured the World Under-17 Championship to become the first African nation to win a world tournament. Eleven years later, the Super Eagles, as the team is nicknamed, were the stars of the Atlanta Olympics thanks to their attacking verve, team spirit and will to win. Featuring talented players such as Celestine Babayaro, Emmanuel Amunike and Daniel Amokachi, Nigeria beat Hungary 1-0 and Japan 2-0, before losing to Brazil 1-0 in the group stages. They then beat Mexico 2-0 in the quarter-finals to set up a second meeting with Brazil. That match is considered to be the finest in Olympic history. With just 13 minutes to go, Nigeria were losing 3-1. But the Africans pulled one goal back before their captain, Nwankwo Kanu, scored a last-gasp equalizer. In a frenetic period of extra time, Kanu struck again to seal a 4-3 victory. Another great comeback in the final saw Nigeria win gold by defeating Argentina 3-2, thanks to an 89th-minute goal by Amunike.

◄ *Daniel Amokachi scored the second of Nigeria's three goals against Argentina in the 1996 Olympic final.*

ITALY
Founded: 1898

Italy and Uruguay emerged as the leading sides during the first decade of the World Cup. The Italians chose not to enter the first tournament, in 1930, but were hosts of the second, where they were managed by Vittorio Pozzo, who was nicknamed the Old Maestro. Pozzo deployed several *oriundi* – Argentinians of Italian descent – including Raimundo Orsi and the captain, Luisito Monti. His side also included one of the world's finest attackers of the inter-war years in Giuseppe Meazza. Italy won the 1934 World Cup under Pozzo's leadership and also triumphed at the 1936 Olympics. Recognizing the fact that his side was ageing, the wily Pozzo introduced more and more youngsters, so that by the time of the 1938 World Cup only two members of the 1934 team,

Meazza and Giovanni Ferrari, remained. Pozzo's overhaul of the side proved a triumph, as Italy beat the highly fancied French, Brazilian and Hungarian teams to reclaim the trophy and make Pozzo the only manager in history to have won two World Cups.

> **FACTFILE** In the semi-final of the 1938 World Cup, the string of Giuseppe Meazza's shorts broke and they fell to the ground just as he went to take a penalty. Holding his shorts up with one hand, Meazza calmly stroked the penalty home past the bemused Brazilian goalkeeper, Valter.

▲ *Italy's national team, including star striker Giuseppe Meazza (front row, centre) pose before the 1938 World Cup. The Italians comfortably beat Hungary 4-2 in the final.*

ENGLAND
Founded: 1863

As an England player, Alf Ramsey's last match had been the 6-3 demolition by Hungary in 1953 – the game that punctured English belief in its footballing superiority. On the back of managing Ipswich Town from the lowly Third Division South to the league championship in 1962, Ramsey was named England manager later that year. By the 1966 World Cup he had assembled a powerful team with a strong spine – Gordon Banks in goal, Jackie Charlton and Bobby Moore in central defence, Bobby Charlton in midfield and, up front, Roger Hunt and the free-scoring Jimmy Greaves (who was injured during the tournament and replaced by Geoff Hurst). Propelled by goals mainly from Hunt and Bobby Charlton, and by a miserly defence that did not concede a goal until the semi-final, England beat Mexico, France, Argentina and Portugal. In the final at Wembley, a memorable hat-trick by Geoff Hurst and a goal from Martin Peters saw England beat West Germany 4-2 to win the trophy (see pages 68–69). After reaching the semi-finals of the 1968 European Championships, England were one of the favourites for the 1970 World Cup. In the quarter-final they were leading 2-0 with just 20 minutes left to play, before West Germany struck back to win 3-2.

▲ England's captain Bobby Moore (left) and keeper Gordon Banks hold aloft the World Cup at Wembley.

◀ Gao Hong makes a save during training before the final of the 1999 Women's World Cup between China and the USA.

SAUDI ARABIA
Founded: 1959

Saudi Arabia began to take football seriously in the 1970s, luring foreign coaches and developing its leading clubs, such as Al-Ahly, Al-Hilal and Al-Ittihad. In the 1980s, the national team won two Asian Cups and the World Under-16 Youth Cup. At the 1994 World Cup, the Saudis lost narrowly to Holland before beating Morocco 2-1 in the first all-Arab nation tie at the World Cup finals. In their next game, against Belgium, Saeed Owairan scored the goal of the tournament. Picking up the ball deep in his own half, he sped upfield, skipping a number of tackles before slotting the ball home past Michel Preud'homme. The goal took the Saudis into the last 16 of the World Cup for the first time, where they lost to Sweden. Two years later, they won the Asian Cup and almost defended their title in 2000, reaching the final but losing 1-0 to Japan.

◀ Saeed Owairan at the 1994 World Cup.

CHINA (WOMEN)
First international match: 1983

While the USA, Norway and, more recently, Germany have vied for the title of the leading team in women's international football, all contenders for the crown have had to overcome the considerable and consistent threat of the Chinese. Dubbed the Steel Roses, China have dominated women's football in their own continent, winning seven consecutive Asian Women's Championship titles from 1986 onwards. In 1997, the Chinese recorded their biggest-ever victory, crushing the Philippines 16-0. At the heart of the team throughout much of the 1990s were world-class players such as goalkeeper Gao Hong, dynamic midfielder Liu Ailing, and the high-scoring Sun Wen. On the world stage, the Steel Roses have endured agonizingly close defeats, losing the 1996 Olympic final by a single goal and the 1999 World Cup final in a penalty shootout, both to the USA. In the latter tournament, China reached the final thanks to an unbeaten group record and a 5-0 mauling of the World Cup holders, Norway.

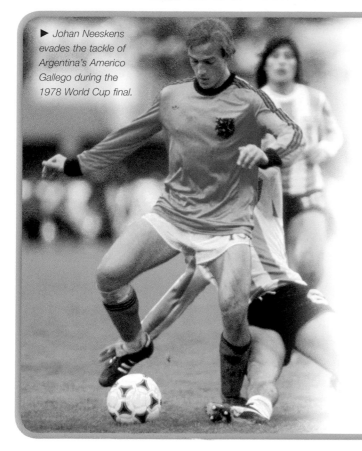

▶ Johan Neeskens evades the tackle of Argentina's Americo Gallego during the 1978 World Cup final.

HOLLAND
Founded: 1889

Rinus Michels, a former centre-forward for Holland, masterminded a revolution in Dutch football in the mid-1960s. First at club side Ajax, and then with the national team, he developed a system in which all his players were comfortable on the ball and would switch positions, often with devastating results. Called 'total football' (see page 61), the system revolved around such world-class talents as Johan Cruyff, Johan Neeskens and Ruud Krol. With Michels at the helm, the Dutch powered to the 1974 World Cup finals, scoring 14 goals and conceding just one in qualifying. They soared through the rounds, demolishing Argentina 4-0 and beating Brazil 2-0 on the way to the final against West Germany. Despite taking a one-goal lead within 80 seconds, Holland suffered heartbreak, losing 2-1. Two years later, they reached the semi-final of the 1976 European Championships, going out to the eventual winners, Czechoslovakia, in extra time. The Dutch entered the 1978 World Cup without Cruyff, but could still call upon many of the 1974 squad, including Neeskens, Krol and strikers Johnny Rep and Robbie Rensenbrink. They reached the final again, this time losing 3-1 to Argentina. Considered the most talented team never to win the World Cup, the Dutch enthralled millions of fans with their exploits and flair.

MEXICO
Founded: 1927

Having reached the quarter-finals of the two World Cups it has hosted (1970 and 1986), the football-mad nation of Mexico had much to cheer in the 1990s, when its national team dominated the continental championships, the CONCACAF Gold Cup. In the inaugural competition of 1991, Mexico lost to the USA at the semi-final stage, but in the next three competitions they were unstoppable. They were rampant in 1993, beating Canada 8-0 and Jamaica 6-1, before humbling the USA 4-0 in the final. At the 1996 Gold Cup, they defeated invited guests Brazil to win the title and, four years later, beat the USA again to secure a hat-trick of wins. At the heart of Mexico's authoritative displays was the defender Claudio Suarez, nicknamed the Emperor for his commanding performances. Suarez made his national debut in 1992 and notched up his 172nd cap in the 2004 Copa America game against Ecuador. Mexico's success was also underpinned by a succession of great attackers, including Hugo Sanchez, Luis Garcia, Carlos Hermosillo and Luis Hernandez.

FACTFILE At the 1998 World Cup, Mexican striker Cuauhtemoc Blanco amazed spectators and bewildered defenders with the trick of jumping over tackles with the ball clenched between his feet.

▶ Mexico's Luis Hernandez is tackled by Dietmar Hamann of Germany at the 1998 World Cup. Hernandez and Carlos Hermosillo are the joint top scorers for Mexico, with 35 goals each.

BRAZIL

Founded: 1914

The 1958 World Cup signalled the arrival of Pelé and the start of a magnificent era for Brazil, who enchanted fans of the beautiful game as they won three out of four World Cups. The side that claimed the 1970 World Cup is considered by many people to be international football's greatest team. In attack, few nations before or since have been able to field a side so blessed with flair, composure and skill on the ball, as well as superb vision and movement off it. Opposition teams sometimes tried to mark Pelé out of the game, but this would only give space and opportunities to marvellous players such as centre-forward Tostao, the bustling Roberto Rivelino (who had one of the most fearsome shots in world football), the midfield general Gerson or the powerful winger Jairzinho. At the back, high-class players such as Carlos Alberto and centre-back Wilson Piazza maintained a solid defence, but this side was all about attack. After going a goal down to Czechoslovakia in their first match at the 1970 World Cup, Brazil responded by scoring four times. They scored three to beat Uruguay in the semi-final and four in the final, in which they outclassed a strong Italian side with one of the greatest displays of attacking football. Brazil dazzled with their wit and invention, and the 4-1 scoreline was completed by a marvellous team move ending in a thunderous shot by Carlos Alberto (see below). In his last match for

▲ *Brazil's team that beat England at the 1970 World Cup. Back row, left to right: Carlos Alberto, Brito, Wilson Piazza, Félix, Clodoaldo, Everaldo, Mario Zagalo (coach); front row: Jairzinho, Roberto Rivelino, Tostao, Pelé, Paulo Cesar.*

Brazil, Pelé was chaired off the field by his team-mates after his part in the victory. The departure of other members of the side meant that by the 1974 World Cup, only Rivelino and Jairzinho remained from the team that had captured the imagination of millions.

FACTFILE In 1970, Brazil's manager, Mario Zagalo, became the first person to have both played in and managed a World Cup-winning team. He had played in Brazil's 1958 and 1962 World Cup triumphs.

Alberto

Pelé

Jairzinho 2

Jairzinho 1

Rivelino 2

FACTFILE Idriss Carlos Kameni was just 16 when he played in goal for Cameroon in the 2000 Olympic final. He was a hero as early as the fifth minute, when he saved a Spanish penalty. Cameroon went on to win gold in a penalty shootout, making their coach, Jean-Paul Akono, the first African manager to win a major world football competition.

► Cyril Makanaky (left) clears the ball under pressure from Colombia's Carlos Valderrama during Cameroon's 2-1 victory at the 1990 World Cup. The Africans were the talk of the tournament, defeating World Cup holders Argentina in the group stage.

MATCH ACTION

In the 1970 World Cup final against Italy, right-back Carlos Alberto scored one of the finest ever team goals. The move started in the Brazilian half with a series of passes and some highly skilled dribbling from defender Clodoaldo. He released Roberto Rivelino, who fired a pass down the touchline. Jairzinho controlled the ball instantly and cut infield, shielding the ball from Italian defenders before feeding Pelé. Pelé spotted a run by a team-mate on his right and nonchalantly rolled the ball diagonally into the penalty area. Marauding down the right flank, Carlos Alberto met the pass with a booming right-foot shot that sent the ball crashing low into the corner of the net.

FACTFILE Brazil's first international match was in July 1914, when they played English league side Exeter City. In 2004, the 1994 Brazilian World Cup-winning side played a rematch against Exeter, winning the game 1–0.

Clodoaldo 1

Clodoaldo 2

Rivelino 1

CAMEROON
Founded: 1960

Cameroon threatened a major shock at the 1982 World Cup, drawing against Italy (the eventual winners) and Poland, yet failing to reach the second round by a hair's breadth. In 1990, a team led by Roger Milla lit up the tournament, winning a tough group containing the Soviet Union, Argentina and Romania, beating Colombia in round two and taking England to extra time before losing 3-2. Recently, many of Cameroon's footballers have played for Europe's top clubs – Geremi at Real Madrid, Samuel Eto'o at Barcelona and Salomon Olembe at Marseille, for example. After a disappointing 1998 World Cup, Cameroon roared back in 2000. They won the African Nations Cup, beating Nigeria. They then triumphed at the Olympics, stunning Brazil in the quarter-finals, Chile in the semis and Spain in the final to win gold.

LONGEST UNBEATEN INTERNATIONAL RUNS (IN GAMES)

36	Brazil 1993–96	27	Colombia 1992–94
31	Argentina 1991–93	24	Brazil 1975–78
	Spain 1994–98		Ghana 1981–83
30	France 1994–96	23	Brazil 1981–82, 1997–98
	Hungary 1950–54		Czechoslovakia 1974–76
29	Brazil 1970–73		West Germany 1978–81

CLUB SIDES

BARCELONA
Spain
Founded: 1899
Stadium: Nou Camp

With their own bank, radio station and one of the most impressive stadiums in the world, Barcelona can easily claim to be one of the world's largest football clubs. Despite being overshadowed in Europe by fierce rivals Real Madrid, Barcelona's domestic achievements are impressive – their sixth-place finish in the Spanish league, La Liga, in 2003 was their worst since 1942. The club have won 17 league titles, finished runners-up 21 times and top the list of Spanish Cup winners, with 24 victories. They have also won the European Cup-Winners' Cup four times – more than any other team. Barcelona smashed the world transfer record in 1973 when they paid £922,000 for Dutch maestro Johan Cruyff. Fifteen years later, he returned as the club's manager, taking over from Terry Venables. In his first season, Cruyff helped steer the club to second place in La Liga and to a 2-0 victory over Sampdoria to collect the European Cup-Winners' Cup. Dutchman Ronald Koeman and Denmark's Michael Laudrup were signed to play alongside Spanish stars such

▲ *Barcelona players, including Ronaldo (with the trophy), stand on the winner's podium after beating Paris Saint Germain to win the 1997 Cup-Winners' Cup.*

as keeper Andoni Zubizarreta and midfielder José Bakero. In 1991, Barcelona won the first of four league titles in a row, and a year later they celebrated their first European Cup success, beating Sampdoria at Wembley in front of around 40,000 jubilant Spanish fans.

KASHIMA ANTLERS
Japan
Founded: 1991
Stadium: Kashima Soccer Stadium

The former factory team of Sumitomo Metals Industries, Kashima Antlers were formed in time to enter the inaugural J-League competition in 1993. Their name comes from the literal translation of Kashima, meaning 'deer island'. Little was expected of the side, which lacked the pedigree of Japanese teams such as

▲ *Kashima's Yasuto Honda celebrates with the J-League trophy in 2000.*

Yokohama Marinos and Verdy Kawasaki. The Antlers' management team was ambitious, however, recruiting Brazilian World Cup star Zico, first as a player and later as technical director. Zico's fellow countrymen Mazinho, Jorginho and Bismarck – along with talented Japanese players such as Atsushi Yanagisawa, Tomoyuki Hirase and Yasuto Honda – helped take the Antlers to four J-League titles and three Japanese Cups between 1996 and 2002.

AL-AHLY
Egypt
Founded: 1907
Stadium: Mukhtar El-Tetsh

Cairo-based Al-Ahly are the dominant football club in Egypt and one of the most successful teams in North Africa. Having won the first Egyptian league competition in 1949, they held on to the title until 1960, when they lost out to fellow Cairo side and fierce rivals Zamalek. Although Zamalek won two African Champions League titles during the 1980s, the decade was especially glorious for Al-Ahly. At home, they won five of the seven Cup of Egypt trophies and seven out of a possible ten league titles between 1980 and 1989. Abroad, Al-Ahly won the African Champions League twice, in 1982 and 1987, and were runners-up in 1983. They also won the African Cup-Winners' Cup three times in a row from 1984 to 1986. Al-Ahly's success led to them being named as the CAF African Club of the 20th Century.

> **FACTFILE** Two of Al-Ahly's youngest stars during the 1990s were the twins Hossam and Ibrahim Hassan, the most-capped players in Egyptian football. The brothers were idolized as they helped Al-Ahly to four league titles, but turned from heroes to villains when they sensationally quit the club to join rivals Zamalek in 2000.

▲ Flamengo's Ze Carlos da Silva performs a spectacular overhead kick during the 2003 Brazilian Cup final against Cruzeiro.

FLAMENGO
Brazil
Founded: 1895
Stadiums: Gávea, Maracana

Brazil is full of famous football sides, including Vasco da Gama, São Paulo, Botafogo and Corinthians. Flamengo are the most heavily supported of them all, having recorded 42 attendances of 100,000 or more at their games. Many gifted players have worn the side's distinctive black-and-red striped shirts. One of the greatest was Léonidas da Silva, known as the Black Diamond and the star of the 1938 World Cup. After a successful period in the 1950s, when the team won three Rio state league titles and earned the nickname the Steamroller, Flamengo had to wait more than 25 years for their next great era. Inspired by Zico and his strike partner, Nunes, the side won the Rio Championship (the Carioca) in 1978, 1979 and 1981, and the Brazilian National Championship in 1980, 1982 and 1983. In 1981, they captured the Copa Libertadores and a month later went on to claim the World Club Cup, beating Liverpool 3-0.

MANCHESTER UNITED
England
Founded: 1878
Stadium: Old Trafford

Sir Alex Ferguson, the Premiership's longest-serving and most successful manager, led Manchester United to a unique treble in English football when they won the Premiership, the FA Cup and the Champions League in 1999. Forty years earlier, a Manchester United side managed by Sir Matt Busby – another Scot who became a knight – had captured the hearts and minds of supporters everywhere. The story began in the mid-1950s. Great things were expected of the young 'Busby Babes' side that had won two league titles (in 1956 and 1957) and included, among other talents, the young England stars Roger Byrne and Duncan Edwards. But in 1958, a tragic plane crash in Munich killed 23 people

◄ Bobby Charlton (left) celebrates after scoring the opening goal in Manchester United's defeat of Benfica to win the European Cup in 1968.

on board, including eight members of the Manchester United first team. Busby had to build a new side, which contained tough defenders like Nobby Stiles, young midfielders such as Brian Kidd, and two survivors from the Munich crash, Bobby Charlton and central defender Bill Foulkes. Although often playing in midfield, Charlton formed a glittering attacking trio with Denis Law and George Best. Busby's side won the league title in 1965 and 1967, but the pinnacle of their achievements came in the 1968 European Cup. After beating Real Madrid in the semi-final, Manchester United faced Benfica in the final. Two goals from Charlton, one from Best and one from the 19-year-old Kidd secured a memorable 4-1 victory. The Red Devils, as the team is nicknamed, had become the first English side to win the European Cup.

◄ Manchester United winger Ryan Giggs (left) speeds past Bayern Munich's Stefan Effenberg during the 1999 Champions League final.

INTERNAZIONALE (INTER MILAN)
Italy
Founded: 1908
Stadium: Giuseppe Meazza (San Siro)

Also known as Inter Milan, Internazionale were formed by a group of former AC Milan players. During the rule of dictator Benito Mussolini, the club was forced to change its name to Ambrosiana-Inter, but switched it back in 1942. Argentinian coach Helenio Herrera joined Inter in 1960 and pioneered a new tactical system, playing a sweeper behind a back four and using fast-moving defenders to build attacks. Known as the *catenaccio* (doorbolt) system, it was seen as negative and defensive by some. Yet with fast, attacking full-backs such as the outstanding Giacinto Facchetti, the commanding Spanish midfielder Luis Suarez and creative attackers Alessandro Mazzola and Angelo Domenghini, the team flourished. Inter won Serie A in 1963, 1965 and 1966 and also triumphed over Real Madrid in 1964 and the mighty Benfica in 1965 to win the European Cup twice. They added the World Club Cup to their list of honours in 1964 and 1965, beating Independiente of Argentina by a 3-0 aggregate score on both occasions. But it was not until the 1990s that Inter were able to add to their European glories, winning the UEFA Cup in 1991, 1994 and 1998.

▲ *Sparta Prague's Radoslav Kovac is challenged by Michael Chrysostomos of Cypriot side APOEL Nicosia during a Champions League qualifier in 2004.*

SPARTA PRAGUE
Czech Republic
Founded: 1893
Stadium: Letná

One of the grand clubs of Eastern European football, Sparta have been known by a series of different names, from Kralovske Vinohrady (King's Vineyard) through AC Sparta, Spartak Sokolovo and Sparta Bratrstvi. The club have dominated the domestic game, winning 22 Czech Cups and 30 league championships. They have also finished as league runners-up no less than 20 times since the professional Czech league began in 1925. The first great Sparta side competed admirably in Europe in the late 1920s and 1930s, winning the Mitropa Cup (the forerunner of the European Cup) in both 1927 and 1934. A number of Sparta players also featured in the Czechoslovakia side that finished runners-up in the 1934 World Cup. These included star striker Oldrich Nejedly, who was the tournament's leading scorer with five goals. Sparta had several more great eras, notably in the early 1960s and the beginning of the 1990s, when they competed in the first Champions League competition in 1991–92. Despite memorable victories over Olympique Marseille, Dynamo Kiev and Barcelona, Sparta narrowly failed to qualify for the final.

◄ *Luiz Suarez, Inter Milan's elegant midfielder, on the ball in 1967. Inter broke the world transfer record to buy the Spaniard, paying £142,000 in 1961.*

SANTOS
Brazil
Founded: 1912
Stadium: Vila Belmiro

Santos are most famous as being Pelé's club. They had won few honours before he began playing for them in 1956, aged only 15. During his 19 years at the club, Santos won the São Paulo Championship ten times and the Copa Libertadores twice, in 1962 and 1963. They also won the World Club Cup in those years, the first with an extraordinary 5-2 win away at Benfica, which included a sensational hat-trick from Pelé. Santos have fared less well in the years since, but a number of bright young stars emerged at the turn of the century. The club took a gamble on many of these players in the 2002 Brazilian National Championship, fielding a side with an average age of just 22. With 17-year-old midfielder Diego and 18-year-old striker Robinho especially prominent, Santos rolled back the years and delighted many neutral fans by winning the competition.

▲ *Young Santos striker Robinho (left) skips past Corinthians' Vampeta during a Brazilian National Championship game in 2002. Robinho subsequently moved to Real Madrid.*

BOCA JUNIORS
Argentina
Founded: 1905
Stadium: La Bombonera

Best known in Europe as the club for which Diego Maradona played, Boca Juniors were founded by a group of Italian immigrants and an Irishman, Patrick MacCarthy. With their Buenos Aires neighbours River Plate, they form one of the fiercest rivalries in world football. Boca have the edge in the derby matches between the two sides and have won three more Copa Libertadores than River. Boca had a strong resurgence at the end of the 20th century. Beginning in May 1998, they went 40 league games unbeaten to set an Argentinian record. The run helped them to win the Clausura and Apertura league titles in 1999, a feat that was followed by three Copa Libertadores triumphs, in 2000, 2001 and 2003. They also won the World Club Cup in 2000 and 2003.

DICK, KERR LADIES
England
Founded: 1917
No stadium

W. B. Dick and John Kerr owned a rail and tram equipment-making factory in Preston, northwest England. During World War I, women began to work in factories, taking the jobs of the men serving in the war. In 1917, the women at Dick, Kerr challenged their male colleagues to a game of football and went on to organize matches against male and female opposition to raise money for war charities. By 1920, Dick, Kerr Ladies were playing matches to sell-out crowds. One fixture against St Helen's Ladies attracted 53,000 spectators to Everton's Goodison Park. In 1921, at the peak of their popularity, Dick, Kerr Ladies played 67 games and a tour of the USA the following year saw the team win three and draw three out of nine matches against male sides. The Football Association felt threatened by a team which, in some cases, was drawing bigger crowds than the men's game. In 1921, the FA banned all women from playing football on the pitches of its member clubs. Incredibly, the ban remained in force for 50 years. As a result, support for women's football dwindled, and by 1926 Dick, Kerr Ladies had disbanded. Yet the team left an important legacy by showing that women could play football in a competitive, entertaining fashion.

◀ *The Dick, Kerr Ladies attack the penalty area during a floodlit game against Heys of Bradford in 1919.*

AC MILAN
Italy
Founded: 1899
Stadium: Giuseppe Meazza (San Siro)

AC Milan's first period of notable success came in the 1950s, when a trio of Swedish stars – Gunnar Gren, Nils Liedholm and Gunnar Nordahl – followed by Uruguayan striker Juan Alberto Schiaffino, helped them to four Serie A titles. Nordahl remains the club's highest scorer, with an amazing 210 goals in 257 games. The 1960s saw AC Milan emerge as one of the leading clubs in Europe, winning two European Cups and a Cup-Winners' Cup trophy. A period of decline followed, which included an enforced relegation in 1980 as a result of a betting scandal. Milan's fortunes were revived by the arrival of a new chairman, Silvio Berlusconi, in 1986. The wealthy media tycoon and future Italian prime minister appointed Arrigo Sacchi as coach the following year. An exciting team was assembled, which included the superb Dutch trio of Ruud Gullit, Marco van Basten and Frank Rijkaard, alongside the home-grown talents of Franco Baresi, Roberto Donadoni and Paolo Maldini. Milan won Serie A in 1988 and went on to win it five times during the 1990s. Starting in 1991, Milan went unbeaten in Serie A for an incredible 58 games, a run that included thrashings of Foggia (8-2) and Fiorentina (7-3).

▲ *George Weah scores for AC Milan during a 1997 derby match against Internazionale. Weah was bought as a replacement for Marco van Basten.*

The side also put five goals past Sampdoria, Lazio, Pescara and Napoli (twice). In Europe, Milan beat Real Madrid 5-0 and then Steaua Bucharest 4-0 in the final to collect the European Cup in 1989 – a competition they won again in 1990, 1994 and 2003. The Italians narrowly lost the 1993 final to French club Olympique Marseille, who were later stripped of the trophy following an investigation into corruption.

RIVER PLATE
Argentina
Founded: 1901
Stadium: Monumental

River Plate are one of Argentina's leading sides. In the late 1930s, they moved to a wealthy suburb of Buenos Aires which, along with a team of expensive players, led to their nickname, the Millionaires. River are renowned for their attacking style. In the late 1940s, their powerful forward line became known as *La Maquina* (the Machine), and the club has produced a succession of world-class attackers, including Omar Sivori, Mario Kempes, Hernan Crespo, Javier Saviola and the legendary Alfredo di Stefano. River Plate have won a total of 32 Argentinian league titles, yet it was not until 1986 that they triumphed in the Copa Libertadores. The team had made the final twice previously (in 1966 and 1976) before a side featuring Norberto Alonso, Juan Gilberto Funes and the great Uruguayan striker Enzo Francescoli beat America Cali of Colombia. River continued their habit of making the Copa Libertadores final in years ending in six with their second win, again versus America Cali, in 1996.

◄ *Paraguayan striker Nelson Cuevas (left) is congratulated by Gaston Fernandez after scoring River Plate's first goal in a 3-2 victory over Colón in 2004.*

KAIZER CHIEFS
South Africa
Founded: 1970
Stadium: Johannesburg Athletics Stadium

Kaizer Motaung played for South Africa's oldest and most famous club for black footballers, the Soweto-based Orlando Pirates. In 1968, he moved to the USA to play for the Atlanta Chiefs in the newly formed NASL. On returning to South Africa, he founded the Kaizer Chiefs (named after Motaung and his former US team) with ex-Orlando Pirates team-mates Zero Johnson, Ratha Mokgoatlheng, Msomi Khoza and Ewert Nene. Featuring a mixture of promising youngsters and experienced veterans, the Chiefs soon made their mark. They won the Life Cup in 1971 and 1972, and the BP Top Eight Cup in 1974. In the same year, they claimed their first South African league title. Tragedy struck in 1976, with the death of captain Ariel Kgongoane in the Soweto uprising and the killing of Ewert Nene, but the Chiefs went on to win the league in 1977 and 1979.

▲ *Patrick Mabedi (left) of Kaizer Chiefs tackles Vikash Dhorasoo of Olympique Lyonnais during the 2003 Peace Cup competition, held in South Korea.*

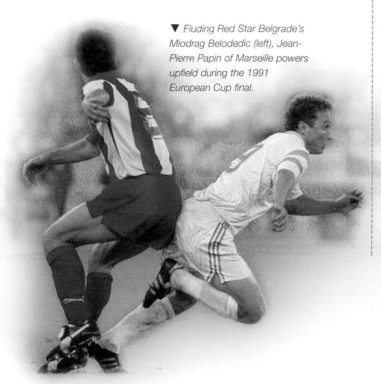

▼ *Eluding Red Star Belgrade's Miodrag Belodedic (left), Jean-Pierre Papin of Marseille powers upfield during the 1991 European Cup final.*

MOST CONSECUTIVE LEAGUE CHAMPIONSHIPS

14	Skonto Riga (Latvia)	1991–2004
13	Rosenborg (Norway)	1992–2004
10	BFC Dynamo (East Germany)	1979–88
10	Dinamo Tblisi (Georgia)	1990–99
9	Al-Ahly (Egypt)	1949–51, 1953–54, 1956–59
9	Celtic (Scotland)	1966–74
9	Dynamo Kiev (Ukraine)	1993–2001
9	Rangers (Scotland)	1989–97

OLYMPIQUE MARSEILLE
France
Founded: 1899
Stadium: Vélodrome

Arguably the best known French club side, Olympique Marseille boast an intensely passionate support. After a flurry of league titles at the start of the 1970s (helped by Yugoslavian striker Josip Skoblar, who scored a record 44 goals in the 1970–71 season), Marseille found success hard to come by. New chairman Bernard Tapie arrived in 1985 and invested heavily, bringing in expensive stars

such as Enzo Francescoli, Jean-Pierre Papin, Didier Deschamps and the Ghanaian midfielder Abedi Pele. Papin had the greatest impact, showing an incredible appetite for goals and becoming the French league's leading scorer for an astonishing five consecutive seasons from 1988 to 1992. The team rampaged through the domestic league, winning five championships in a row from 1989 to 1993. Marseille were agonizingly close to becoming the first French club to win the European Cup, going out in the semi-finals to Benfica in 1990 and losing on penalties in the final to Red Star Belgrade the following year. In 1993, a header by Basile Boli sent Marseille fans into ecstasy as they beat AC Milan 1-0 to win the trophy. Then it all went horribly wrong. Shortly after their victory, Marseille were found guilty of match-fixing a French league game against Valenciennes. They were stripped of the European Cup and their 1993 league title, as well as being relegated, while Tapie was eventually imprisoned for corruption. Marseille spent the rest of the 1990s battling to regain their status, with a certain degree of success – in 1999 they were runners-up in both the French league and the UEFA Cup.

► Brazilian legend Romario (left), in Fluminense colours, challenges for the ball with Paulo Baier of Goias during a 2004 Brazilian National Championship game.

FLUMINENSE
Brazil
Founded: 1902
Stadiums: Laranjeiras, Maracana

Founded in 1902, Fluminense have traditionally been supported by the middle classes, while their fierce Rio de Janiero rivals Flamengo drew support from the working class. Derby games between the two always guarantee big crowds. One 'Flu v Fla' derby in 1963 attracted a world-record attendance for a club match, with 177,656 supporters crammed inside the enormous Maracana Stadium. Fluminense also contest Rio's oldest derby, the *Classico Vovô* (Grandpa Derby), with Botafogo, co-founders of the Rio league. Despite being the home club of a series of Brazilian footballing legends, including Didi during the 1950s and Carlos Alberto and Roberto Rivelino in the 1960s and 1970s, Fluminense have always disappointed on the international stage. They have never won a major South American competition, nor even reached a final. However, they have achieved much in Brazil, winning the Rio Championship title 28 times. One of their most impressive runs occurred in the 1980s, when the Tricolores – so nicknamed for their traditional green, red and white colours – won three Rio Championships in a row from 1983 to 1985. With Paraguay's star striker Julio César Romero leading the line, Fluminense also won the Brazilian National Championship in 1984.

ARSENAL
England
Founded: 1886
Stadium: Highbury (Emirates Stadium from 2006)

First known as Dial Square FC, Arsenal were formed by workers from the Royal Arsenal munitions factory in Woolwich, south London – hence their nickname, the Gunners. After a move to the north of the city in 1913, the club's rise to the top of the English game coincided with the appointment of Herbert Chapman as manager in 1925. Chapman was highly innovative both on and off the pitch, and he built a counter-attacking team featuring inside-forwards Alex James and David Jack, and winger Cliff Bastin, whose 178 goals for the club remained a record for over half a century. Arsenal were league runners-up in Chapman's first season and went on to win the title in 1931 with a points total that would not be beaten for 30 years. Runners-up in 1932, they then claimed three league titles in a row (1933–35) and two FA Cups (1930 and 1936). Despite a league and FA Cup double in 1971,

> **FACTFILE** Under Herbert Chapman, 'The Arsenal' became just 'Arsenal', allegedly to make them appear at the top of an alphabetical list of Division One clubs. Chapman also successfully campaigned for Gillespie Road underground station, close to the ground, to be renamed Arsenal.

▲ Arsenal players congratulate Thierry Henry after his goal against Fulham. Henry scored 37 goals in all competitions in both 2002–03 and 2003–04.

the closest Arsenal have come to their earlier dominance has been under French manager Arsène Wenger. With a team boasting Thierry Henry, Dennis Bergkamp and Patrick Vieira, they have won three Premiership titles (1998, 2002 and 2004), finished runners-up five times and also won four FA Cups. Arsenal went unbeaten through the 2003–04 league season, eventually recording a total of 49 league matches without defeat, a record in English football.

▲ *Alessandro del Piero of Juventus lines up an overhead kick during the 2003 Champions League final against AC Milan.*

JUVENTUS
Italy
Founded: 1897
Stadium: Delle Alpi

Juventus are one of the most famous clubs in the world. Formed by a group of high-school students in the city of Turin, they played in pink shirts before a club official visited England in 1903. He was so taken by Notts County's strip of vertical black-and-white stripes that he took a set of the shirts back to Italy, where they became Juve's official home colours. The 'Old Lady of Turin' has enjoyed many successful spells, including five consecutive league titles from 1931 to 1935 and a 1980s team that won Serie A four times. Juve beat Liverpool to win the 1985 European Cup, but the victory was overshadowed by the Heysel Stadium tragedy in which 39 fans lost their lives. Financed by the extremely wealthy Agnelli family, the owners of the Fiat motor company, Juventus spent lavishly on recruiting top-class players in the 1990s. Throughout the decade, many of the world's finest footballers arrived at Turin to play for the club. These included Roberto Baggio, Gianluca Vialli, Attilio Lombardo, Fabrizio Ravanelli, Angelo di Livio, Alessandro del Piero and Christian Vieri. After capturing the UEFA Cup twice in the early 1990s, Juve won an Italian league and cup double in 1995, and beat Ajax to win the Champions League in 1996. They lost the final of that competition in 1997 and 1998, but their devoted fans could console themselves with Serie A titles in both years.

STEAUA BUCHAREST
Romania
Founded: 1947
Stadium: Ghencea

Formed by the Romanian Army, Steaua Bucharest had built a formidable team by the mid-1980s. The side included the superb goalkeeper Helmut Ducadam, Miodrag Belodedici (one of the finest sweepers in Europe), goal machine Marius Lacatus in attack and Romania's greatest player, Gheorghe Hagi. In August 1986, the club began an unbeaten run that is unique in Romanian football. They did not suffer a defeat for three league seasons, conceding 63 goals but scoring a staggering 322. The team made history abroad too, beating Spanish giants Barcelona in the final of the 1986 European Cup to become the first East European club to lift the prestigious trophy. In the early 1990s, after three seasons as runners-up in the Romanian league, Steaua began another incredible run, winning six consecutive domestic titles between 1993 and 1998.

> **FACTFILE** Legendary Steaua player Marius Lacatus spent 20 years at the club. In 2004, he became coach of rivals Stiinta Craiova. The Craiova fans were so angry that Lacatus resigned after just eight hours.

GALATASARAY
Turkey
Founded: 1905
Stadium: Ali Sami Yen

Turkey's three biggest clubs – Galatasaray, Fenerbahçe and Besiktas – are all based in Istanbul and their passionate supporters are fierce and occasionally violent rivals. Galatasaray have won the league title 15 times (one fewer than Fenerbahçe) and the Turkish Cup 14 times (ten more than Fenerbahçe). They are the best-known Turkish club abroad, partly through their competitive performances in Europe during the 1990s. Visiting foreign teams often encounter an intimidating atmosphere – from 'Welcome to Hell' banners displayed at the airport by fans, to a stadium that turns into a cauldron of colour and noise on match nights. Galatasaray went unbeaten at home in Europe from 1984 to 1994, the year in which they drew 3-3 at Old Trafford to knock Manchester United out of the Champions League. In 2000, they won their first major European trophy by beating Arsenal to win the UEFA Cup.

▲ *Striker Hakan Sukur has made more than 300 appearances for Galatasaray, scoring almost 200 goals.*

BAYERN MUNICH
Germany
Founded: 1900
Stadium: Allianz Arena

Germany's most famous club was formed in 1900 from rebels who had split from their former club, MTV 1879. The new team beat their old side 7-1 in the first match between the clubs. Although Bayern won a league title in 1932, by the early 1960s they were one of West Germany's less fashionable clubs and did not merit a place in the Bundesliga when it was formed in 1963. They achieved promotion soon after, and by the late

▶ *Bixente Lizarazu (right) battles Valencia's Gaizka Mendieta in the 2001 Champions League final. Bayern won the title on penalties.*

1960s were a dominant force in the domestic game. At the helm were future footballing legends such as Sepp Maier, Franz Beckenbauer and Gerd Müller, who was the Bundesliga's top scorer in seven seasons (1967, 1969–70, 1972–74 and 1978). With that squad, Bayern won German Cups in 1966 and 1967, and a European Cup-Winners' Cup in 1967. In the early 1970s, Bayern's stars were joined by more world-class players such as Paul Breitner and Uli Hoeness. The team won three Bundesliga titles in a row and three consecutive European Cups from 1974 to 1976. In 1976, Bayern's international reputation was sealed when they won the World Club Cup, beating Belo Horizonte of Brazil. Until 2005, Bayern and TSV 1860 shared the Olympic Stadium in Munich, but both clubs now play at the Allianz Arena, which will host matches at the 2006 World Cup.

▲ *Werner Roth rounds the Atlético Madrid goalkeeper as Bayern Munich power to a 4-0 victory to win the 1974 European Cup final replay. Bayern had salvaged a 1-1 draw in the first match with a goal in the last minute of extra time.*

BENFICA
Portugal
Founded: 1904
Stadium: Estadio da Luz

Benfica remain Portugal's most famous and successful club, despite the long periods of glory enjoyed by rivals Porto and Sporting Lisbon. Their greatest era was undoubtedly the 1960s, which began under the management of Hungarian Bela Guttmann. The side played with a mix of pace, power and skill, typified by the midfielder Mario Coluna and the brilliant Eusebio. Benfica began the decade by defeating Barcelona 3-2 to win the 1961 European Cup. The following year, facing the mighty Real Madrid in the final, they found themselves 3-1 down to a Ferenc Puskas hat-trick, but fought back to beat the Spanish giants 5-3. They featured in five European Cup finals during the 1960s and won eight out of ten league championships. Defending another league title in the 1972–73 season, Benfica went unbeaten through 30 league matches, scoring 101 goals in the process.

▲ *Benfica pose before the 1968 European Cup final, having beaten Juventus in the semi-finals. Amazingly, their toughest opponents were Northern Irish side Glentoran in the first round – Benfica sneaked through on the away goals rule.*

ASANTE KOTOKO
Ghana
Founded: 1935
Stadium: Kumasi Sports Stadium

Asante Kotoko, nicknamed the Porcupines, developed out of a team formed in the 1920s by Kwesi Kuma, a taxi driver. In 1967, the club won the first of three back-to-back league titles and reached the final of the African Champions League. Despite two draws against Tout Puissant Englebert of Zaire (now the Democratic Republic of Congo), the Ghanaian club were declared the losers when they refused a play-off to decide the contest. In 1970, the two clubs met again in the final. This time, Asante Kotoko secured a 2-1 away win (after a 1-1 draw at home) to become the first Ghanaian side to win the African Champions League. The club were runners-up in the 1971 and 1973 competitions, and won the 1972 Ghanaian league title.

NACIONAL
Uruguay
Founded: 1899
Stadium: Centenario

Nacional are engaged in a see-saw battle for supremacy in Uruguayan football with Peñarol, the side with which they share the country's biggest stadium. Since 1992, Nacional have won five league championships. One of their greatest eras, however, was in the late 1960s. Led by Argentinian striker Luis Artime, they won three league titles in a row from 1969 to 1971, made the final of the Copa Libertadores in 1969 and won that competition in 1971. Nacional again claimed South America's biggest club prize in 1980 and 1988, and each time went on to win the World Club Cup.

◄ Nacional's Denis Mila (left) and Victor Esparrago (right) tussle with Martin O'Neill of Nottingham Forest in the 1980 World Club Cup. Nacional won 1-0.

ANDERLECHT
Belgium
Founded: 1908
Stadium: Constant vanden Stock

▲ Belgian striker Enzo Scifo on the ball for Anderlecht against PSV Eindhoven – the team for which Luc Nilis, Scifo's World Cup team-mate, played.

It took 39 years from the club's formation for Anderlecht to win their first Belgian league championship. Since then, the Brussels-based side have made up for lost time, winning a staggering 27 league titles – 14 more than the second most successful side in Belgium, Club Brugge. In addition, Anderlecht have been runners-up 18 times. Such consistency has seen the club qualify to play in a major European competition every year from 1964 to 2005. The 1970s were a golden era for Anderlecht. They were runners-up in the 1970 Inter-Cities Fairs Cup, losing 4-3 over two legs to Arsenal. By the mid-1970s, under the management of Raymond Goethals, Anderlecht's team boasted many quality players. A strong midfield, featuring Frankie van der Elst, Ludo Coeck and Arie Haan, played behind talented attacking duo Benny Nielsen and Robbie Rensenbrink. The club contested three European Cup-Winners' Cup finals in a row, beating West Ham 4-2 in 1976, but losing to Hamburg the following year. Anderlecht bounced back to knock the same German side out of the 1977–78 competition on their way to the final, where they thrashed Austria Vienna 4-0. The team also added two European Supercups to their trophy cabinet by beating Bayern Munich in 1976 and Liverpool in 1978.

HIT THE NET

www.soccerlinks.net/pages/index.html
A huge collection of web links to more than 5,000 official and unofficial club websites, searchable by continent and country.

www.eurotopfoot.com/clubgb.php3
This website ranks 120 European clubs according to their performances in European competitions and provides profiles of each of the featured clubs.

www.expertfootball.com
A comprehensive football website, featuring a history of the game, profiles of teams and players, the latest news and transfer rumours, plus a forum for fans.

ESPERANCE SPORTIVE TUNIS

Tunisia
Founded: 1919
Stadium: El-Menzah

▲ *Esperance's Karim Ouji and Ali Zitouni celebrate reaching the semi-finals of the 2004 African Champions League.*

With a distinctive strip that gave them their nickname – the Blood and Golds – Esperance have long been one of the leading clubs in Tunisia and North Africa. Back-to-back Tunisian league wins in 1993 and 1994 paved the way for their 1994 African Champions League triumph where, in front of a delirious home crowd, they beat the Egyptian holders Zamalek 3-1. In 1997, Esperance began a record-breaking league run. Seeing off the challenge of leading rivals such as Etoile Sportive du Sahel and Club Africain, the team captured an incredible seven straight league championships. Before this feat, no Tunisian club had won more than three league titles in a row. Many of the side's most prominent players – including Radhi Jaidi, Brazilian-born José Clayton and long-serving club captain Khaled Badra – were part of the Tunisian national side that won the 2004 African Nations Cup on home soil.

MOSCOW SPARTAK

Russia
Founded: 1922
Stadium: Lokomotiv

Although Moscow Dynamo are the most famous Russian team outside the country, their local rivals Moscow Spartak have claimed more silverware, winning 12 Soviet league titles and ten Soviet Cups. They also made the semi-finals of European competitions two times in the early 1990s. Unfortunately, Spartak's greatest team (of the late 1940s and early 1950s) peaked in the days before major European competitions existed. Spartak have dominated the Russian league since its formation in 1992, winning the title nine times in its first ten seasons.

▲ *Spartak Moscow's Senegalese defender Baye Ali Ibra Kebe (right) tackles Liverpool's Jamie Carragher during a Champions League match in 2002.*

PEÑAROL

Uruguay
Founded: 1891
Stadium: Centenario

Along with Nacional, Peñarol dominate Uruguayan football. Peñarol are marginally the more successful, with more than 45 league titles. In head-to-head meetings up to the start of 2004, Peñarol lead their rivals by 175 wins to 150. The club's first golden era came in the 1960s. Led by Ecuadorian striker Pedro Spencer, the side won three Copa Libertadores (1960, 1961 and 1966) and two World Club Cups (against Benfica in 1961 and Real Madrid in 1966). Peñarol's side of the 1980s added to this tally, winning two more Copa Libertadores and, in 1982, beating Aston Villa to win a third World Club Cup. Peñarol hold a number of Copa Libertadores records: the largest win (11-2 against Valencia of Venezuela in 1970), the highest aggregate win (14-1 versus Everest of Ecuador in 1963) and the most consecutive participations in the competition (15 between 1965 and 1979).

▼ *Peñarol players celebrate their winning goal against fierce rivals Nacional to claim the 1999 Uruguayan Championship.*

AJAX
Holland
Founded: 1900
Stadium: Amsterdam ArenA

Coach Rinus Michels arrived at Ajax in the 1964–65 season, just in time to save them from relegation. (The team finished 13th out of 16). Michels went on to develop the concept of 'total football' (see page 61), which would have a major impact at both club and international level. Signs of a renaissance at Ajax began to show as early as 1966, when the team won the Dutch league and shocked Liverpool 5-1 in the European Cup. Three years later, Ajax became the first Dutch side to reach the final of that competition, where they lost to AC Milan. Spurred on by Dutch rivals Feyenoord winning the European Cup in 1970, Ajax went on to claim the trophy for the next three years with the help of such legends as Johan Cruyff, Arie Haan, Ruud Krol and Johan Neeskens. Playing an electric style of fluid football with the emphasis firmly on attack, they were crowned Dutch league champions six times in eight seasons (1966–68, 1970, 1972–73) and won the European Supercup and World Club Cup, both in 1972. Ajax also supplied the bulk of the players for the Dutch side that finished runners-up at the 1974 World Cup. By the mid-1970s, however, Neeskens, Cruyff and the coach Michels had moved to Spain and Ajax entered a period of decline. But through a comprehensive and much-copied youth system, they were eventually able to replace their former stars with several new waves of talent, including Frank Rijkaard, Dennis Bergkamp and the de Boer brothers, Frank and Ronald.

▼ *Twins Frank and Ronald de Boer, together with strikers Nwankwo Kanu and Finidi George, take a lap of honour after Ajax's 1-0 victory against AC Milan in the final of the 1995 Champions League.*

LIVERPOOL
England
Founded: 1892
Stadium: Anfield

In 1959, Liverpool were struggling in the English second division and had been knocked out of the third round of the FA Cup by amateur side Worcester City. Then Bill Shankly arrived as manager.

He was a passionate, no-nonsense Scot who went on to build a successful Liverpool side that won the league championship three times and lifted the UEFA Cup in 1973. A year later he resigned, and Bob Paisley – Shankly's assistant for 15 years – was promoted to manager. Paisley's Liverpool won 19 major trophies in nine years, making him the most successful British manager of the 20th century.

The club won six league titles and three League Cups thanks to a watertight defence, a quick, accurate passing game and intelligent attacking by players such as Kevin Keegan, Steve Heighway, John Toshack and Kenny Dalglish. A UEFA Cup win in 1976 was followed by European Cup triumphs in 1977 and 1978, making Liverpool the first British side to successfully defend the trophy. In 1981, the club beat Real Madrid to win the European Cup for a third time, and a fourth win came (after penalties) in 1984 against Italian side Roma.

> **FACTFILE**
> Between January 1978 and January 1981, Liverpool set an all-time record of 85 home games unbeaten in all competitions. Included in this run were an incredible 63 home league matches in a row.

◄ *Liverpool's Ray Kennedy (far left), Graeme Souness and Alan Hansen close down Flamengo star Zico during the 1981 World Club Cup.*

CELTIC
Scotland
Founded: 1888
Stadium: Celtic Park

Celtic, along with their Glasgow-based rivals Rangers, have dominated Scottish football for decades. However, Celtic had not won the league title for 11 years before the arrival of Jock Stein as manager in 1965. Stein developed a home-grown side, all of whom hailed from Glasgow and the surrounding area. The team was full of youth and pace, and had an adventurous style of play. These qualities were typified by the tricky winger Jimmy Johnstone, marauding full-back Tommy Gemmell, prolific strikers Steve Chalmers, Bobby Lennox and Willy Wallace, and a defensive rock in Billy McNeill, the captain. Celtic began an astonishing run from 1966, winning nine Scottish league championships in a row and completing a Scottish Cup and league double five times during that period. Yet they contested the 1967 European Cup final as underdogs to a powerful Internazionale side that had won two of the previous three European Cups. Against the odds, Celtic recovered from a goal down to beat the Italians 2-1, becoming the first British side to win the biggest club prize in European football. The 'Lions of Lisbon' narrowly failed to repeat their achievement when they reached the 1970 European Cup final, going down 2-1 to Dutch side Feyenoord. It would be 33 years before the Scottish club reached their next European final, losing 3-2 to Porto in the 2003 UEFA Cup final.

▶ *Winger Jimmy Johnstone (left) scored 130 goals for Celtic on the way to nine league championships, five League Cups and four Scottish Cups with the club.*

▲ *Colo Colo's Rodolfo Madrid gets away from Alfredo Moreno of Argentinian side Boca Juniors during a Copa Libertadores match in 2003.*

COLO COLO
Chile
Founded: 1925
Stadium: David Arellano

With around 60 per cent of the country's football fans following them, Colo Colo are easily the most heavily supported and successful of all the Chilean club sides. The team has won a record 23 league championships (11 more than fierce rivals Universidad de Chile) as well as the Chilean Cup – the *Campeonato de Copa* – ten times. Under their coach Arturo Salah, Colo Colo captured league titles in 1986 and 1989, before former Yugoslavia under-20 coach Mirko Jozic took up the manager's post during the 1990 season. The team completed a sequence of three league titles in a row in 1991, the same year that they enjoyed fantastic success abroad. In 1973, Colo Colo had been the first Chilean side to contest a final of the premier South American club cup competition, the Copa Libertadores. In 1991, the club went one stage further, beating the mighty Argentinian side River Plate in the semi-finals and the cup holders Olimpia 3-0 on aggregate to win the trophy. Under Jozic, they would win a further league title in 1993, while one member of the 1991 team, Jaime Pizarro, would go on to manage them to league success in 2002.

▲ *Dynamo Kiev pose with the 2003 Ukrainian Cup after beating the holders – and Kiev's most competitive rivals in Ukrainian football – Shakhtar Donetsk.*

DYNAMO KIEV
Ukraine
Founded: 1927
Stadium: National Sport Komplex Olimpiyskiy

Originally the football team of the Soviet secret police, Dynamo Kiev were the first club outside Moscow to win the Soviet league championship. A player in that 1961 side, Valery Lobanovsky, became Kiev's coach 13 years later. He led the club through its greatest era, which began spectacularly with back-to-back Soviet league titles. In 1975, Kiev won the Cup-Winners' Cup, becoming the first Soviet side to win a European competition. They also beat Bayern Munich 3-1 to win the European Supercup. In total, Lobanovsky (in three separate spells) managed Kiev to eight league titles, six Soviet Cups and two European Cup-Winners' Cups. In 1991, after the break-up of the Soviet Union, Kiev played in the newly formed Ukrainian league. They have dominated the competition, winning the title in every year except 2002 and 2005.

REAL MADRID
Spain
Founded: 1902
Stadium: Bernabeu

Real Madrid are one of the world's most famous and successful sides. They have won 29 Spanish league titles, 12 more than rivals Barcelona and 20 more than their neighbours, Atlético Madrid. They have also captured 11 European trophies and three World Club Cups. In the 1940s and 1950s, Real's president, Santiago Bernabeu, began to transform the club with foreign signings and a huge desire to win the newly formed European Cup competition. Real did not disappoint, capturing not only the first European Cup, in 1956, but the next four as well. The team included two of the world's outstanding attacking talents in Ferenc Puskas and Alfredo di Stefano, as well as pacy winger Paco Gento, central defenders Marcos Marquitos and Juan Zarraga, and attacking midfielder Hector Rial. From 1957 to 1965, Real remained unbeaten at home in 121 Spanish league matches and won five La Liga titles in a row (1961–65). A new-look side captured the European Cup for a sixth time in 1966.

Today, Real are one of the world's richest clubs, with a habit of buying football's most famous players such as Zinedine Zidane, Ronaldo and David Beckham. With these stars, known as *galacticos*, Real won the 2001 and 2003 Spanish league titles, and have taken their total of European Cup / Champions League triumphs to nine – more than any other side.

▲ *Real Madrid's victorious team pose with the 1960 European Cup after one of the greatest ever displays of attacking football (see pages 14–15).*

◀ *After wins in 1998 and 2000, Fernando Hierro lifts Real's third Champions League trophy in 2002 – adding to the club's tally of six European Cups between 1956 and 1966.*

SNAPSHOT
THE WORLD CUP COMES HOME

France entered the 1998 World Cup under intense pressure. The tournament was to be held on French soil, they had failed to qualify for the previous World Cup and critics claimed that the squad lacked a striker of true international class. What they did have, however, was the world's most creative midfielder in Zinedine Zidane, a strong defence and a battery of hard-working midfielders and attackers. France powered through their group, winning all three games. In the second round, veteran defender Laurent Blanc scored the first golden goal at the World Cup, to beat Paraguay. Further victories over Italy and Croatia took *Les Bleus* to a final against the mighty Brazil, led by Ronaldo. More famous for his mesmerizing ball skills on the ground, Zidane scored two headed goals against a subdued Brazilian team, and an injury-time strike by Emmanuel Petit completed a 3-0 victory. The World Cup had been the brainchild of a Frenchman back in the 1920s. Now, at last, the cup had come home. *Les Bleus* were on top of the world.

France's Zinedine Zidane (number ten) rises high to score with a header in the 1998 World Cup final.

FOOTBALL DREAMS

From Beijing to Buenos Aires, Manchester to Mexico City, millions of children, teenagers and adults play football for fun, sport and exercise. Many are content to take part at an amateur level, but for some, the dream of emulating the stars they read about, watch and worship is a passion.

YOUNG DREAMS

Promising players often emerge at an early age in school and local teams. In most countries, young footballers can play at a regional, county or state level in organized youth team competitions. Major football clubs run youth sides and football academies, and also send scouts to watch games in the hope of spotting new talent. Young players may be invited to an open day or trial, where scouts and coaches can observe them in action at close hand. A club may then offer a contract or a place at its youth academy to a promising player. Famous academies exist at clubs such as Bayern Munich, Manchester United and Porto. The most famous is De Toekomst, the youth academy of Dutch side Ajax. It has been responsible for producing truly great footballers such as Johan Cruyff, Marco van Basten, Dennis Bergkamp, Patrick Kluivert and, more recently, up-and-coming stars such as Rafael van der Vaart and Wesley Sneijder.

▲ Freddy Adu was born in Ghana, but is now a US citizen. Here, aged 14, he shoots past Sierra Leone's keeper at the 2004 Under-17 World Championship.

YOUTH TEAMS AND COMPETITIONS

As young players approach the pinnacle of the game, there are international matches for schoolboys and schoolgirls as well as under-17 and youth competitions. These reach a peak with FIFA's Under-17 World Championship and the World Youth Championship. The latter competition began in 1977; at the 1991 tournament, Portugal swept to the title with a midfield containing teenagers João Pinto, Rui Costa and Luis Figo. Ten years later, Argentina won the trophy thanks to the goals of Javier Saviola. The young striker was the top scorer at the tournament with 11 goals, ahead of rising Brazilian player Adriano and France's Djibril Cissé. FIFA's Under-17

> **FACTFILE**
> Internazionale offered 750,000 US dollars (about £460,000) to sign Freddy Adu in 2000. The offer was rejected by his mother – Adu was just ten years old.

▲ Young Chinese footballers perform wheelbarrow exercises. They are part of a group of 27 teenagers, known as the 2008 Star Team, who are expected to form the core of China's side at the next Olympics.

World Championship has also thrown up a number of stars. The 1997 competition, for example, showcased the talents of the up-and-coming Ronaldinho, Spanish goalkeeper Iker Casillas and Germany's Sebastian Deisler. Some young players are thrown into action with the adults in the reserve side or first team at a professional club. One of the youngest was Freddy Adu, who in 2004 came on as a substitute for US club DC United in their game against San Jose Earthquakes. He was just 14 years old.

HANDLING REJECTION

For millions of wannabes, the hope of playing professional football remains just a dream. As players rise through the footballing ranks, the vast majority find that their talents are surpassed by others and they are unable to progress further. Some talented young footballers are rejected because coaches believe their slight build or lack of height would put them at a disadvantage. As youngsters, Kevin Keegan and Allan Simonsen were rejected by major clubs for being too small, yet both went on to star for club and country and win the coveted European Footballer of the Year award. Other players are turned down because their levels of fitness are not high enough. As a 16-year-old, the great Michel Platini was rejected by French club Metz after medical checks revealed he had poor breathing and a weak heart.

Rejection is hard to take for many junior players, but some are able to use such a setback to spur themselves on and prove their doubters wrong. Young England star Shaun Wright-Phillips was discarded by Nottingham Forest at 15 for being too small and not good enough. He eventually signed for Manchester City, the club that released 14-year-old Ryan Giggs from its academy. The great Dino Zoff trialled at Internazionale, whose coaches were unimpressed. The same thing happened at Juventus, but the young keeper was not put off – he worked hard at his game and was eventually signed by Udinese. More than 20 years later, he captained Italy to the World Cup trophy.

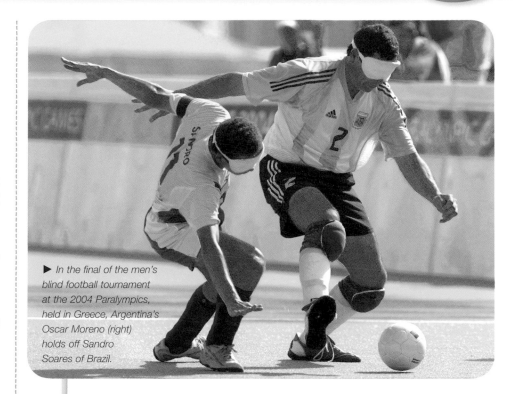

▶ In the final of the men's blind football tournament at the 2004 Paralympics, held in Greece, Argentina's Oscar Moreno (right) holds off Sandro Soares of Brazil.

▼ Souleymane Maman (right), playing for Belgian side Royal Antwerp, gets away from Mohammed Diallo of Beveren. Maman came on as a substitute for his national team, Togo, in a 2002 World Cup qualifying match against Zambia. He was just 13 years old.

FOOTBALL FOR ALL

Football can be enjoyed in all climates and conditions and by people of all ages and abilities. It is also played competitively by footballers with disabilities that range from being wheelchair-bound to having impaired hearing. In 2005, Great Britain, Iran and Germany were the football medallists at the Deaflympics, held in Australia. Amputee football is played by outfield players using crutches, but no artificial leg, and by goalkeepers who are single-arm amputees. Since 1984, the Paralympics has included a seven-a-side football competition for people suffering from cerebral palsy and brain injuries.

The game is played largely according to FIFA's seven-a-side rules, but with bigger goals, no offsides and two 30-minute halves. Football for blind and visually impaired athletes uses a special ball. It contains tiny ball bearings that make a distinctive sound as the ball moves. Teams consist of four blind outfield players, a keeper who can be partially sighted, and five substitutes. In 2004, the sport made its debut at the Paralympics, with teams from South Korea, France and Argentina amongst others. The sides contested 50-minute games, with Brazil emerging as gold medallists after a dramatic penalty shootout in the final.

> **FACTFILE** Francesc 'Cesc' Fabregas was signed by Arsenal from Barcelona in 2003. He became Arsenal's youngest ever first-team player at the age of 16 years and 177 days.

▶ Eric Cantona controls the ball during a beach football match. The sport is popular around the globe – in May 2005, spectators flocked to the first beach soccer World Cup, in Rio de Janeiro, Brazil.

A PRO'S LIFE

Viewed from the outside, a professional footballer's life appears glamorous, exciting and rewarding. But behind the appearances in top matches, on television shows and at celebrity events, lies much hard work and sometimes frustration and disappointment.

MAKING THE FIRST TEAM

Signing as a youngster for a big club is every aspiring footballer's dream, but, in truth, a young player in this position is only halfway towards his or her goal. Competition for one of the 11 starting places is intense. Many young players do not make the grade and have to move elsewhere – often down a division or two – to play first-team football. 'If you're good enough, you're old enough' is a motto used by some coaches who have thrust exceptionally talented youngsters into first-team action for their club or country. Cameroon striker Samuel Eto'o, for example, first played for his country the day before his 16th birthday. England's Wayne Rooney made his Premiership debut just months after leading Everton to the final of the

FA Youth Cup. He later became England's youngest international player at the age of 17 years and 111 days. In contrast, the majority of promising young players have to wait far longer for their first-team debut, often spending a number of seasons in their club's junior or reserve sides.

LOANED OUT

Increasingly in a number of major leagues, players are loaned out to other clubs to gain experience. Loan spells can be relatively short and to a lower-division club in the same country, such as David Beckham's six-week loan spell at Preston North End when he was a Manchester United youngster. They can also be for longer periods and to a club in a different country, such as Tottenham Hotspur's 18-month loan of Egyptian striker Mido from Italian club Roma. Many players who are frustrated by a lack of opportunities seek a loan or permanent move elsewhere to play first-team football. This is not just limited to young, inexperienced footballers. Real Madrid's Spanish striker Fernando Morientes has scored 24 times for his national side, but could not get into the Real first team ahead of Raúl and Ronaldo. He went on loan for the 2003–04 season to Monaco, where his nine goals helped take the club to the Champions League final. On his return to Real, however, first-team action was again in short supply and in 2004 he moved permanently to Liverpool.

◀ Fernando Morientes cannot hide his delight as he scores for Monaco. The goal knocked Real Madrid – the team that sent him on loan – out of the 2003–04 Champions League.

TRAINING, INJURIES AND RECOVERY

A typical week for a footballer involves training, resting, going to club functions and travelling to one or more games. Training usually involves a mixture of fitness, strength and flexibility exercises to boost a player's stamina, pace and sharpness. Players also practise skills and tactics – improving their heading or working on free kicks, for example. In Europe, footballers have for years eaten a healthy, scientifically managed diet. Britain, in contrast, was slow to catch on. Even in the 1970s and 1980s, a pre-match meal was often as heavy as steak, egg and chips.

Injuries occur fairly often in football. An English FA study of the 1997–98 and 1998–99

> **FACTFILE** Spanish goalkeeper Santiago Canizares missed the 2002 World Cup after dropping a bottle of aftershave on his foot.

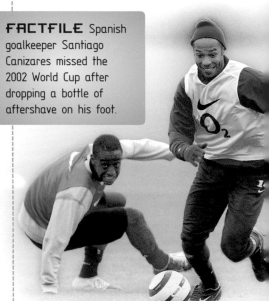

▲ Thierry Henry gets away from a defender at Arsenal's training ground before a Champions League match against Rosenborg in 2004.

▲ Gary Neville and Wayne Rooney in training for England. Players train hard and often, following a programme worked out by their coaches.

▲ *Ronaldo works in the gym to strengthen his injured knee. Recovery from an operation or a serious injury can be a difficult time, as players miss key games and face a long period of training.*

◄ *Top players are constantly in the public eye. Here, David Beckham signs autographs at an open training session. To attend, each fan donated £4 to charity.*

seasons recorded over 6,000 injuries, mostly to knee and ankle joints or leg muscles. At the end of March 2005, 80 players in Spain's top division were out with an injury, including Zinedine Zidane and Henrik Larsson. In Serie A, that figure was 101, including Pavel Nedved at Juventus, AC Milan's Andriy Shevchenko and Adriano, Alvaro Recoba, Edgar Davids, Christian Vieri and Dejan Stankovic at Internazionale.

Injured players are treated by a club's doctor and physiotherapist. They are sent to the best consultants and surgeons to ensure as quick a recovery as possible. This can take weeks or months and usually involves long days in the gym, gentle training and intensive sessions with the physio. Injured players are painfully aware that their place in the team has been filled. A young footballer may have seized the chance well, making it harder for the injured player to return.

A career in football can be short, with players retiring by their early thirties (although goalkeepers can play on into their late thirties). Serious injuries are what professional footballers fear most. Every year, an average of 50 English league players are forced to retire because of injury.

REWARDS AND RESPONSIBILITIES

Football's top players are paid handsomely and treated as celebrities in a similar way to music and movie stars. Some use their celebrity to publicize good causes, to help coach and inspire young people or to visit hospitals, schools and charities. Just like showbusiness stars, footballers have to deal with the media. A club may ask players to give interviews for website features or to co-operate with newspapers and television companies to promote an upcoming game or new kit, for example. What can be harder for young footballers to handle is the way in which the press can

▶ *Goalkeeper Fabien Barthez shields the ball from motor-racing legend Michael Schumacher during a charity match in Monte Carlo. The money raised went to a number of children's charities.*

invade their private lives. Photographers and reporters may besiege a player's home and follow their family and friends. Footballers are seen as important role models for young people and any wrongdoing, such as being fined for speeding, snubbing autograph hunters or partying, attracts much negative television and newspaper attention.

THE PLAYERS' STAGE

Without stadiums, football would still be played, but games would be far quieter, less passionate and exciting affairs. Stadiums spring into life on match days, when they are transformed from empty, silent steel and concrete structures into a seething sea of noise and colour.

GREAT STADIUMS

England and Scotland boasted the world's first great stadiums. Glasgow's Hampden Park was built in 1903; in 1937, almost 150,000 spectators were admitted to watch an international match between Scotland and England. The biggest crowd at London's Wembley Stadium – which was built in just 300 days – was its first, for the 1923 FA Cup final. More than 200,000 people crammed inside, spilling onto the pitch and forcing the kick-off to be delayed.

The mighty Maracana Stadium in Rio de Janiero, Brazil, is almost completely round. It holds the official world record for a football crowd – in 1950, around 199,850 people watched a World Cup game there between Brazil and Uruguay. Mexico City's Azteca

▲ A staggering 114,000 spectators, all standing, cram into London's Crystal Palace to watch the 1901 FA Cup final between Tottenham Hotspur and Sheffield United.

is the only stadium to have hosted two World Cup finals (1970 and 1986). Many of the world's biggest football arenas were built to host the World Cup or European Championships – from the Centenario in Uruguay, the venue for the first World Cup

in 1930, to Portugal's new Estadio da Luz that hosted the final of Euro 2004. The 2002 World Cup saw the most venues ever used for the tournament, with ten stadiums in South Korea and ten in Japan providing venues for the 32 teams.

BEHIND THE SCENES

The forgotten people of football are often the staff who run a stadium and ensure that the day of a match goes smoothly. We tend to think of them only when there is a problem such as crowd trouble or a pitch that is unfit for play. The club or stadium owner liaises with police and local authorities and employs stewards to prevent pitch invasions, violence and other problems. Box office staff do their best to ensure that tickets are sold and distributed correctly, while turnstile operators and sellers of programmes and food and drink all work at

▼ At Euro 2004, Fabien Barthez saves a David Beckham penalty in the Estadio da Luz in Lisbon, Portugal. The 65,000-capacity arena is Benfica's home ground.

▶ Groundstaff in traditional dress prepare the goal nets at the National Stadium in Lagos, Nigeria, before the opening game of the 1999 World Youth Championship.

a ground on a match day. At the 2006 World Cup, tickets will contain tiny microchips that can be read by scanners, easing crowd congestion and helping to prevent ticket fraud.

The groundstaff are in charge of the goals, the pitch and its markings. They work especially hard when the pitch is in poor condition because of bad weather – clearing snow, thawing out the pitch or soaking up excess moisture. On the day of the game, or sometimes earlier, the match referee examines the pitch carefully and talks to the groundstaff before deciding whether the game can go ahead.

▲ A groundsman gives the pitch a close cut at Newcastle United's St James Park stadium. Pitch care is vital at all top-level clubs.

STADIUM INNOVATION

Stadium tragedies have occurred all over the world (see pages 104–105), prompting many governments and football authorities to bring in far stricter rules on stadium design, capacities and crowd control. In the past 30 years, new safety laws and innovations in architecture have led to major changes in the design of football stadiums. Despite fans feeling a strong emotional attachment to a ground, dozens of clubs have abandoned their old stadium in or near the centre of a town or city. The money raised from the sale of the land is used to build a new stadium on the outskirts. Many of these stadiums form part of a hotel, leisure or shopping complex. A famous example is the Stade

> **FACTFILE** Azerbaijan's national stadium is named after Tofik Bakhramov, the linesman who famously awarded England's controversial third goal in the 1966 World Cup final.

> **FACTFILE** At the 1986 World Cup, eagle-eyed officials spotted that the pitch markings at the edge of the penalty area for the France–Hungary game were in the wrong place. They had to be hastily repainted.

de France in Paris, which was built to host the final of the 1998 World Cup. It features 17 shops and 43 cafes and restaurants for its 80,000 spectators.

Notably, the USA staged the first indoor World Cup qualifier (at the Seattle Kingdome) and the first indoor World Cup finals match (at the Pontiac Silverdome). Stadiums with a sliding roof have become more and more popular, allowing the venue to host music concerts and other indoor events. The Amsterdam ArenA was opened in 1996 as Ajax's new ground. The first European stadium with a retractable roof, it seats 51,859 spectators. The Millennium Stadium in Cardiff, Wales, and the Oita 'Big Eye' Stadium in Japan also have sliding roofs. Inside a new stadium, fans may find a removable pitch, corporate boxes for business entertaining and giant screens that replay action from the game. Germany's Arena Auf Schalke, opened in 2001, has 540 video screens throughout the stadium and a giant video cube suspended from the roof. With four 36m² video screens, it is the first of its kind in Europe.

TOP TEN LARGEST FOOTBALL STADIUMS

POPULAR NAME	LOCATION	CAPACITY
Saltlake	Kolkata, India	120,000
Azteca	Mexico City, Mexico	106,000
Azadi	Tehran, Iran	100,000
Nou Camp	Barcelona, Spain	98,600
Maracana	Rio de Janeiro, Brazil	95,095
San Siro	Milan, Italy	85,700
Soccer City	Soweto, South Africa	85,000
Olimpiyskiy	Kiev, Ukraine	83,160
Olimpico	Rome, Italy	82,556
Mineiro	Belo Horizonte, Brazil	81,897

▲ Munich's Allianz Arena will be completed for the 2006 World Cup. The 66,000-seat stadium has a see-through roof and walls. Lights will enable the colour of the stadium to change, depending on which team is playing.

SUPPORTERS AND TEAMS

Dreams are not only held by players and coaches. Everyone connected to a club or national side dreams that their team will achieve glory and success, and this especially includes the most loyal, passionate and vocal group of all – the fans.

FOLLOWING A TEAM

For millions of supporters, following their club or national side is a lifelong passion. Fans may chant for a manager to leave or be unhappy with certain players or the team's form, but their love of the club tends to remain. Dedicated fans go to great lengths to follow their side, putting up with poor weather and long hours of travelling to away games. Many fans spend much of their income every season on getting to as many games as possible and buying replica shirts and other merchandise – from T-shirts and scarfs to club-branded toothpaste and credit cards. Do these supporters get a fair deal for their time, effort and expenditure? To many casual or non-fans, the answer appears to be no. Entertainment and the 'right' result are never guaranteed, and ticket prices have soared at all-seater

▼ *Mascots are a feature at many football games. These British mascots are taking part in the 2002 Mascot Grand National, which was won by Oldham Athletic's Chaddy the Owl.*

TOP TEN AVERAGE ATTENDANCES IN EUROPE (2003–04)		
1	Borussia Dortmund	79,600
2	Real Madrid	69,200
3	Manchester United	67,640
4	Barcelona	67,585
5	AC Milan	63,245
6	Schalke 04	61,140
7	Internazionale	58,350
8	Celtic	58,180
9	Bayern Munich	55,470
10	Newcastle United	51,965

stadiums, sometimes pricing ordinary fans out of the game. Yet, being a loyal football fan is rarely a decision made with the head. It is all about heart and emotion. Every loyal fan loves to feel the rush of excitement as they approach their home ground, chant with the crowd and witness the start of a match. What comes next is a 90-minute rollercoaster ride of highs and lows, ending at the final whistle and followed by a post-match examination of what went right and wrong, before hope and expectancy build for the next game.

◀ *Facepainted Greek fans celebrate their team's surprise triumph at the 2004 European Championships.*

FANS AND THE MEDIA

Few stadiums hold more than 60,000 spectators, but the rise of television coverage has opened up the game to millions of new fans. Some supporters, however, criticize TV for concentrating on the top teams and moving matches to different days and new starting times. TV companies spend a fortune on buying the rights to show live games and highlights from the top leagues. Back in the studio, famous ex-players and managers comment on the action, while

HIT THE NET

www.stadiumguide.com
Information on the leading football stadiums in Europe and elsewhere, including the venues for Euro 2008.

www.expertfootball.com/history/soccer_derby.php
A pair of webpages looking at some of the world's greatest derby matches.

http://fifaworldcup.yahoo.com/06/en/p/cs/index.html
Profiles of the world's most famous stadiums, including the Azteca, the San Siro and Munich's Olympic Stadium.

FACTFILE With a Dutch mother and a Belgian father, fan Raymond Brul had a problem at Euro 2000. In the end, he showed his support for both nations by painting half his car in Dutch team colours and half in Belgian colours.

▲ Pelé's 1970 World Cup shirt was auctioned in 2002 for a record £157,750, beating the sum paid for Geoff Hurst's 1966 World Cup shirt by £66,000.

► Fans of Turkish club Galatasaray drum up a fearsomely loud atmosphere before their side's 2002 Champions League match against Barcelona.

reporters and statisticians provide interviews and highly detailed analysis of matches.

Coverage of football in other media has boomed, too. Fans manage their own sides in computer simulations or fantasy football leagues, while results, news and video clips are sent to their mobile phones. They can read about their club in books, magazines and fanzines. More recently, the rise of radio phone-ins and online messageboards has allowed fans to voice their opinions on games, players, managers and referees.

MORE THAN A GAME

Fans look forward to certain matches in particular – a clash between two teams at the top of the league table, for example. In a knockout cup competition, a game between a small club and a top side allows fans to dream of a famous giantkilling victory. Sometimes, even a draw in such matches goes down in history, such as Latvia's 0-0 result against Germany at Euro 2004.

The most anticipated and passionate of all games tend to be derby matches between two neighbouring sides. Most clubs have some form of derby match, but certain rivalries have passed into football folklore. Among them are the Buenos Aires derby between Boca Juniors and River Plate, the Peñarol-Nacional clash in Uruguay, the Milan derby between Internazionale and AC Milan and, in Greece, the battle between Olympiakos and Panathinaikos. The most intense derby in Britain is between the two Scottish 'Old Firm' sides – Rangers and Celtic. For some fans, beating their rivals in a derby can be even more important than league or cup success.

Some of the biggest derbies are not between neighbouring sides, but between the top clubs in the country. Spain's *Superclassico*, for example, is contested by two teams 500km apart – Real Madrid in the heart of the country and Barcelona on the east coast.

WHEN FANS TURN BAD

Sometimes, the passion of fans at a derby or other match can turn violent. Fighting between fans has occurred since football's early days, but it became known as the 'English disease' in the 1960s and 1970s as hooliganism flared up around the country. In 1995, a match between England and the Republic of Ireland had to be abandoned after 27 minutes when English fans rioted. At the 1998 World Cup and Euro 2000, England supporters fought running battles with other nationalities. More recently, hooliganism at English clubs has declined dramatically thanks to CCTV cameras, undercover police operations, all-seater stadiums and police forces working with clubs to identify, ban and even jail hooligans. Such techniques are being adopted in other countries where fan violence is a problem. In 2000, two Leeds United supporters were stabbed to death in Turkey by Galatasaray fans, while in 2002, two men died when Russian fans went on the rampage in Moscow after a World Cup defeat to Japan. The final of the 2000 African Women's Championship was abandoned when South African fans rioted after a controversial Nigerian goal. Yet, for all the incidents reported in the media, the vast majority of football fans never cause trouble.

◄ AC Milan keeper Dida is struck by a flare thrown by Internazionale supporters during a Champions League quarter-final in 2005. Referee Markus Merk abandoned the game and AC Milan were awarded a 3-0 win.

THE FOOTBALL INDUSTRY

Football is extremely big business. The world's largest clubs are valued in hundreds of millions of pounds and generate more than £50 million per year in income. But the pressure to achieve success has seen many clubs fall deeply into debt, with some facing the threat of going out of business.

BIG BUSINESS

The leagues of Germany, Italy, England, Spain and France are the wealthiest in the world, generating £3.9 billion in income during 2002–03. But within these leagues there are huge differences in spending power. In summer 2004, for example, Bayern Munich spent £17 million on new players, £11 million more than Hamburg, Germany's next highest spenders. Money is no guarantee of success, however. Manchester United and Real Madrid are the richest clubs in the world, yet neither won a league or Champions League title in the 2003–04 and 2004–05 seasons. Some other big spenders in recent years have also won relatively little – Serie A clubs Internazionale, Sampdoria and Lazio, for example.

Less wealthy clubs can still succeed in football. In 1997, Spain's Villareal were bottom of the second division, had just three members of staff and a stadium that held 3,500 fans. The club, based in a small town with only 40,000 people, has since reached the Spanish first division and in 2004 reached the semi-final of the

FACTFILE
In 1991, Manchester United were valued at £18 million. In 2005, to buy control of the club, American businessman Malcolm Glazer had to spend £790.3 million.

FACTFILE In 1999, Romanian club Nitramonia Fagaras were so cash-stricken that they could not pay a £14,000 gas bill. They had to transfer two players, Gabor Balazs and Ioan Fatu, to Gazmetan Medias (the gas company's football club) as payment.

▲ Argentina's Carlos Tevez scores against Paraguay in the 2004 Olympic football final. One of the game's hottest properties, Tevez was sold by Boca Juniors to Corinthians in 2004 for over £10 million, a record fee in South America.

UEFA Cup. Porto do not figure in the list of the world's top 20 richest clubs, but in 2004 they won the biggest club prize in Europe, the Champions League.

MONEY MATTERS

In the past, football clubs received almost all of their money from selling programmes, tickets, and food and drink. Today, these items often contribute less than a third of all the money a club generates in a year. Sales of merchandise and deals with advertisers may make up around a third of a club's income (sometimes more for the biggest clubs). The largest part of a club's income comes from the sale of broadcasting rights to television in particular, but also to radio and the internet. In 2002–03, 55 per cent of the money earned by Serie A clubs came from the sale of media rights.

Some clubs have succeeded through the backing of a wealthy company or individual who spends many millions on the team. In under three seasons, Roman Abramovich has spent

TRANSFER MILESTONES

YEAR	FEE	PLAYER
1905	£1,000	Alf Common (Sunderland to Middlesbrough)
1929	£10,000	David Jack (Bolton to Arsenal)
1952	£52,000	Hans Jeppson (amateur to Napoli)
1961	£142,000	Luis Suarez (Barcelona to Internazionale)
1968	£500,000	Pietro Anastasi (Varses to Juventus)
1975	£1.2m	Giuseppe Savoldi (Bologna to Napoli)
1985	£5m	Diego Maradona (Barcelona to Napoli)
1992	£10m	Jean-Pierre Papin (Marseille to AC Milan)
1996	£15m	Alan Shearer (Blackburn Rovers to Newcastle United)
1998	£21m	Denilson (São Paolo to Real Betis)
1999	£32m	Christian Vieri (Lazio to Internazionale)
2001	£45.62m	Zinedine Zidane (Juventus to Real Madrid)

▲ *Fans survey the wide range of merchandise for sale at the Nihondaira Stadium, one of the two homes of Japanese J-League side Shimizu S-Pulse.*

over £200 million buying players for Chelsea, while the Agnelli family – owners of car-makers Fiat – has financed Juventus for many years. Some clubs sell shares in the company that runs them, with mixed success. Share prices are sensitive to the performance of the team. When Borussia Dortmund were knocked out of the Champions League in 2003–04, for example, the value of the club fell by more than 15 per cent. In 2005, this famous club was on the brink of bankruptcy.

Many clubs, big and small, have run up huge debts through excessive transfer fees and wages, the collapse of TV deals or bad management. The entire debts of the Bundesliga clubs are estimated at £400 million. In Spain, the debt of Real Madrid alone is believed to be over £160 million. Some clubs, such as Colo Colo and River Plate, have been forced to sell their best players. Others have dropped down the leagues or, like Fiorentina or Czech side Bohemians, gone bankrupt. Fans of smaller clubs have sometimes banded together to buy their clubs and try to turn them around.

► *Real Madrid bought Luis Figo, David Beckham and Zinedine Zidane for £100 million – almost a million times the £110 it cost Bolton Wanderers to put together their entire 1958 FA Cup-winning side.*

FACTFILE
In 2004, David Beckham was believed to have a personal fortune of £65 million.

PLAYER MOVEMENT

Players have always moved from club to club, and for a century the best players have often cost some sort of transfer fee. In the 2004–05 season, Chelsea could field a starting 11 that cost more than £150 million in transfer fees. Fees spiralled from the mid-1980s, reaching a peak with the sale of Zinedine Zidane for more than £45 million in 2001. Since then, transfers have tended to drop in value. Part of the reason is that many clubs now face growing debts and lower income from media rights and other sources, making them unwilling to spend beyond their means. In 1995, a ruling by the European Court of Justice – the Bosman ruling – made it easier for players to move from club to club at the end of their contracts on a free transfer. This has pushed up players' wages, as many top footballers choose to see out their time at one club and leave for nothing in order to gain a big signing-on fee or higher wages elsewhere.

RICH REWARDS?

More of a football club's money is spent on buying and paying players than on any other expenditure. In 2002–03, Manchester United spent £79 million on wages, more than any other Premiership team. The yearly salary of a footballer in the English top division averages more than £400,000. The rewards for top players are similar in the world's richest leagues, which are all in Europe. Players employ agents to handle transfer moves, from which they may receive five per cent or more of the overall fee plus a signing-on bonus. Advertising and endorsing products, sponsorship deals and writing books and newspaper columns can greatly boost the income of a player.

In 2005, David Beckham, for example, was believed to be earning almost £15 million per year in endorsements. But in the lower divisions of the top leagues and in smaller leagues around the world, the rewards are much smaller and job security for players can be poor.

◄ *Walter Strutz, chairman of Mainz, despairs as his side misses out on promotion to the German Bundesliga. For clubs everywhere, playing in the top division – where the financial rewards are greatest – is a major goal.*

FOOTBALL NIGHTMARES

Football has a dark side. With passions running high on and off the pitch and with so much at stake in big matches, the game has sometimes lurched into a nightmare world of cheating, abuse, violence and even death.

CUT OFF IN THEIR PRIME

A number of players have died suddenly through on-pitch collisions or because of a medical problem. In 1973, Pedro Berruezo died of heart failure while playing for Sevilla. Thirty years later, during a Confederations Cup match against Colombia, Cameroon's 28-year-old midfielder Marc-Vivien Foe collapsed, and died shortly afterwards. A year later, in 2004, Hungarian international Miklós Fehér suffered a fatal heart attack while playing for Benfica.

Plane crashes have wiped out entire football teams, including Bolivia's most popular team, The Strongest, in 1969, the Soviet (now Uzbek) team of Pakhtakor Tashkent in 1979, and 18 members of the Zambian national squad in 1993. Other air crashes have devastated club sides, such as the 1958 Munich disaster that killed eight Manchester United players and 11 officials and journalists.

▲ In the 1940s, Torino won four league titles in a row. When their aircraft crashed in 1949, 18 players died, comprising most of the Italian national side.

MATCH-FIXING AND CHEATING

In 1909, George Parsonage was banned for life after asking for a £50 signing-on fee when he joined Chesterfield (the maximum allowed was £10). This looks quaint compared to today's examples of corruption, bribery and match-fixing. In 1999, the former head coach of Romania's Dynamo Bucharest, Vasile Ianul, was sentenced to 12 years in prison for stealing £1.6 million from the club, while Marseille president Bernard Tapie was jailed in 1997 for bribing players and officials. German football was rocked in 2004 when referee Robert Hoyzer owned up to fixing matches and being in league with a Croatian gambling syndicate. But Germany is far from alone – there were match-fixing allegations and illegal payments to players and managers in England during the 1990s, while six Italian players were banned in 2004 for their role in gambling-related match-fixing. An attempt to fix a game on the pitch occurred when Chile were being outplayed by Brazil in a 1989 World Cup qualifier. Goalkeeper Roberto Rojas cut himself with a razor blade hidden in his glove and pretended to have been injured by an object thrown from the crowd. The game was abandoned, but video footage proved Rojas' cheating. He was banned and Chile were prevented from qualifying for the 1994 World Cup.

STADIUM DISASTERS

Crumbling stadiums, overcrowding, poor safety rules and bad crowd control have caused many stadium disasters. The worst ever football tragedy occurred in Lima, Peru, in 1964 when over 300 fans were killed and more than 500 injured in panic stampedes and riots. In a 1982 European Cup match in Moscow, 340 people died, most by

FACTFILE

In 1999, the owner of Doncaster Rovers, Ken Richardson, was sent to prison for four years for conspiring to burn down the club's main stand.

▲ Fans pay tribute to Colombian defender Andres Escobar. The scorer of an own goal in a 2-1 loss to the USA at the 1994 World Cup, Escobar was murdered in his home country ten days later, shot 12 times by an unknown gunman.

▲ Emergency workers tend to a victim of a tragedy at South Africa's Ellis Park in 2001. Four major stadium disasters occurred in Africa in that year. Altogether, they took the lives of more than 200 people.

◄ Newcastle United players and Aston Villa's Gareth Barry try to separate brawling team-mates Kieron Dyer and Lee Bowyer in April 2005. Both players had fallen foul of the authorities before and been criticized as poor role models for youngsters.

FACTFILE In November 2004, the mother of Brazilian star Robinho was kidnapped and only released 41 days later. The mothers of two more Brazilian star players were kidnapped shortly afterwards.

crushing, when police tried to force fans out of a crowded section of the stadium and down an icy staircase. Two major disasters occurred in 1985 – a wooden stand at Bradford City's ground caught fire, killing 56 people, while the European Cup final also ended in tragedy. A wall collapsed at the Heysel Stadium in Belgium and a riot flared when some Liverpool fans charged at Juventus supporters. One Belgian and 38 Italian spectators died as a result.

POOR ROLE MODELS?

Footballers are highly esteemed as role models to the young, but some have abused their position and been convicted of crimes. In 2004, English striker Lee Hughes was jailed for six years for causing death by dangerous driving. Other players have behaved violently on and off the pitch. In 2001, a mass brawl broke out at a match between Roma and Galatasary, while in a 1993 cup game between South America's Gremio and Peñarol, four players from each

▲ At Liverpool's Anfield ground, fans lay tributes to the 96 people who died during the 1989 FA Cup semi-final at Hillsborough Stadium.

side were sent off. Footballers have also fought with fans. Manchester United's Eric Cantona, for example, kung-fu kicked a Crystal Palace supporter in 1995; and in March 2005, Malaga's Paulo Wanchope scuffled with his club's fans.

Like athletes in other sports, footballers are tested for illegal drug use. In 2003, Rio Ferdinand received an eight-month ban for failing to attend a drugs test, while a year later Adrian Mutu tested positive for cocaine. Diego Maradona remains football's most

notorious drugs cheat. He was sent home from the 1994 World Cup after testing positive for the stimulant ephedrine; in recent years, Maradona has fought an addiction to cocaine. Many other footballers have battled against alcohol addiction, from former England captain Tony Adams to George Best and Brazilian legend Garrincha.

RACISM AND INTIMIDATION

Some fans, players and managers have been found guilty of racially insulting or abusing opponents. Racism in football was thought to be on the wane, with non-white footballers making up a fifth or more of the total number of players in many European leagues. Anti-racism campaign work has been carried out by many clubs, governments and groups such as FARE (Football Against Racism in Europe). However, the racist chanting aimed at England's black players at the Bernabeu Stadium during a 2004 Spain-England game and similar incidents of racial abuse in Italy, Spain, England and Eastern Europe prove that much work still needs to be done. Violence and intimidation can occur on and off the pitch; sometimes, match officials are the target. In 2000, a French first division game between Metz and Strasbourg was abandoned after an assistant referee was hit by a firecracker. In 2005, referee Luiz Carlos Silva was drawn into a fist fight after being attacked on the pitch by a fan during the Brazilian derby between America MG and Atlético Mineiro.

▲ Referee Anders Frisk was hit by an object thrown by Roma fans during a 2004 Champions League match against Dynamo Kiev. Frisk abandoned the game at half time and UEFA awarded Kiev a 3-0 victory. In 2005, Frisk retired from refereeing after he and his family received death threats.

SNAPSHOT
GREECE WIN EURO 2004

Greece began Euro 2004 as rank outsiders, never having won a match in the finals of the European Championships. Short on superstars yet superbly organized by their 65-year-old German manager, Otto Rehhagel, the Greeks made their mark at once. They beat the hosts, Portugal, 2-1 in the opening match of the tournament. Greece stuttered through their next two group games before springing more surprises in the knockout phase. First they defeated the holders, France, by a single goal and then beat the highly rated Czech Republic by a silver goal in extra time. Meeting Portugal in the final at Lisbon's Estadio da Luz, the Greeks were indebted to their goalkeeper, Antonis Nikopolidis, who made a string of crucial saves to ensure that Angelos Charisteas' goal, a header in the 57th minute, would take them to glory.

Portuguese defenders look on in disbelief as Angelos Charisteas scores the header that would win Greece the Euro 2004 title. It was Charisteas' third strike of the championships.

THE WORLD CUP

Friendlies or charity matches are entertaining, but for a football match to have meaning it has to be part of a wider competition. Football has spawned hundreds of different competitions, but none can compete in global interest and prestige with the World Cup. From small beginnings with 13 competing countries, it has grown to the point where 193 nations attempted to qualify for the 2002 competition, the final of which was watched by around one billion people.

▼ Sepp Blatter and Franz Beckenbauer

▲ Argentina's goalkeeper, Juan Botasso, makes a despairing dive, but fails to stop Hector Castro scoring Uruguay's fourth goal in the 1930 final.

HOPING TO HOST

Six nations expressed an interest in hosting the first World Cup, held in 1930. Until Japan and South Korea hosted it in 2002, the tournament had always been staged in Europe or the Americas, but the competition now moves around the globe – in 2010, the World Cup will be held in Africa for the first time. In July 2000, Germany was awarded the 2006 World Cup, six years after tabling its bid. Bidding countries must prepare in great detail, making presentations and receiving official inspections from FIFA before a decision is made.

URUGUAY 1930

Final
Uruguay 4 • Argentina 2
Semi-finals
Uruguay 6 • Yugoslavia 1
Argentina 6 • USA 1
Games 18 **Goals** 70
Goals per game 3.89

It took 19 minutes for France's Lucien Laurent to write his name in the record books as the scorer of the first World Cup goal. France beat Mexico 4-1, but it was their only victory and, like Belgium and Romania, they went out at the group stage. Four European sides made the long trip to South America by boat, but only Yugoslavia reached the semi-finals. They and the USA were thrashed in the semis, by Uruguay and Argentina respectively. Argentina boasted the best forward of the competition, Guillermo Stabile, but Uruguay – on home soil and as reigning Olympic champions – were firm favourites. In the final, they came back strongly after Argentina had taken a 2-1 lead, to become the first World Cup winners.

ITALY 1934

Final
Italy 2 • Czechoslovakia 1
Semi-finals
Italy 1 • Austria 0
Czechoslovakia 3 • Germany 1
Games 17 **Goals** 70
Goals per game 4.12

In 1934, the South American teams had not forgotten the lack of European entrants for the first World Cup. As a result, world champions Uruguay chose not to defend their title, while Brazil and Argentina sent understrength sides to Italy. Yet 32 nations, mostly European, were keen to enter the competition. With 16 places available, qualification matches began in June 1933. Italy's 4-0 win over Greece marked the first and only time that a World Cup host has had to play a qualifier to get into the finals. Egypt were the first nation outside of the Americas or Europe to qualify, but following one round of knockout games, the eight remaining teams were all European. After a 7-1 thrashing of the USA, Italy's goals dried up and they only just sneaked past Spain and Austria on their way to the final. In that match, Italy's Luisito Monti (formerly of Argentina) became the only player to have appeared in a World Cup final for different countries. Against a battling Czech side, a goal five minutes into extra time from Italy's Angelo Schiavio secured the Jules Rimet trophy for the hosts.

▼ Coach Vittorio Pozzo is carried aloft by triumphant Italian players after masterminding their 1934 World Cup campaign.

FRANCE 1938

Final

Italy 4 • Hungary 2

Semi-finals

Italy 2 • Brazil 1

Hungary 5 • Sweden 1

Games 18 **Goals** 84

Goals per game 4.67

With the threat of war looming over Europe, Spain and Austria were forced to pull out of the tournament. But the 1938 World Cup did feature the first team from Asia, the Dutch East Indies (now Indonesia), as well as a Cuban side that sprang a major shock by beating Romania in a replay. Sweden thrashed Cuba 8-0, but were then on the receiving end of a 5-1 semi-final mauling by the first great Hungarian side. The other semi-final saw one of the great managerial blunders when the Brazil coach, Adhemar Pimenta, either because of arrogance or through injury fears, rested his star player, Léonidas da Silva. Léonidas had lit up the tournament, most notably in an epic 6-5 thriller against Poland in which he became the first player to score four goals in a World Cup finals match, only for Poland's Ernest Wilimowski to do the same five minutes later. Without the tournament's top scorer, Brazil crashed to defeat against Italy, who went on to become champions for the second time.

▶ *Léonidas da Silva twists and turns at the 1938 World Cup. An outrageously skilful attacker, the Brazilian was one of the first players to master the overhead kick.*

FACTFILE Dr Ottorino Barassi, the vice president of the Italian FA, smuggled the World Cup out of a bank in Rome and hid it to prevent the Nazis from stealing the trophy. For much of World War II, football's greatest prize lay in a shoebox under Barassi's bed.

▲ *Brazilian keeper Moacir Barbosa gathers the ball during a 1950 group game against Yugoslavia. The match, watched by more than 142,000 spectators in the Maracana, ended in a 2-0 victory to Brazil.*

BRAZIL 1950

Final pool

Uruguay 5 pts • Brazil 4 pts

Sweden 2 pts • Spain 1 pt

Games 22 **Goals** 88

Goals per game 4.00

The only World Cup to feature a final pool of four instead of a final, the 1950 tournament started poorly. Scotland and Turkey withdrew, only 13 nations attended and the mighty Maracana Stadium was not ready to host the first match. But the competition built in excitement and drama as the goals flowed, often from the boots of the hosts who, after topping their group, ran rampant in the final pool stages, scoring seven against Sweden and six against Spain. Before that point, there had been several notable shocks, including the USA's 1-0 defeat of a highly rated England team. The final pool format could have been an anticlimax, but the outcome went down to the very last game, with Uruguay and Brazil separated by one point and playing in front of around 199,850 fans. Despite falling a goal behind to the favourites, Uruguay won the match 2-1 to lift the World Cup once more.

FACTFILE At the 1930 World Cup, not one of the 18 games was drawn. Neither was there a play-off game to decide third place.

WORLD CUP GOLDEN BOOT WINNERS

1930	Guillermo Stabile, Argentina (8 goals)
1934	Oldrich Nejedly, Czechoslovakia (5)
1938	Léonidas da Silva, Brazil (8)
1950	Ademir Menezes, Brazil (9)
1954	Sandor Kocsis, Hungary (11)
1958	Just Fontaine, France (13)
1962	Garrincha, Brazil; Vava, Brazil; Valentin Ivanov, USSR; Leonel Sanchez, Chile; Florian Albert, Hungary; Drazan Jerkovic, Yugoslavia (4)
1966	Eusebio, Portugal (9)
1970	Gerd Müller, West Germany (10)
1974	Gregorz Lato, Poland (7)
1978	Mario Kempes, Argentina (6)
1982	Paolo Rossi, Italy (6)
1986	Gary Lineker, England (6)
1990	Salvatore Schillaci, Italy (6)
1994	Hristo Stoichkov, Bulgaria; Oleg Salenko, Russia (6)
1998	Davor Suker, Croatia (6)
2002	Ronaldo, Brazil (8)

SWITZERLAND 1954

Final

West Germany 3 • Hungary 2

Semi-finals

West Germany 6 • Austria 1

Hungary 4 • Uruguay 2

Games 26 **Goals** 140

Goals per game 5.38

As home to the headquarters of FIFA, which was celebrating its 50th birthday, Switzerland was an obvious host for the 1954 tournament. It featured newcomers such as Turkey, South Korea and the western half of a divided Germany (which had been barred from the 1950 competition). The fans saw plenty of drama and goals, none more than in Austria's 7-5 defeat of Switzerland (the highest-scoring game in the history of the World Cup finals). Hungary, boasting the incredible talents of Ferenc Puskas, Sandor Kocsis and Nandor Hidegkuti, were the most rampant side, scoring an incredible 27 goals in just five matches. At their third World Cup, Uruguay thrashed Scotland 7-0 and beat England 4-2 to reach the semi-finals. They were the only team never to have been beaten in the World Cup until they came up against Hungary, who won 4-2 and went into the final as favourites. West Germany, however, overturned the odds to record a highly emotional victory.

◀ *Pelé chases the ball during Brazil's exciting semi-final against France. The tie was poised at 2-1 to Brazil before Pelé scored three goals in 21 minutes.*

first ever 0-0 draw. Yet it was the two smaller British nations, Wales and Northern Ireland, who qualified for the quarter-finals, with the Irish sensationally beating a strong Czechoslovakian team. Free-scoring France and Brazil quickly emerged as the favourites, and their semi-final clash was an epic in which the 17-year-old Pelé blasted a hat-trick in Brazil's victory. France had to be content with a 6-3 mauling of West Germany to secure third place. Just Fontaine's four goals in that game propelled him to the Golden Boot with 13 goals in total, a record to this day. The hosts, Sweden, had quietly and efficiently seen off some very strong sides – including Hungary, the Soviet Union and West Germany – to reach the final, but they were no match for Brazil. In a rematch of the pair's third-place play-off at the 1938 World Cup, Brazil triumphed 5-2 to win the tournament for the first time.

FACTFILE Vava's goal in the 1962 final (to add to his pair of goals in the 1958 final) make him the only player to have scored in the finals of successive World Cups.

SWEDEN 1958

Final

Brazil 5 • Sweden 2

Semi-finals

Brazil 5 • France 2

Sweden 3 • West Germany 1

Games 35 **Goals** 126

Goals per game 3.60

Fifty-five countries entered the 1958 qualifying tournament and some big names, including Italy, Holland, Spain and Uruguay, failed to qualify. All four UK home nations (Scotland, England, Northern Ireland and Wales) reached the finals – the only time this has happened. England had lost key players in the Munich aircrash (see page 79), but were the only team to hold a rampant Brazilian side to a draw and to stop them scoring. It was the World Cup's

◀ *Hungary's Zoltan Czibor outjumps Ottmar Walter of West Germany in the 1954 final. Czibor scored to put Hungary 2-0 up, but found himself on the losing side after a heroic comeback by the Germans.*

▲ *Argentina's Jorge Albrecht (left) and Uwe Seeler of West Germany struggle for the ball in 1966. Seeler played in each of the four World Cups sandwiched between West Germany's victories in 1954 and 1974.*

CHILE 1962

Final

Brazil 3 • Czechoslovakia 1

Semi-finals

Brazil 4 • Chile 2

Czechoslovakia 3 • Yugoslavia 1

Games 32 **Goals** 89

Goals per game 2.78

Chile was a controversial choice to host the World Cup, with its small population and its infrastructure damaged by an earthquake in 1960. As it turned out, most of the problems happened on the pitch. A series of bad-tempered matches occurred in the first round, including the infamous 'Battle of Santiago', during which armed police invaded the pitch three times to split up warring Chilean and Italian players. Chile made it through to a semi-final against Brazil by beating the Soviet Union, while two strong Eastern European sides, Yugoslavia and Czechoslovakia, battled it out in the other semi-final. The Brazilians lost Pelé to injury after only two games, but in Garrincha and Vava they had two of the best players of the tournament. Brazil duly won the final with a team featuring eight World Cup-winners from the 1958 tournament.

ENGLAND 1966

Final

England 4 • West Germany 2

Semi-finals

England 2 • Portugal 1

West Germany 2 • Soviet Union 1

Games 32 **Goals** 89

Goals per game 2.78

The 1966 World Cup was a well-organized tournament and the first to feature a mascot (World Cup Willie). West Germany and Portugal were the most free-scoring sides in a competition characterized by defensive play. Two enormous shocks occurred early on – Brazil were eliminated by Portugal and newcomers North Korea knocked out Italy with a stunning 1-0 victory. The North Koreans won the support of many neutral fans, and their quarter-final meeting with Portugal was a classic. North Korea were 3-0 up within 20 minutes before Portugal, inspired by the tournament's

▲ *Portugal's star striker, Eusebio, walks off in tears after his team is eliminated from the 1966 World Cup following a 2-1 defeat by England.*

eventual top scorer, Eusebio, hit back to win 5-3. In the semi-final, Eusebio's 82nd-minute strike could not stop England going through to meet West Germany in what proved to be an epic final. The Germans went ahead, then England scored twice to lead until a surprise last-minute German goal took the game into extra time. Geoff Hurst scored two more goals to secure a dramatic victory for the host nation (see pages 68–69).

> **FACTFILE** Two pairs of brothers have played on winning sides in a World Cup final – Fritz and Ottmar Walter of West Germany (1954) and England's Jack and Bobby Charlton (1966).

MEXICO 1970

Final

Brazil 4 • Italy 1

Semi-finals

Brazil 3 • Uruguay 1

Italy 4 • West Germany 3

Games 32 **Goals** 95

Goals per game 2.97

For many seasoned football observers, the 1970 World Cup remains the best. Much of the brutal, physical play seen in the 1962 and 1966 tournaments was absent. In its place were fascinating tactical and skilful contests between the world's greatest sides. Although the tournament was the first to feature red and yellow cards, no player was sent off, and some of the games have passed into football legend. These include a chess-like battle between Brazil and England that the South Americans narrowly won 1-0; Italy's 4-1 defeat of Mexico; and the Italians amazing 4-3 victory against West Germany in the semi-final. But the final tops the list. Brazil had powered through the rounds, with star players such as Jairzinho (who set a record by scoring in all six of Brazil's games), Pelé and Rivelino exhibiting great attacking flair. In the final they were unstoppable, recording their third World Cup win and claiming the Jules Rimet trophy for good.

▼ *Brazilian striker Tostao holds off Italy's Roberto Rosato during the 1970 World Cup final. Tostao suffered a freak eye injury before the tournament and only last-minute surgery enabled him to play.*

WEST GERMANY 1974

Final

West Germany 2 • Holland 1

Third-place play-off Poland 1 • Brazil 0

Games 38 **Goals** 97

Goals per game 2.55

Ninety-nine nations attempted to qualify for the 1974 tournament, which would see the winners lift a new trophy – the FIFA World Cup. Spain, France and England all failed to reach the tournament, while Zaire, Haiti, East Germany and Australia made their debuts. Changes to the competition format meant that there would be no semi-final games. Instead, the winners of the two second-round groups would contest the final and the group runners-up would play off for third place. Holland, exhibiting their brand of 'total football', swept aside Bulgaria (4-1), Uruguay (2-0), Brazil (2-0) and Argentina (4-0) to top Group A and reach the final. Poland were the surprise team of the tournament. Propelled in part by the goals of striker Gregorz Lato, they came second in Group B after narrowly losing 1-0 to West Germany. The West Germans had taken time to reach top gear, but with Franz Beckenbauer pulling the strings and the prolific Gerd Müller in fine form, they made the final. There, they overcame the setback of a first-minute Dutch goal from a penalty to win the World Cup for a second time.

▼ Peru's Teofilo Cubillas (centre) runs at Argentina's defence during his side's controversial 6-0 defeat. Cubillas scored five goals at the 1978 World Cup, matching his tally at the 1970 competition.

ARGENTINA 1978

Final

Argentina 3 • Holland 1

Third-place play-off Brazil 2 • Italy 1

Games 38 **Goals** 102

Goals per game 2.68

A colourful and at times controversial tournament, the 1978 World Cup may have lacked some standout stars, but it was rarely short of footballing drama. The hosts found themselves in the toughest of groups with France, Hungary and a young Italian side that beat them, but Argentina made it through to the second group stage. Tunisia caused a shock by drawing with holders West Germany and beating Mexico 3-1 to become the first African side to win a World Cup finals game. Austria, with their star striker Hans Krankl, played strongly in the early stages, beating Spain, Sweden and West Germany. But they were crushed 5-1 by a Dutch squad lacking Johan Cruyff, who had pulled out of the tournament for family reasons. Scotland's campaign promised much, but went badly wrong when they failed to beat Iran and lost to Peru. They then roused themselves, however, to beat Holland 3-2. In the second group stage, Italy, Argentina, Brazil and Holland emerged as frontrunners. Much controversy centred on the Argentina-Peru game. The last match in Group B, it would determine whether Argentina or Brazil reached the final. Peru had played well in the early stages of the tournament, winning their group ahead of Holland. Their 6-0 loss to Argentina was suspicious and meant that Brazil were knocked out without having suffered a defeat, while Argentina progressed to the final, in which they beat Holland.

FACTFILE On 14 June 1974, Carlos Caszely of Chile became the first player to receive a red card in a World Cup tournament.

◄ Germany's defence, marshalled by legendary goalkeeper Sepp Maier and the incomparable Franz Beckenbauer (far right), holds firm against a Dutch attack in the 1974 World Cup final.

SPAIN 1982

Final

Italy 3 • West Germany 1

Semi-finals

Italy 2 • Poland 0

West Germany 3 • France 3 (5-4 penalties)

Games 52 **Goals** 146

Goals per game 2.81

In 1982, the format of the tournament changed again so that 24 countries would appear at the finals. Teams played in six groups of four, with the top 12 sides playing in four groups of three to determine the semi-finalists. Belgium surprised the holders, Argentina, beating them and El Salvador to win their group, while England topped theirs ahead of France. The two surprise teams were Northern Ireland, who beat Spain to reach the second round, and Algeria, who had stunned fans by winning their match with West Germany. Poland made the semi-finals, but the hosts went out after winning just one match. The toughest second-round group, containing Brazil, Argentina and Italy, saw the Italians go through, beating Brazil in a 3-2 thriller. At the semi-final stage, West Germany beat France in an equally exciting encounter, but could not stop the Italians from winning their third World Cup.

▶ In 1982, an Algerian fan waves banknotes in protest as West Germany and Austria conspire to achieve a result which took both European teams through at the expense of Algeria. All final group matches are now played simultaneously to give teams an equal chance.

MEXICO 1986

Final

Argentina 3 • West Germany 2

Semi-finals

Argentina 2 • Belgium 0

West Germany 2 • France 0

Games 52 **Goals** 132

Goals per game 2.54

Colombia had been due to host the 1986 World Cup, but troubles in that country meant they had to withdraw. When Mexico stepped in, they became the first nation to host the tournament twice. More than 120 nations battled for the 24 places in the finals, in which Canada and Iraq both made their debuts. Morocco became the first African nation to reach the second round when they won a group that

FACTFILE The fastest sending-off in World Cup history occurred in 1986, when Uruguay's José Batista was dismissed against Scotland after just 55 seconds.

contained Portugal, Poland and England. Denmark looked promising until they were thrashed 5-1 by Spain, while Belgium squeezed past the Soviet Union 4-3 in one of the best games of the tournament. The quarter-finals were extremely tight affairs. Three went to penalty shootouts, while the fourth game saw England face Argentina. Maradona arrived at the World Cup as the world's most expensive player and a heavily marked man. His incredible dribbling and scoring skills made him the best player of the tournament. In the quarter-final, his two goals (one a deliberate handball, the other a magnificent solo effort – see pages 56–57) sank England and he repeated the feat against Belgium in the semi-final. In the final, West Germany went 2-0 down, rallied to 2-2, but were beaten by an 88th-minute goal from Argentinian midfielder Burruchaga.

▲ Marco Tardelli (left) charges away after scoring Italy's second goal in the 1982 World Cup final against West Germany. Team-mates Claudio Gentile and Gabriele Oriali are equally jubilant.

◀ Argentina's Diego Maradona is in ecstasy as the side he captained and inspired triumphs over West Germany in the 1986 final.

ITALY 1990

Final

West Germany 1 • Argentina 0

Semi-finals

West Germany 1 • England 1 (4-3 penalties)

Argentina 1 • Italy 1 (4-3 penalties)

Games 52 **Goals** 115

Goals per Game 2.21

This well organized and attended World Cup is remembered for moments of great theatre, from veteran Cameroon striker Roger Milla's dance at the corner flag to Costa Rica's joy at defeating both Scotland and Sweden to qualify for the second round. Sadly, the tournament also saw much negative football and a record number of bookings (164), as well as 16 sendings-off. Every previous winner of the World Cup made it through the group stages, with Cameroon the talk of the tournament after their defeats of Romania and Colombia set up a quarter-final against England. Cameroon went 2-0 up, but two Gary Lineker penalties and a third England goal in extra time saw every neutral's favourite team go out. Holland arrived as European Champions, but failed to win a match, while Brazil and the Soviet Union had similarly disappointing tournaments. Both semi-finals were tense games that went to penalty shootouts, but the final was deeply forgettable. West Germany beat Argentina courtesy of an 85th-minute penalty, while Pedro Monzon was the first of two sendings-off for Argentina and the first player to be red-carded in a World Cup final.

▼ Italian goalkeeper Walter Zenga concedes a headed goal to Argentina's Claudio Caniggia in the 1990 semi-final.

USA 1994

Final

Brazil 0 • Italy 0 (3-2 penalties)

Semi-finals

Brazil 1 • Sweden 0

Italy 2 • Bulgaria 1

Games 52 **Goals** 141

Goals per game 2.71

Some people feared that the crowds at the 1994 World Cup would be small in a country where male football is not a dominant sport. But they were proved wrong by a lively tournament attended by an average of 70,000 spectators per game. Attacking play had been encouraged by the adoption of both the backpass rule (see page 24) and three instead of two points for a win during the group-stage games. Despite losing many players since the break-up of the Soviet Union, Russia recorded the biggest win of the tournament, 6-1 against Cameroon, with Oleg Salenko scoring five goals – the most by one player in a single World Cup match. Maradona exited the tournament when he failed a drugs test, but plenty of other stars were on display. The Republic of Ireland caused the biggest shock of the group stages by beating Italy 1-0, but Saudi Arabia's win against Belgium and Bulgaria's defeat of Argentina came close. The Bulgarians had a marvellous tournament, knocking out Germany and finishing fourth overall. European sides dominated the quarter-finals, taking seven out of the eight places, yet it was Brazil who beat Holland, Sweden and Italy to lift the World Cup trophy for a record fourth time.

◄ Bulgaria's Iordan Letchkov (left) beats Germany's Thomas Hassler to score a spectacular diving header at the 1994 World Cup.

WORLD CUP PENALTY SHOOTOUTS

YEAR	TEAMS	PENS
1982	West Germany – France	5-4
1986	West Germany – Mexico	4-1
1986	France – Brazil	4-3
1986	Belgium – Spain	5-4
1990	Rep. Ireland – Romania	5-4
1990	Argentina – Yugoslavia	3-2
1990	Argentina – Italy	4-3
1990	West Germany – England	4-3
1994	Bulgaria – Mexico	3-1
1994	Sweden – Romania	5-4
1994	Brazil – Italy	3-2
1998	Argentina – England	4-3
1998	France – Italy	4-3
1998	Brazil – Holland	4-2
2002	Spain – Rep. Ireland	3-2
2002	South Korea – Spain	5-3

FRANCE 1998

Final

France 3 • Brazil 0

Semi-finals

France 2 • Croatia 1

Brazil 1 • Holland 1 (4-2 penalties)

Games 64 **Goals** 171

Goals per game 2.67

More countries from outside Europe and South America attended the last World Cup of the 20th century, as the number of places was raised from 24 to 32. Newcomers included Jamaica, Japan and South Africa. Iran caused a shock in their first World Cup for 20 years by beating the USA 1-0. Nigeria also upset the odds with a 3-2 defeat of Spain that effectively knocked the European side out of the tournament. Despite 22 red cards (the most ever), the competition was enthralling, with sides including Croatia, Denmark, Brazil, France and Holland playing attacking football. England narrowly went out, losing on penalties to Argentina in one of the games of the tournament. Croatia were the dark horses, progressing quietly and then beating Germany 3-0 in the quarter-final. For the second tournament in a row, Italy were knocked out on penalties, this time to France at the quarter-final stage. A France-Brazil final was an exciting prospect, but Ronaldo was ill before the game and was extremely subdued, as were his team-mates. France won with relative ease, aided by two headed goals from Zinedine Zidane (see pages 92–93).

▶ England's David Beckham is shocked to receive a red card for aiming a kick at Argentinian captain Diego Simeone, who had fouled Beckham moments earlier. Argentina won this 1998 second-round match on penalties.

SOUTH KOREA AND JAPAN 2002

Final

Brazil 2 • Germany 0

Semi-finals

Brazil 1 • Turkey 0

Germany 1 • South Korea 0

Games 64 **Goals** 161

Goals per game 2.52

The 2002 competition was the first to be held in Asia and the first to be hosted by two nations. An amazing 193 countries attempted to qualify for the 32 places on offer and there were surprise failures to reach the finals by Holland, Yugoslavia, Uruguay and Colombia, while China appeared at their first tournament. The shocks began in the opening game, when France – the World Cup holders and European Champions – were sensationally beaten 1-0 by Senegal. France then lost to Denmark and went out of the

▶ Turkey's Hakan Sukur (right) tangles with South Korea's Lee Min-Sung during the 2002 third-place play-off.

World Cup with just one point. They were joined by Russia and also by European heavyweights Poland and Portugal, who finished in the bottom two places of Group D behind the USA and South Korea. Cheered on by passionate home crowds, the South Koreans were the story of the tournament, knocking out Italy, Spain and Portugal on the way to the semi-finals. The USA beat Mexico to make the quarter-finals, as did Senegal, who beat Sweden before losing to Turkey. The Turks lost narrowly to Brazil in the semi-final, but claimed third place overall. In the final, Brazilian striker Ronaldo put memories of 1998 behind him, scoring two goals against Germany and winning the Golden Boot.

were all knocked out in the quarter-finals, leaving the USA, Norway, Sweden and Germany in the semi-finals. Around 65,000 spectators watched the final, in which the USA beat Norway with a goal from Michelle Akers just three minutes from full time.

◄ *Sisleide do Amor Lima, better known as Sissi, brings the ball down for Brazil. At the 1999 Women's World Cup, the veteran midfielder tied with China's Sun Wen for the Golden Boot award.*

THE WOMEN'S WORLD CUP

After much lobbying from the women's football associations, the FIFA Women's World Cup was launched in China in 1991. Since then, interest in the women's game has boomed, with the tournaments attracting millions of television viewers.

CHINA 1991

Final USA 2 • Norway 1
Although there were several mismatches at the tournament (in particular Sweden's 8-0 thrashing of Japan), the first Women's World Cup was a great success and proof that women's football had a major global audience. China, Denmark, Chinese Taipei and Italy

SWEDEN 1995

Final Norway 2 • Germany 0
The 1995 tournament started with a shock, as an up-and-coming Brazilian women's team beat the hosts, Sweden, in the opening game. The 25 games that followed saw plenty of goals. Brazil were thrashed 6-1 by Germany, who then lost a 3-2 thriller to Sweden. The USA and China shared the spoils in an epic 3-3 encounter and Norway powered through their group, putting 17 goals past Canada, England and Nigeria, before knocking out the USA at the semi-final stage. In the other semi-final, Germany beat China in a close-fought game. Sweden's Ingrid Jonsson became the first woman to referee a FIFA final, in which Norway scored two first-half goals to secure the world crown.

USA 1999

Final USA 0 • China 0 (5-4 penalties)
The 1999 Women's World Cup – featuring 16 teams and 32 games – was a huge success, with large crowds and heavy media coverage. Nigeria, propelled by their star player Mercy Akide, became the first African nation to reach the quarter-finals, where they lost narrowly to Brazil in extra time. The USA, with Mia Hamm, Brandi Chastain and Tiffeny Milbrett all playing superbly, had to come from behind against

a strong German team, before overcoming Brazil in the semi-finals. In contrast, China cruised to the final – their 5-0 mauling of cup-holders Norway was an awesome spectacle. The final, played in front of more than 90,000 fans at the Rose Bowl, was a very tense affair. Like the 1994 men's final at the same venue, the game went to penalties, with Briana Scurry saving Ying Liu's spot kick to see the USA win the shootout 5-4.

USA 2003

Final Germany 2 • Sweden 1
An epidemic of the SARS virus prevented China from hosting the World Cup for a second time and the tournament was moved to the USA at the last minute. By way of compensation, China retained its automatic qualification to the 2003 competition as host nation, and will host the 2007 tournament. The 2003 World Cup was predicted to be a successful swansong for many of the USA's veteran players. However, a vibrant, attacking German side – headed by the tournament's leading scorer, Birgit Prinz – knocked them out at the semi-final stage. In a memorable final, a golden goal by subsitute Nia Kuenzer secured Germany their first Women's World Cup.

▲ *Germany's captain, Bettina Wiegmann, holds aloft the 2003 Women's World Cup. Germany were by far the best side at the competition, scoring 25 goals (11 more than any other team) on the way to their first World Cup triumph.*

not qualifying for a World Cup. England fans still wince at their team's failure to reach the 1974, 1978 and 1994 tournaments, while Holland failed to qualify for six World Cups in a row before 1974, and also missed out on the 2002 competition. Before the 2006 tournament, Portugal had only managed to reach three World Cups (1966, 1986 and 2002). Brazil are the only country to have successfully qualified for and attended every single World Cup tournament.

◄ Commins Menapi of the Solomon Islands is the hero after his side achieve a shock result during 2006 World Cup qualifying, holding Oceania's leading team, Australia, to a 2-2 draw.

HIT THE NET

www.fifaworldcup.yahoo.com/06/en
FIFA's homepage for the 2006 World Cup is packed with news, plus features on qualifying and organization.

www.worldcup-history.com
An in-depth statistical guide to every World Cup, searchable by player, team or tournament.

www.planetworldcup.com
Find out about World Cup tournaments, with results, statistics and stories.

▲ FIFA president Sepp Blatter hosts the preliminary draw for qualifying places for the 2006 World Cup.

WORLD CUP QUALIFICATION

For the teams that contested the first World Cup qualifying campaign in 1933–34, it was all or nothing – a single knockout match determined who made it to the finals. Since then, the number of countries aiming for World Cup glory has risen considerably, and qualifying campaigns have grown much longer. To qualify for the 1998 World Cup, for example, Jamaica played a gruelling 20 matches. For the 2002 World Cup, there were over 770 qualifying games. Each football confederation (see pages 12–13) organizes its own qualifying contests to fill the places it is given at the World Cup. For the 2006 tournament, the number of places awarded were: Europe (14), Africa (5), Asia (4.5), South America (4.5), CONCACAF members (3.5) and Oceania (0.5). The half places are decided by a pair of home and away play-off games between teams from different confederations for the right to appear at the World Cup.

Qualifying is a highly competitive drama in itself, and national managers rarely survive

GERMANY 2006

Like the 2002 World Cup, the 2006 competition in Germany will feature 32 teams. In the past, the holders usually gained automatic entry along with the hosts. This time round, Brazil also have to qualify for the competition. The successful teams will appear in eight groups of four teams, with the top two sides qualifying for the knockout stages – second round, quarter-finals, semi-finals and the final. Lasting a month, the 2006

World Cup will be played in 12 stadiums. The opening match will be held in the futuristic new Allianz Arena in Munich (see page 99), while the final will be played in Berlin's refurbished Olympic Stadium. Organizing a World Cup is an enormous task involving thousands of people and costing hundreds of millions of pounds. Germany has to build stadiums, provide facilities for the media and teams and deal with 3.2 million fans, the majority of whom will be foreign tourists.

THE EUROPEAN CHAMPIONSHIPS

The European Championships started life in 1958 as the UEFA European Nations Cup, but struggled to find enough nations to compete. Today, however, the competition is the largest international football competition behind the World Cup. Like that tournament, it is held every four years.

HUMBLE BEGINNINGS

Henri Delaunay, secretary of the French FA and the first general secretary of UEFA, had suggested a European tournament back in 1927. Regionalized European competitions such as the Balkan Cup and the Home Internationals for the four countries that comprise the UK took place, but a complete European-wide competition did not begin until 1958, with the final held in France in 1960. The early tournaments saw teams play a series of qualifying rounds, with the four winners progressing to play a mini tournament consisting of semi-finals and a final. The standout match in the first competition was the semi-final between France and Yugoslavia. France were ahead 4-2 when Yugoslavia scored in the 75th, 78th and 79th minutes to win 5-4. The Yugoslavs lost

to the Soviet Union in the final and would also lose to Italy in the 1968 final. Strong teams from Eastern Europe dominated the early competitions – the Soviet Union reached the semi-final or final of each tournament between 1960 and 1972, while Hungary, Yugoslavia and Czechoslovakia also performed well. The Czechs had a sparkling 1976 competition. In just four days, they beat the two 1974 World Cup finalists, West Germany and Holland, to win the title.

FACTFILE Midfielder Michel Platini holds the record for the most goals scored in a European Championships. He scored nine of France's 14 goals in the 1984 competition.

CHANGING FORMATS

From 1968, qualifying took place in groups rather than rounds of knockout matches; the format of the competition has continued to change since. By the 1980 tournament in Italy, eight teams were taking part in the finals. Belgium were the story of that competition, winning a very tough group containing England, Italy and Spain before losing narrowly to West Germany in the final. The 1980s saw two highly gifted and entertaining sides, France and Holland, win the European Championships. Throughout the 1980s and early 1990s, however, many top sides failed to reach the finals, which dented the competition's prestige. England, Holland and Italy all failed to make the 1984 tournament; France failed to qualify for the 1988 Championships; and neither Italy nor Spain were present in 1992. With the countries of Eastern Europe dividing into smaller states in the early 1990s, the numbers of competing sides boomed and UEFA expanded the format so that 16 teams contested the finals of Euro 96.

HOSTS AND WINNERS

YEAR	HOST	FINAL
1960	France	USSR 2-1 Yugoslavia
1964	Spain	Spain 2-1 USSR
1968	Italy	Italy 2-0 Yugoslavia (after replay)
1972	Belgium	West Germany 3-0 USSR
1976	Yugoslavia	Czechoslovakia 2-2 West Germany (5-3 penalties)
1980	Italy	West Germany 2-1 Belgium
1984	France	France 2-0 Spain
1988	West Germany	Holland 2-0 USSR
1992	Sweden	Denmark 2-0 Germany
1996	England	Germany 2-1 Czech Republic
2000	Belgium / Holland	France 2-1 Italy
2004	Portugal	Greece 1-0 Portugal

▶ Slavisa Jokanovic (left) of Yugoslavia tangles with Spain's Alfonso during a truly epic encounter at Euro 2000. Alfonso scored in injury time to secure Spain a 4-3 victory after they had been 3-2 down with just moments to play.

EURO 92

The 1990s began in a colourful fashion for the Championships, as the Faroe Islands recorded a shock 2-0 victory over Austria in a qualifying match. The 1992 tournament saw perhaps the biggest surprise win in the competition's history. Denmark had failed to qualify, most of its players were on holiday and the team's manager was decorating his kitchen when news emerged of Yugoslavia's disqualification and Denmark's invitation to join. Inspired by Brian Laudrup, Flemming Povlsen and Peter Schmeichel in goal, the Danes set about their task with relish, beating France to qualify from Group A. In a dramatic semi-final against Holland, a heroic penalty save by Schmeichel saw them through to the final, where they beat Germany to win the most unlikely of crowns.

EURO 96 AND 2000

Euro 96 got off to a strong start, with Paul Gascoigne scoring the goal of the tournament against Scotland, the Czech Republic stunning Italy with a 2-1 win and Croatia effectively knocking the holders, Denmark, out of the competition. England then sprang a surprise, mauling the fancied Dutch team 4-1, before losing a semi-final penalty shootout to Germany. In the final, Germany defeated the Czech Republic with a golden goal, the first to decide a major football competition. Euro 2000 was co-hosted by Holland and Belgium – the first time two countries had jointly held the competition. The Dutch side scored the highest number of goals in a finals match, thrashing Yugoslavia 6-1. The Yugoslavs' two other games were among the most entertaining in the tournament – a 3-3 draw with Slovenia and a 4-3 defeat to Spain. The Spanish impressed, but fell to the eventual winners, France, in the semi-final.

▲ Denmark's players line up before their Euro 92 match against Sweden, which they lost 1-0. The under-prepared Danes rallied superbly, however, qualifying from their group and winning the title.

> **FACTFILE** Spanish leader General Franco, a critic of communism, refused the Soviet team entry into Spain to play their qualifying game for the 1960 competition. The Soviets were awarded a win.

EURO 2004

Euro 2004 began with 50 nations taking part in the qualifying competition. The first round threw up a series of surprises as Spain and Italy were knocked out; the same fate befell Germany, who drew with minnows Latvia in their group. In Group A, Russia beat Greece thanks to a Dmitri Kirichenko goal scored after just 67 seconds – the fastest in the history of the European Championships. The Czech Republic and France topped their groups unbeaten, but both were knocked out by a hard-working, well-organized Greek team, as were Spain. The Greeks also beat Portugal twice (in the first and last games of the competition) to win the trophy. The 2008 European Championships, to be held in Austria and Switzerland, are likely to conjure up just as many surprises and moments of drama as previous tournaments.

▲ Czech Republic striker Milan Baros was the top scorer at Euro 2004, with five goals.

▶ England's Paul Gascoigne celebrates at Euro 96, held high by Gary Neville. Gascoigne had just scored the goal of the tournament – a superb volley against Scotland.

▶ Zlatan Ibrahimovic of Sweden lays off the ball ahead of Italy's Giuseppe Favalli in a 1-1 draw at Euro 2004. Italy failed to reach the quarter-finals despite beating Bulgaria in their next group match.

THE OLYMPICS

Until the emergence of the World Cup, the Olympics provided football's leading world competition. Football appeared in the 1896 games as an exhibition event and became a full Olympic sport twelve years later. With the exception of the 1932 Los Angeles games, it has featured at every Olympics since. The competition was boosted in the 1990s by the admittance of professional stars and the emergence of African football, which produced two Olympic gold medallists in Nigeria and Cameroon.

AMATEURS ONLY

For most of its history, Olympic football was played by amateurs only. The rise of professional football in the 1920s meant that many of the world's best professionals were unable to appear at the games. State-run teams from Eastern Europe dominated the Olympics after World War II – from 1952 to 1988, every Olympic winner came from Eastern Europe with the exception of the 1984 French side, while Hungary remain the only team to have won football gold three times. But as the Olympics began to accept professional athletes in other sports, so it changed the rules for football.

Professionals who were part of their national under-23 team appeared at the 1992 games. In 1996, the rule was relaxed to allow each side to field three professional players over the age of 23. At Sydney 2000, Chile, led by 33-year-old striker Ivan Zamorano, won bronze. Zamorano's six goals made him top scorer at the games.

FACTFILE The 1952 Olympics produced three amazing games. Egypt caused a shock by beating Chile 5-4. Luxembourg eclipsed that with a 5-3 win over England. Yugoslavia led the Soviet Union 5-2 with just 14 minutes to go, but the game ended as a thrilling 5-5 draw.

EMERGING PLAYERS

Great professional players have emerged from the Olympics. For example, French midfielder Michel Platini and Mexican legend Hugo Sanchez burst onto the international scene at the 1976 Montreal games. The 1996 Brazil team included Rivaldo and Ronaldo. The 1952 Olympics in Helsinki, Finland, saw the arrival of a stunningly good Hungarian side. Featuring players such as Ferenc Puskas, Nandor Hidegkuti and Sandor Kocsis, the Hungarians conceded two goals but scored 20 on their way to the gold medal. These players went on to form the core of the Hungarian side that lit up international football through the 1950s (see page 70).

▲ Celestine Babayaro of Nigeria in action during the gripping 1996 Olympic semi-final against Brazil. Nigeria won 4-3 and went on to beat Argentina 3-2 in the final to become the first African side to win a major international tournament.

▶ Cameroon celebrate winning gold at the 2000 Olympics. The African side defeated Brazil and Chile to reach the final, where they beat Spain in a penalty shootout.

FACTFILE Records of the first games at the 1896 Olympics are vague, but appear to have been between two Greek teams and a Denmark side that won 15-0 in the final. One Greek team fielded five British men all with the surname Whittal.

OLYMPIC WOMEN

Women's football finally became part of the Olympics at the 1996 Atlanta games, after many years of lobbying for inclusion. With no time for a qualifying competition, the top eight nations at the 1995 Women's World Cup were invited to take part, with the exception of England, who were ineligible to compete. The final saw China beaten 2-1 by the USA in front of 76,481 spectators, a world record for a women's sporting event. The five powerhouse nations of women's football – the USA, Germany, Norway, China and Brazil – have since won all the medals between them. But the qualification system now in place will ensure that Asia, Africa and Oceania are all represented at future Olympics.

▲ *The US team celebrate winning gold at the 2004 Olympics. Mia Hamm (front row, second from right), the most famous player in women's football, announced her retirement shortly after receiving the gold medal.*

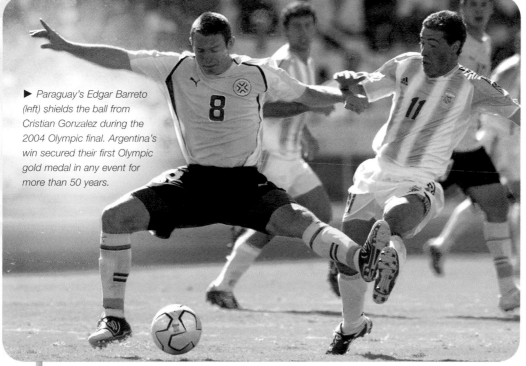

▶ *Paraguay's Edgar Barreto (left) shields the ball from Cristian Gonzalez during the 2004 Olympic final. Argentina's win secured their first Olympic gold medal in any event for more than 50 years.*

THE 2004 GAMES

There were plenty of shocks in the men's competition in Athens. Mali beat the hosts, Greece, 2-0 in the preliminary rounds, while Iraq caused a sensation with a thrilling 4-2 win over Portugal. The Iraqis were knocked out in the semi-finals by Paraguay, who managed to defeat Italy, Japan and South Korea along the way. In a cagey final with just five shots on target, Paraguay lost 1-0 to their South American neighbours, Argentina. In the women's competition, China were crushed 8-0 by Germany, a women's Olympic record. A young Brazilian side bounced back from a 2-0 loss to the USA to defeat Mexico 5-0 and then Greece 7-0. But the ageing US team managed to beat first Germany and then Brazil to win Olympic gold for the second time.

OLYMPIC GOLD MEDALLISTS

MEN

1908	Great Britain
1912	Great Britain
1920	Belgium
1924	Uruguay
1928	Uruguay
1936	Italy
1948	Sweden
1952	Hungary
1956	Soviet Union
1960	Yugoslavia
1964	Hungary
1968	Hungary
1972	Poland
1976	East Germany
1980	Czechoslovakia
1984	France
1988	Soviet Union
1992	Spain
1996	Nigeria
2000	Cameroon
2004	Argentina

WOMEN

1996	USA
2000	Norway
2004	USA

THE COPA AMERICA

The oldest continental cup competition, the Copa America has been played under a bewildering array of names and formats ever since the first competition, a three-way affair between Argentina, Uruguay and Chile in 1910. One thing has remained constant – its status as a major footballing prize for the nations of South America.

▲ Brazil's players charge across the pitch after beating Argentina in a penalty shootout to win the 2004 Copa America.

CUP DOMINATION

The Copa America has had to contend with clubs reluctant to release players and the increasing popularity of international club competitions. Yet it still maintains a strong appeal. Its largest ever audience, 170,000 fans, crammed into the Maracana in 1989 to watch Brazil beat Uruguay in the final. There have been 42 Copa America competitions, eight of which have been unofficial, but are counted for the records. The tournament has been dominated by the big three South American nations of Argentina, Brazil and Uruguay. Fifteen Copas passed until another country, Peru, won it. Since then, Argentina (with 15 titles) and Uruguay (with 14) have maintained a strong grip. Brazil have won six times; Paraguay and Peru have twice been the victors; and Bolivia and Colombia have each won one tournament.

INVITED GUESTS

In 1993, the Copa was expanded to 12 sides, including two invited teams from the CONCACAF federation, Mexico and the USA. Mexico have since competed in four further Copa Americas and have proved to be tough opponents, finishing as runners-up twice (in 1993 and 2001) and recording two third-place finishes. Costa Rica, Japan and South Korea have all competed in the Copa America. Another CONCACAF guest, Honduras, caused a sensation at the 2001 competition, knocking out Brazil 2-0 in the quarter-finals, losing to Colombia in the semi-finals, but beating Uruguay to claim third place. The 42nd Copa, held in Peru in 2004, saw Argentina lose to Mexico after beating Ecuador 6-1, yet still make the final, in which they lost to Brazil.

FACTFILE Two players have scored 17 Copa goals – Norberto Mendez (Argentina) and Zizinho (Brazil).

◄ Colombia's Gerardo Bedoya (right) fights for the ball with Ricky Garcia of Honduras during a 2001 Copa America semi-final. Colombia won the match and went on to beat Mexico in the final.

COPA AMERICA WINNERS

1910*	Argentina	1949	Brazil
1916*	Uruguay	1953	Paraguay
1917	Uruguay	1955	Argentina
1919	Brazil	1956*	Uruguay
1920	Uruguay	1957	Argentina
1921	Argentina	1959*	Argentina
1922	Brazil	1959	Uruguay
1923	Uruguay	1963	Bolivia
1924	Uruguay	1967	Uruguay
1925	Argentina	1975	Peru
1926	Uruguay	1979	Paraguay
1927	Argentina	1983	Uruguay
1929	Argentina	1987	Uruguay
1935*	Uruguay	1989	Brazil
1937	Argentina	1991	Argentina
1939	Peru	1993	Argentina
1941*	Argentina	1995	Uruguay
1942	Uruguay	1997	Brazil
1945*	Argentina	1999	Brazil
1946*	Argentina	2001	Colombia
1947	Argentina	2004	Brazil

*unofficial tournament

THE AFRICAN NATIONS CUP

The first African Nations Cup, held in 1957, was contested by just three of Africa's nine independent nations at the time – Sudan, Ethiopia and the eventual winners, Egypt. Since then, the number of independent African countries has risen sharply. At the 2002 tournament, 48 teams competed to qualify for 16 places at the finals.

AFRICAN NATIONS CUP WINNERS

Year	Winner	Year	Winner
1957	Egypt	1982	Ghana
1959	Egypt	1984	Cameroon
1962	Ethiopia	1986	Egypt
1963	Ghana	1988	Cameroon
1965	Ghana	1990	Algeria
1968	Congo-Kinshasa	1992	Ivory Coast
1970	Sudan	1994	Nigeria
1972	Congo-Brazzaville	1996	South Africa
1974	Zaire	1998	Egypt
1976	Morocco	2000	Cameroon
1978	Ghana	2002	Cameroon
1980	Nigeria	2004	Tunisia

◄ Tunisia and Morocco contest the final of the 2004 African Nations Cup.

FACTFILE In 1998, Egyptian coach Mahmoud al-Gohari became the first person to have won the African Nations Cup as both a player (in 1959) and as a manager.

UPS AND DOWNS

The African Nations Cup has had to endure its ups and downs, with poor playing facilities in some countries, hostilities between nations and major controversies. These continue into the modern era. Nigeria, one of Africa's top sides, were expelled from the 1998 tournament after they had refused to travel to the 1996 competition. Since the early 1990s, the best teams in the competition have relied on calling back as many of their foreign-based stars as possible. In 2000, for example, Nigeria's team contained just one player based in his home country. At the same tournament, the Ivory Coast's goalkeeper, Alain Gouamene, set a record with his seventh African Nations tournament appearance and his 24th game.

WINNERS AND LOSERS

A qualifying stage for the African Nations Cup was introduced in 1968, with eight places up for grabs. This was increased to 12 in 1992 and 16 for the 1998 competition (including the hosts and the defending champions). Champions have come from around the continent – from Africa's northernmost country, Morocco (winners in 1976), to its southernmost nation, South Africa, who returned from the international wilderness to win an emotional competition in 1996. Five tournament finals have ended in exciting penalty shootouts, none more tense than in 1992, when an epic shootout saw the Ivory Coast beat Ghana 11-10.

Three sides – Egypt, Ghana and Cameroon – head the winners' table, with four victories each. One of the most unlucky nations has to be Zambia, who lost an entire team in a tragic 1993 plane crash (see page 104), yet miraculously reached the final the following year. They lost the final, however, and remain a team with three third places, two second places, but no trophy win. Tunisia, with two runners-up spots and one third place, were in a similar position until the 2004 Nations Cup, when they won the title, beating Senegal, Nigeria and Morocco along the way.

► Mahamadou Diarra of Mali (left) goes past Senegal's Henri Camara at the 2004 African Nations Cup.

THE ASIAN GAMES AND ASIAN CUP

Asia is the one continent that has two major football competitions for its nations – the Asian Games and the Asian Cup. Both tournaments are held every four years, but in cycles that keep them two years apart.

THE ASIAN GAMES

The Asian Games is a multi-sport competition in which football is just one of a number of events. In the first tournament, football featured alongside weightlifting, cycling and basketball, and was played in games lasting 80, not 90, minutes. India, Burma (now Myanmar) and Taiwan dominated the early competitions, with South Korea finishing runners-up three times in a row. The South Koreans have also shared the title twice, after the final was drawn. Penalty shootouts were later introduced to decide the winner and Iran beat North Korea 4-1 on penalties to capture the 1990 title. After a self-imposed

▲ Iran's Yahya Golmohammadi (left) and keeper Ebrahim Mirzapour run a lap of honour after a shock defeat of Japan to win the 2002 Asian Games.

exile from the Asian Games in the mid-1990s, Iran powered to victories in 1998 and 2002. By the 2002 games, the tournament had been altered to become an under-23 competition, with sides allowed to field up to three over-age players. The 2006 competition in Qatar will feature football alongside more than 35 other sports.

THE ASIAN CUP

First held in Hong Kong with just four competing sides, the Asian Cup has grown greatly in importance. Qualification for the 12-team tournament held in Lebanon in 2000 attracted 42 countries. The footballing gap between rich and poor Asian nations was highlighted when Kuwait recorded the

◄ Zheng Zhi (left) of China and Japan's Takayuki Suzuki jump for a header during the 2004 Asian Cup final, held in Beijing. Japan took the trophy with a 3-1 victory.

highest ever victory in qualifying, trouncing Bhutan 20-0. However, the gradual emergence of higher-quality sides from the former Soviet Republics, smaller Gulf states such as Bahrain and Qatar, and countries in southeast Asia promises to make future tournaments more competitive. In recent years, the frontrunners have come from the Middle East (Iran and Saudi Arabia, for example) or the Far East (including Japan, South Korea and China). Iran, Japan and Saudi Arabia are the competition's most successful teams, winning the cup three times each, while Israel were a major force in the early years. They competed in the final of the first four Asian Cups, winning in 1964. In 1975, however, Israel were expelled from the Asian Football Confederation, and joined UEFA in 1992.

China became hosts for the first time in 2004, when the tournament was expanded to include 16 teams. There were plenty of surprise results, with much-fancied sides Saudi Arabia and Qatar finishing bottom of their groups, while Uzbekistan won all their group games. The final, between Japan and China, attracted enormous interest. The match was broadcast live to 60 nations; in China alone, the television audience was more than 250 million.

ASIAN GAMES AND ASIAN CUP WINNERS

GAMES WINNERS		CUP WINNERS	
1951	India	1956	South Korea
1954	Taiwan	1960	South Korea
1958	Taiwan	1964	Israel
1962	India	1968	Iran
1966	Burma	1972	Iran
1970	Burma and South Korea	1976	Iran
		1980	Kuwait
1974	Iran	1984	Saudi Arabia
1978	North Korea and South Korea	1988	Saudi Arabia
		1992	Japan
1982	Iraq	1996	Saudi Arabia
1986	South Korea	2000	Japan
1990	Iran	2004	Japan
1994	Uzbekistan		
1998	Iran		
2002	Iran		

THE CONCACAF CHAMPIONSHIP

Of all the footballing regions of the world, North America, Central America and the Caribbean Islands have had the most complex history of competitions. Five different tournaments have been open to them, starting with the CCCF Championship in 1941.

▲ Manley Junior Tabe of Vanuatu releases the ball ahead of New Zealand's Aaron Lines in the 2002 Oceanian Nations Cup.

THE GOLD CUP

For a number of years, competition in the CONCACAF zone was used as a direct way of qualifying for the World Cup. In 1991, the tournament was renamed the Gold Cup, which today features 12 teams at the finals. Every Gold Cup has been hosted by the USA, either alone or jointly with Mexico. Teams from outside CONCACAF have often been invited to play. In 1996, the Brazilian under-23 side lost to Mexico in the final.

South Korea were guests in 2000, but they lost out on a quarter-final place to Canada on the toss of a coin. Canada went on to beat another guest, Colombia, in the final. At the 2002 competition, lots were drawn in a three-way tie for two quarter-final places. Canada and Haiti progressed at the expense of Ecuador, but the tournament was eventually won by the USA for the first time since 1991. The 2005 competition, featuring guest teams Colombia and South Africa, was won by the USA, who beat surprise finalists Panama 3-1 on penalties after a 0-0 draw.

THE OCEANIAN NATIONS CUP

Oceania's competition is the smallest and youngest of the continental championships. It has been held seven times since its birth in 1973, when the small Pacific island of Tahiti made it to the final, only to be beaten by New Zealand. In 1996, it was decided to stage the competition every two years. The 2004 tournament threw up a major surprise as the Solomon Islands defeated New Zealand and eventually finished runners-up to Australia.

GOLD CUP WINNERS

1991	USA
1993	Mexico
1996	Mexico
1998	Mexico
2000	Canada
2002	USA
2003	Mexico
2005	USA

▲ Hernan Medford (left) of Costa Rica is fouled by Guatemala's Gustavo Cabrera. Costa Rica were Gold Cup runners-up in 2002.

▲ Mexican captain Pavel Pardo celebrates with the CONCACAF Gold Cup in 2003 after his side's 1-0 victory over Brazil in the final.

FOOTBALL LEAGUES

Clubs compete in leagues that are made up of several divisions. Rules, numbers of teams and the length of a league season vary around the world. Many top leagues – in Spain, Italy, France and Germany, for example – have 18 or 20 teams.

NUMBERS AND BREAKS

The top divisions of Romania, Russia and Japan each contain 16 teams. In Sweden and Poland the figure is 14, in Slovakia it is ten and in Latvia just eight. In most leagues, sides play each other twice, home and away, during a season. In Denmark, the 12 teams play each other three times. Scotland's top division has an unusual format – there are 12 teams, but the season lasts for 38 games. Sides play each other

three times, before the league turns into two groups of six for a further round of matches. Some leagues – in Argentina, Mexico and Japan, for example – are split into two short seasons every year. League teams in Spain, France, Bulgaria, Hungary and some other countries take a midwinter break, while in northern European nations such as Russia, Norway and Finland, the league season begins in the spring.

PROMOTION AND RELEGATION

While leagues in South Korea and the USA guarantee each team a place for the following season, most leagues have a system of promotion and relegation, with top and bottom sides switching places for the new season. In Uruguay, relegation and promotion are determined by the performance of teams over two seasons. In Austria and Scotland, one side is promoted and one relegated each season. In Hungary, the Czech Republic and the Ukraine, two

▼ *Toluca (in yellow) battle with Tigres in the Mexican league. Toluca won the 2002–03 Clausura, or winter, championship – their fourth league title since 1998.*

▲ *Jefferson Farfan of PSV Eindhoven runs between Feyenoord's Karim Saidi and Bruno Basto during a Dutch first division league match in 2004.*

▲ *South Korean Ahn Jung-Hwan, playing for Japanese side Yokohama F Marinos, celebrates his winning goal in a J-League encounter against Kashima Antlers.*

▼ *Celtic's Bobo Baldi lunges for the ball, held by Dado Prso of Rangers, during a derby between Scotland's two most successful sides.*

HARD FALLERS

Just as clubs can rise, so can they fall. In the 2004–05 season, 11 former champions of the English league (with 28 titles between them) played outside the top division. A slide down the divisions can be gradual or sudden. Napoli were home to Diego Maradona and one of Italian football's aristocrats, winning the league title in 1987 and 1990 and finishing runners-up in the two intervening years. Yet, by the early 2000s they were bankrupt and playing in Serie C, two divisions down from the top flight.

Rarely, however, has a downturn been more dramatic than that experienced by Manchester City or Tasmania 1900 Berlin. In 1937, Manchester City were the English league champions. In the following season, they scored 80 league goals, more than any other side, but were relegated. Tasmania 1900 Berlin were joint first in the early stages of the 1965–66 Bundesliga season. By the end, they were bottom and holders of a series of unenviable records for a season, including: fewest wins (two), most losses (28), most goals against (108) and lowest points total (eight).

teams go up and down, while in Germany, France, Spain and Portugal it is three.

In Greece, the third-place team in the second division contests a play-off with the team finishing 13th in the first division to decide who will play in the top division the following season. Other nations, such as Italy and England, hold a play-off series featuring semi-finals and a final to determine which of four teams will be promoted along with others that won automatic promotion above them. In Italy, play-offs are also used to determine which side joins three other relegated teams from Serie A. Play-off systems are criticized for turning a whole season into a lottery over one, two or three games, but many people think they maintain interest and generate high drama.

FAST RISERS

Some leagues have been dominated by a small number of teams throughout their history. For 43 seasons from 1932, the Uruguayan league title was won by either Peñarol or Nacional (Defensor were champions in 1976). Scotland's Glasgow Rangers hold the world record for the most league championships, with a staggering 51 titles, 12 more than their arch rivals, Celtic. In some leagues, small teams have risen dramatically from humble beginnings to become champions or contenders. In Europe, the now mighty Bayern Munich were not considered successful enough to join the Bundesliga in the early 1960s, but since then they have become one of the pillars of German football.

FACTFILE
The Isles of Scilly, off the coast of southwestern England, are home to the Scillonian League, the world's smallest. Woolpack Wanderers and Garrison Gunners are the only two sides to contest the league, as well as two cup competitions.

► *River Plate's Paraguayan striker Nelson Cuevas is challenged by defender German Re of Newell's Old Boys during an Argentinian first division match in Buenos Aires.*

SERIE A

Serie A has long had a reputation as the ultimate test for the world's top players. For decades, South American stars have played for its clubs; they were joined in the 1990s by great talents from Africa and Asia. Some clubs are now struggling with severe financial problems as a result of their lavish spending on players. Winning Serie A is sometimes referred to as the *scudetto* (small shield), as the champion's strip the following season bears a small coat of arms in Italian colours. Sometimes, the quality of the league has meant that a team which is successful abroad has struggled domestically. The best example of this is Internazionale, who won the UEFA Cup in the 1993–94 season, but could only manage 13th place in the league. Juventus are the most successful Serie A club, with 28 titles, followed by AC Milan (17), Internazionale (13) and Genoa (nine). In 2004, Serie A was expanded from 18 to 20 teams.

◄ *Francesco Totti of Roma (in red) clashes with Emanuele Filippini of Lazio during a Serie A derby match in 2005. Lazio won 3-0.*

LA LIGA

The Spanish league banned foreign players between 1963 and 1973, but since then it has been the home of some of the world's greatest footballers, from Johan Cruyff and Diego Maradona to current stars Ronaldo, Ronaldinho, Raúl, Luis Figo and Roy Makaay. These players find themselves in a highly competitive league. While Barcelona romped to the 2005 title and Real Madrid won in 2001 and 2003, Atlético Madrid, Valencia and Deportivo la Coruña have all taken the title since 1995. In recent seasons, Athletic Bilbao, Real Sociedad and Mallorca have managed top-three placings. La Liga has two professional divisions and, below them, a series of amateur divisons. Unlike other national leagues, the reserve sides of the major clubs play in the lower divisions, not in a separate reserves league. Real Madrid and Barcelona remain La Liga's most wealthy and successful clubs, with 46 titles between them.

▼ *Carlos Marchena (left) of Valencia challenges Real Zaragoza's Fernando Soriano. In the 2003–04 season, Valencia won the Spanish league title and the UEFA Cup.*

THE BUNDESLIGA

After the division of Germany into East and West following World War II, the West German Bundesliga was first contested in 1965. In 1991, after reunification, two sides from the former East Germany were admitted into the top division. Since then, eastern sides have struggled – only Hansa Rostock were a regular presence in the Bundesliga until they were relegated in 2005. Bayern Munich are by far the most successful Bundesliga club, with 18 titles, followed by Borussia Mönchengladbach (five), Werder Bremen (four) and Hamburg

▲ *Werder Bremen display the German Bundesliga trophy after winning the 2003–04 title. They secured a league and cup double two weeks later.*

and Borussia Dortmund (three). Hamburg are nicknamed the Dinosaur and are the only side to have competed in every season of the league. The Bundesliga was one of the last major leagues to adopt a system of three points for a win (in 1995) and Bayern Munich's 1997–98 total of 78 points remains the highest. Werder Bremen came close with 74 points in 2003–04, propelled by 27 league goals from Brazil's Ailton. His tally was the highest since the early 1980s, but still short of the record 40 goals Gerd Müller scored for Bayern in 1971–72. Müller's total of 365 Bundesliga goals is unlikely to be beaten for many years.

◀ *Dutchman Arjen Robben (left) of Chelsea and France's Robert Pires (of Arsenal) are two of the Premier League's most exciting foreign imports.*

THE ENGLISH PREMIER LEAGUE

In the early 1990s, England's first division clubs broke away from league control to form the Premier League. Money has flooded into the top clubs' coffers and a wide gap has opened up between established sides and newly promoted teams, who find it very hard to stay up. At the top of the table, Manchester United have won eight out of a possible 13 titles and never finished lower than third. Their battle for league supremacy with Arsenal was eclipsed in 2004–05 by a Chelsea team coached by José Mourinho and financed by Russian billionaire Roman Abramovich. Although some way short of its claim to be the best league in the world, the Premiership is highly popular – its all-action style attracts millions of viewers worldwide.

LE CHAMPIONNAT

Despite having produced some of the world's greatest players, the French league has traditionally not been as well funded as others in Europe. Its home-grown stars, such as Michel Platini, Zinedine Zidane and Thierry Henry, usually move abroad. Despite this, French teams appear to be on the up, reaching the final of both the Champions League and the UEFA Cup in 2004. The French league is highly competitive. Between 1983 and 2003, only three sides – Auxerre, Monaco and Paris Saint Germain – played

▼ *Bay Area CyberRays' Brandi Chastain scores in a WUSA league game. The world's only professional women's league ran for just three seasons, although hopes for a relaunch remain.*

in the top division every season. Saint Etienne head the list of league winners, with ten titles, but in recent years Lyon have become a major force. In 2005, they became only the second team (after Marseille) to win Le Championnat four times in a row.

ASIAN LEAGUES

The first professional league in Asia was South Korea's K-League, which began with just five teams in 1983. Featuring no relegation, it now has 13 teams and was won by Suwon Samsung Bluewings in 2004. The K-League's most successful side is Seongnam Ilhwa Chunma, with six titles (1993–95 and 2001–03). Japan's J-League kicked off in 1993 and now has two divisions, J1 and J2. Kashima Antlers have won four titles, while in 2004 Yokohama F Marinos became the first club to win three J-league championships in a row. China's professional league has been won three times by Dalian Shide since it started in 1999.

MAJOR LEAGUE SOCCER (MLS)

Early attempts at setting up a professional league in the USA included the heavily financed North American Soccer League (NASL), which ran from 1968–84 and featured global superstars such as Pelé, albeit near the end of their careers. The MLS celebrated the start of its tenth season in 2005 and focuses more on home-grown players and those from the CONCACAF region. The number of MLS teams has fluctuated between ten and twelve, playing in two divisions, Eastern and Western. Unlike most leagues, there is no relegation and promotion. DC United are the most successful MLS side, with four titles.

CLUB CUP COMPETITIONS

In 1872, Wanderers beat Royal Engineers by one goal to nil to win the first FA Cup – the oldest surviving major cup competition. Since that time, hundreds of cup competitions have been introduced all over the world. Some, such as the Asian Supercup and the African Supercup, are contested between the winners of other cup competitions.

▲ Boca Juniors celebrate their penalty shootout victory over AC Milan in the 2003 World Club Cup. Argentinian clubs have won the competition nine times, more than any other nation.

CONTINENTAL CUP COMPETITIONS

Every continent has one or more cup competitions for its best clubs. The two most famous are the Copa Libertadores and the European Champions League (see pages 132–133). The winners of these two competitions play each other to determine the world's best team in the World Club Cup (previously called the Intercontinental Cup). Often seen as a curiosity by neutrals, the World Club Cup has suffered from withdrawals and bad-tempered games, but its staging in Japan from 1980 has kept the competition alive, despite the arrival of the World Club Championship in 2000–01.

In Africa, the African Cup-Winners' Cup and the CAF Cup are only exceeded in prestige by the African Champions Cup, which was first played for in 1964. Egyptian side Zamalek have won the competition five times, while Nigeria's Enyimba recorded back-to-back wins in 2003 and 2004. The Asian Cup-Winners' Cup ran from 1991 to 2002 and was won by Saudi Arabian teams six times. In contrast, the Asian Champions League has seen winners from nine countries. South Korean clubs such as Suwon Samsung Bluewings (winners in 2001 and 2002) and Japanese sides (including 1999 winners Jubilo Iwata) have in recent years been the strongest.

▶ Players from Colombian team Once Caldas are jubilant after defeating Boca Juniors of Argentina to win the Copa Libertadores in 2004. Five months later, however, they lost 8-7 in a penalty shootout to Porto in the World Club Cup.

COPA LIBERTADORES

South America's first international club competition was staged by Chilean club Colo Colo in 1948 and won by Brazilian side Vasco da Gama. However, it was not until 1960 that a regular competition, the Copa Libertadores, was set up. Uruguayan side Peñarol won the first two competitions, but were defeated in the final of the third by Santos, courtesy of two goals from Pelé.

◀ Action from the Asian Champions League 2003 final between Thailand's Tero Sasana club and Al-Ain of the United Arab Emirates. Al-Ain won 2-0.

Since the early competitions, the format of the tournament has changed many times. Today, the Copa Libertadores begins with nine groups of four teams and culminates in a second round, quarter-finals, semi-finals and a pair of games – home and away – between the finalists. It is open to the top sides of each South American nation, but Mexican teams were also invited to compete from 1999–2001. The Copa Libertadores has continually outshone the national team competition – the Copa America – and other South American cups in popularity and passion. Occasionally, this intensity has led to flare-ups on the pitch and in the stands. In the 1971 Copa match between Boca Juniors and Sporting Cristal, for example, a brawl ended in the arrest of most of the players, while Colombia's Atletico Nacional were banned from the 1990 competition after a referee received death threats.

Over the years, the Copa Libertadores has mainly changed hands between teams from Brazil, Argentina and Uruguay. Independiente hold a stunning record of seven final appearances, all ending in wins (1964–65, 1972–75 and 1984); the only teams to have reached the final more often are Peñarol (nine times) and Boca Juniors (eight times). Uruguay's Nacional have won three Copas and been runners-up three times, as have Paraguay's Olimpia, whose most recent victory came in 2002. Colombia's clubs have been among the most unlucky, losing seven out of eight finals before the 2004 Copa. In that year, the small Colombian club Once Caldas beat Brazilian giants Santos and São Paulo and the favourites, Boca Juniors, on their way to becoming the most unexpected winners in the history of the competition.

▶ Charles Coridon (left) of Lens and Samuel Johnson of Gaziantepspor battle for the ball in the 2003–04 UEFA Cup. Lens entered the tournament via UEFA's Fair Play scheme, which awards places to several clubs with the best disciplinary records in Europe the previous season.

CUPS IN EUROPE

Most leagues in Europe have one or more cup competitions for their teams to contest. Among the best known domestic cup competitions are the English FA Cup; the Scottish Cup, which started in 1874; the Spanish Cup, which began in 1902; and the French Cup, which was first played for in 1918. From 1960 until 1999, the winners of national cup competitions in Europe played in the Cup-Winners' Cup. The first and last Cup-Winners' Cups were won by Italian sides (Fiorentina and Lazio), but the most successful team was Barcelona, who lifted the trophy four times. They suffered a surprising loss in the 1969 final to Slovan Bratislava (now in Slovakia), who became the first Eastern European club to win a major continental cup. Since the Cup-Winners' Cup was scrapped, cup winners in Europe's strongest nations have competed for the UEFA Cup.

The UEFA Cup's forerunner began in 1955 as the Inter-Cities Fairs Cup, a competition that took two years to complete. By 1960, the Fairs Cup was played over the course of a year and, for the 1971–72 season, a new trophy and new name – the UEFA Cup – were introduced. In 1972, the European Supercup arrived, and was contested

◀ CSKA Moscow's Venaumin Mandrikin celebrates with the 2005 UEFA Cup as his side become the first Russian club to win a major European trophy, beating Sporting Lisbon 3-1 in the final.

between the victors of the European Champions Cup and the Cup-Winners' Cup. Ajax were the first winners of the Supercup. UEFA Cup winners have so far come from ten nations, with Italian clubs taking the title on nine occasions, German and English sides winning six times and Dutch teams four times. The competition has grown over the years and more than 100 teams now enter the first stages of the competition. Places are granted through winning a national cup, a high league finish, being knocked out of the Champions League group stage or doing well in the Intertoto Cup, another European competition.

EUROPEAN CHAMPIONS

European club competitions date back to 1927, when the Mitropa Cup was first contested by the leading clubs of central Europe. Sparta Prague were its first winners. The last Mitropa Cup was won by Yugoslav side Borac Banja Luka in 1992, but by then the glamour of the Mitropa had long been eclipsed by the mighty European Cup, a competition that is now known as the European Champions League.

◀ *Real Madrid keeper Rogelio Dominguez claims the ball during the 1959 European Cup final against French club Stade de Reims. The game ended 2-0 to Real, who lifted their fourth European Cup in a row.*

▶ *Julius Aghahowa of Shakhtar Donetsk is challenged by Barcelona's Fernando Navarro in a 2004–05 Champions League game. Aghahowa's two goals gave the Ukrainian side a surprise victory.*

EARLY DAYS

The European Champion Clubs' Cup, usually known as the European Cup, developed out of a meeting set up by Frenchman Gabriel Hanot. Italian, Spanish, French and Portuguese club sides were keen to take part, as were teams from many other nations. The first European Cup, held in 1955–56, featured major names such as Real Madrid, Sporting Lisbon, Anderlecht and AC Milan. Clubs that are less well known today also entered – Århus GF and FC Saarbrucken, for example. English league champions Chelsea, however, were forbidden from entering, but Scottish club Hibernian reached the semi-final. The first winners of the trophy were Real Madrid.

CHANGING CHAMPIONS

Real won the first five European Cups, before the tournament hit a golden age of competition in the 1960s, with Benfica, Internazionale and AC Milan all winning the trophy. The 1970s saw both Ajax and Bayern Munich crowned champions three years in a row. English clubs won six European Cups in succession

from 1977, but were banned from European competition for five years after the 1985 Heysel Stadium disaster (see page 105). Italian, Spanish and English clubs have won the cup ten times, while German and Dutch sides have claimed the trophy six times.

As the European Cup grew in intensity, it became harder to successfully defend the title. The last back-to-back winners of the trophy were AC Milan in 1989 and 1990. The first year that the final went into extra time was 1958, while the first penalty shootout in the final was in 1984. The two finals won by Eastern European sides, Steaua Bucharest (1986) and Red Star Belgrade (1991), both went to penalty shootouts.

EXPANSION AND DOMINATION

The format of the European Cup remained almost unchanged for its first 35 years. Teams competed in knockout rounds, playing one match at home and one away. If the scores were tied after the two games, the team with more away goals would go through. For many years, the competition was open only to the league champions of each country. Today, as many as four sides from each top league take part.

▲ *Nottingham Forest celebrate winning their second European Cup title in a row after winger John Robertson's single goal was enough to defeat German side Hamburg in the 1980 final.*

EUROPEAN CUP / CHAMPIONS LEAGUE WINNERS

1956	Real Madrid	1973	Ajax	1990	AC Milan
1957	Real Madrid	1974	Bayern Munich	1991	Red Star Belgrade
1958	Real Madrid	1975	Bayern Munich	1992	Barcelona
1959	Real Madrid	1976	Bayern Munich	1993	Marseille (see p83)
1960	Real Madrid	1977	Liverpool	1994	AC Milan
1961	Benfica	1978	Liverpool	1995	Ajax
1962	Benfica	1979	Nottingham Forest	1996	Juventus
1963	AC Milan	1980	Nottingham Forest	1997	Borussia Dortmund
1964	Internazionale	1981	Liverpool	1998	Real Madrid
1965	Internazionale	1982	Aston Villa	1999	Manchester United
1966	Real Madrid	1983	Hamburg	2000	Real Madrid
1967	Celtic	1984	Liverpool	2001	Bayern Munich
1968	Manchester United	1985	Juventus	2002	Real Madrid
1969	AC Milan	1986	Steaua Bucharest	2003	AC Milan
1970	Feyenoord	1987	Porto	2004	Porto
1971	Ajax	1988	PSV Eindhoven	2005	Liverpool
1972	Ajax	1989	AC Milan		

FACTFILE Manchester United's Ruud van Nistelrooy and José Altafini of AC Milan are the highest goalscorers in one European Cup competition, both with 14 goals.

▲ Stefan Klos of German club Borussia Dortmund holds the Champions League trophy aloft in 1997.

► In the 2005 Champions League final, Liverpool's Luis Garcia celebrates Xabi Alonso's goal that crowned a remarkable comeback. Liverpool had been 3-0 down to AC Milan, but pulled level and then won the penalty shootout.

The competition was revamped as the Champions League in 1992. Group stages were introduced, guaranteeing more games and vast sums of television money for the competing clubs. Champions League success is now essential for the financial health of Europe's top teams. A report in 2005 showed that taking part in the tournament can add 10–20 per cent to a club's total income in a season. For a big side, failure to qualify can be a financial disaster.

The number of games in the Champions League soared from 25 in 1992–93 to 157 in 2002–03. From the 2003–04 season, the number of group stages was reduced from two to one, partly due to criticism that the competition was overblown. Yet, for every one of its critics, there are a thousand fans of the Champions League, as it pits more of the world's elite players against each other than any other club competition.

FACTFILE Up to 2004, only Dutchman Clarence Seedorf has won the European Cup with three different clubs – Ajax (1995), Real Madrid (1998) and AC Milan (2003).

Celebrations get under way in Johannesburg after FIFA's announcement that South Africa is to host the 2010 World Cup.

SNAPSHOT
SOUTH AFRICA 2010

South Africa came agonizingly close to hosting the 2006 World Cup, but lost out to Germany by just one vote. It was a heartbreaking moment for a country that had been thrown out of FIFA in 1976 after hundreds of students were killed in an uprising in the Soweto township. Many other sporting bodies had already barred South Africa from taking part in international competitions because of its policy of apartheid – the segregation of people of different racial backgrounds. After the dismantling of apartheid, the country was allowed back into FIFA in 1992. Four years later, it hosted and won the African Nations Cup. South Africa entered the race to host the 2010 World Cup alongside Egypt, Libya, Morocco and Tunisia. On 15 May 2004, Sepp Blatter, the president of FIFA, revealed the results of the final ballot. Morocco received ten votes, but South Africa triumphed with 14 – and made history by becoming the first African nation to win the right to host football's greatest competition.

▶ *Nelson Mandela, the former president of South Africa, celebrates with the World Cup.*

BRITISH FOOTBALL

Britain is thought of as the birthplace of football – in the late 19th century, pioneering league and cup competitions were set up in England and Scotland. Many of them survive to this day.

CHANGING DIVISIONS

The English league kicked off in 1888, with 12 teams playing in a single division. It was expanded to two divisions of 18 clubs in 1898 and to four divisions containing 92 teams in 1950. Despite several changes in structure – including the creation in 1992 of a Premier League for the top 22 clubs (reduced to 20 teams in 1994) and the rebranding of the football league as the Championship, Division One and Division Two – the figure of 92 clubs linked by promotion and relegation between the divisions remains in place. Three of the sides – Cardiff City, Wrexham and Swansea City – are Welsh, while one England-based club, Berwick Rangers, plays in the Scottish league (which was formed in 1891).

Many clubs have moved to new grounds in the past decade, but only one has moved towns – in June 2004, Wimbledon became Milton Keynes Dons. In protest, Wimbledon supporters set up their own amateur club, AFC Wimbledon, which has successfully begun the long climb up the English league pyramid. Between February 2003 and November 2004, the team recorded the longest unbeaten run in Britain, playing 78 games, winning 69 and drawing nine.

CUP DREAMS

Despite the growing influence of European competitions, the FA Cup and Scottish Cup retain their appeal for clubs and fans alike. A record 660 clubs contested the extra-preliminary rounds of the 2004–05 FA Cup, for example. It is the dream of every non-league and lower league club to reach the third round and have the chance of giving one of the huge teams a run for their money. The histories of the two cups are littered with notable giantkilling acts – as a non-league side, Yeovil Town (now in the English league) beat league opposition 20 times. Despite the gulf in finance and quality of players, teams from lower divisions do still beat higher-placed opponents. The 2004–05 FA Cup saw Oldham knock out Manchester City, Burnley beat Liverpool and Leicester City defeat Charlton Athletic, while first division side Millwall reached the final of the competition in 2004.

At the start of the season, the winners of the FA Cup and the Premier League meet in the Community Shield (formerly the Charity Shield). The first Charity Shield match, in 1908, was between amateur side Queens Park Rangers (the Southern League champions) and Manchester United (the professional league champions). The 2004 game, held at Cardiff's Millennium Stadium, again featured Manchester United, who were beaten by Arsenal. The two sides also met in the last game of the 2004–05 season, the FA Cup final.

FOREIGN IMPORTS

In the past 15 years, foreign players from all over the world have come to play in the Scottish and English leagues. Rangers and Chelsea were the first top-flight teams to field sides containing no British players in a league match, while 101 footballers at the 2002 World Cup played their club football in the English Premiership. Foreign managers were far less common until the mid-1990s. Since then, Wim Jansen (at Celtic), Dick Advocaat (at Rangers), Arsène Wenger (at Arsenal) and José Mourinho (at Chelsea) have all enjoyed major success. The reigns of the first foreign coaches of England and Scotland – Sven-Goran Eriksson and Berti Vogts – have been less smooth, however.

HOME INTERNATIONALS

At international level, three of the four home nations were locked in the same qualifying group for the 2006 World Cup, recalling for older supporters the days of the Home Internationals. Starting in 1883, the British Home Championship saw each side play the other three at least once in a season. Heading the list of winners are England (34 victories), followed by Scotland (24), Wales (seven) and Northern Ireland (three, including the very last competition in 1983–84).

MAGAZINES AND BOOKS

World Soccer Magazine (IPC Media)
The best magazine available for fans of world football, with coverage of all the major and minor leagues as well as news and features on international competitions.

Soccer – Technique, Tactics, Training (Sean Callery, The Crowood Press, 1995)
One of the outstanding books on football's key skills and training techniques.

News of the World Football Annual (Stuart Barnes (editor), HarperCollinsWillow, 2005)
A great-value book, combining a season review with updated historical statistics and facts.

Soccer Rules Explained, Revised and Updated (Stanley Lover, Lyons Press, 2005)
One of the best books on football's laws.

The Man In Black
(Gordon Thomson, Prion Books, 1998)
An interesting and informative look at the referee's world and the history of officials.

100 Years of Football: The FIFA Centennial Book (Weidenfeld & Nicolson, 2005)
A guide to FIFA and the rise of football around the world, packed with rare photos.

Boots, Balls and Haircuts
(Hunter Davies, Cassell Illustrated, 2004)
A thorough and entertaining look at the history of football.

Football in Sun and Shadow
(Eduardo Galeano, Fourth Estate, 2003)
Short, poetic pieces of writing about the emotions of watching and playing football.

So You Think You Know Premier League Football? (Clive Gifford, Hodder, 2004)
Containing more than 1,000 quiz questions.

FACTS AND FIGURES

ENGLISH LEAGUE CHAMPIONS

Clubs from the Midlands and the north dominated the English league from its start, and it was not until 1931 that a southern club, Arsenal, won the title. Doncaster Rovers hold the record for the most wins in a season (33 in 42 games, 1946–47) and the most defeats (34 in 46 games, 1997–98). Liverpool have won 18 league titles, more than any other club, while Manchester United have won the most Premiership titles (eight). Below are the post-war records.

2005 Chelsea
2004 Arsenal
2003 Manchester United
2002 Arsenal
2001 Manchester United
2000 Manchester United
1999 Manchester United
1998 Arsenal
1997 Manchester United
1996 Manchester United
1995 Blackburn Rovers
1994 Manchester United
1993 Manchester United
1992 Leeds United
1991 Arsenal
1990 Liverpool
1989 Arsenal
1988 Liverpool
1987 Everton
1986 Liverpool
1985 Everton
1984 Liverpool
1983 Liverpool
1982 Liverpool
1981 Aston Villa
1980 Liverpool
1979 Liverpool
1978 Nottingham Forest
1977 Liverpool
1976 Liverpool
1975 Derby County
1974 Leeds United
1973 Liverpool
1972 Derby County
1971 Arsenal
1970 Everton
1969 Leeds United
1968 Manchester City
1967 Manchester United
1966 Liverpool
1965 Manchester United
1964 Liverpool
1963 Everton
1962 Ipswich Town
1961 Tottenham Hotspur
1960 Burnley
1959 Wolverhampton Wanderers
1958 Wolverhampton Wanderers
1957 Manchester United
1956 Manchester United
1955 Chelsea
1954 Wolverhampton Wanderers
1953 Arsenal
1952 Manchester United
1951 Tottenham Hotspur
1950 Portsmouth
1949 Portsmouth
1948 Arsenal
1947 Liverpool

SCOTTISH LEAGUE CHAMPIONS

Rangers and Celtic have dominated the Scottish league. In its first year, 1891, Rangers shared the title with Dumbarton; Celtic claimed their first title in 1893. Between them, the two 'Old Firm' sides have won 90 titles and finished runners-up 55 times. The next three most successful sides – Aberdeen, Hearts and Hibernian – have each won the league four times.

2005 Rangers
2004 Celtic
2003 Rangers
2002 Celtic
2001 Celtic
2000 Rangers
1999 Rangers
1998 Celtic
1997 Rangers
1996 Rangers
1995 Rangers
1994 Rangers
1993 Rangers
1992 Rangers
1991 Rangers
1990 Rangers
1989 Rangers
1988 Celtic
1987 Rangers
1986 Celtic
1985 Aberdeen
1984 Aberdeen
1983 Dundee United
1982 Celtic
1981 Celtic
1980 Aberdeen
1979 Celtic
1978 Rangers
1977 Celtic
1976 Rangers
1975 Rangers
1974 Celtic
1973 Celtic
1972 Celtic
1971 Celtic
1970 Celtic
1969 Celtic
1968 Celtic
1967 Celtic
1966 Celtic
1965 Kilmarnock
1964 Rangers
1963 Rangers
1962 Dundee
1961 Rangers
1960 Heart of Midlothian
1959 Rangers
1958 Heart of Midlothian
1957 Rangers
1956 Rangers
1955 Aberdeen
1954 Celtic
1953 Rangers
1952 Hibernian
1951 Hibernian
1950 Rangers
1949 Rangers
1948 Hibernian
1947 Rangers

FA CUP

The FA Cup is the world's longest-running knockout competition. Manchester United are the most successful FA Cup side, with 11 victories, while Preston North End hold the record for the biggest win in an FA Cup game, thrashing Hyde United 26-0 in 1887–88. Below are the post-war winners and runners-up of the FA Cup. An asterisk denotes that extra time was played.

2005 Arsenal 0 Manchester United 0* (5-4 penalties)
2004 Manchester United 3 Millwall 0
2003 Arsenal 1 Southampton 0
2002 Arsenal 2 Chelsea 0
2001 Liverpool 2 Arsenal 1
2000 Chelsea 1 Aston Villa 0
1999 Manchester United 2 Newcastle United 0
1998 Arsenal 2 Newcastle United 0
1997 Chelsea 2 Middlesbrough 0
1996 Manchester United 1 Liverpool 0
1995 Everton 1 Manchester United 0
1994 Manchester United 4 Chelsea 0
1993 Arsenal 2 Sheffield Wednesday 1 (replay after 1-1)
1992 Liverpool 2 Sunderland 0
1991 Tottenham Hotspur 2 Nottingham Forest 1*
1990 Manchester United 1 Crystal Palace 0 (replay after 3-3)
1989 Liverpool 3 Everton 2*
1988 Wimbledon 1 Liverpool 0
1987 Coventry City 3 Tottenham Hotspur 2*
1986 Liverpool 3 Everton 1
1985 Manchester United 1 Everton 0*
1984 Everton 2 Watford 0
1983 Manchester United 4 Brighton and Hove Albion 0 (replay after 2-2)
1982 Tottenham Hotspur 1 QPR 0 (replay after 1-1)
1981 Tottenham Hotspur 3 Manchester City 2 (replay after 1-1)
1980 West Ham United 1 Arsenal 0
1979 Arsenal 3 Manchester United 2
1978 Ipswich Town 1 Arsenal 0
1977 Manchester United 2 Liverpool 1
1976 Southampton 1 Manchester United 0
1975 West Ham United 2 Fulham 0
1974 Liverpool 3 Newcastle United 0
1973 Sunderland 1 Leeds United 0
1972 Leeds United 1 Arsenal 0
1971 Arsenal 2 Liverpool 1
1970 Chelsea 2 Leeds United 1 (replay after 2-2)
1969 Manchester City 1 Leicester City 0
1968 West Bromwich Albion 1 Everton 0*

1967 Tottenham Hotspur 2
Chelsea 1
1966 Everton 3
Sheffield Wednesday 2
1965 Liverpool 2 Leeds United 1*
1964 West Ham United 3
Preston North End 2
1963 Manchester United 3
Leicester City 1
1962 Tottenham Hotspur 3
Burnley 1
1961 Tottenham Hotspur 2
Leicester City 0
1960 Wolverhampton
Wanderers 3
Blackburn Rovers 0
1959 Nottingham Forest 2
Luton Town 1
1958 Bolton Wanderers 2
Manchester United 0
1957 Aston Villa 2
Manchester United 1
1956 Manchester City 3
Birmingham City 1
1955 Newcastle United 3
Manchester City 1
1954 West Bromwich Albion 3
Preston North End 2
1953 Blackpool 4
Bolton Wanderers 3
1952 Newcastle United 1
Arsenal 0
1951 Newcastle United 2
Blackpool 0
1950 Arsenal 2 Liverpool 0
1949 Wolverhampton
Wanderers 3
Leicester City 1
1948 Manchester United 4
Blackpool 2
1947 Charlton Athletic 1
Burnley 0*
1946 Derby County 4
Charlton Athletic 1*

SCOTTISH CUP

The Scottish Cup began in
1873 and for half a century was
won by a wide range of teams
including Renton, Queen's Park
and Vale of Leven. Arbroath
have never won the cup, but
in 1885 they pummelled Bon
Accord 36-0, a record as the
biggest win in British football.

2005 Celtic
2004 Celtic
2003 Rangers
2002 Rangers
2001 Celtic

2000 Rangers
1999 Rangers
1998 Heart of Midlothian
1997 Kilmarnock
1996 Rangers
1995 Celtic
1994 Dundee United
1993 Rangers
1992 Rangers
1991 Motherwell
1990 Aberdeen
1989 Celtic
1988 Celtic
1987 St Mirren
1986 Aberdeen
1985 Celtic
1984 Aberdeen
1983 Aberdeen
1982 Aberdeen
1981 Rangers
1980 Celtic
1979 Rangers
1978 Rangers
1977 Celtic
1976 Rangers
1975 Celtic
1974 Celtic
1973 Rangers
1972 Celtic
1971 Celtic
1970 Aberdeen
1969 Celtic
1968 Dunfermline Athletic
1967 Celtic
1966 Rangers
1965 Celtic
1964 Rangers
1963 Rangers
1962 Rangers
1961 Dunfermline Athletic
1960 Rangers
1959 St Mirren
1958 Clyde
1957 Falkirk
1956 Heart of Midlothian
1955 Clyde
1954 Celtic
1953 Rangers
1952 Motherwell
1951 Celtic
1950 Rangers
1949 Rangers
1948 Rangers
1947 Aberdeen

THE LEAGUE CUP

The League Cup began in
1960 and is open only to the
92 English league clubs. Since
1982, it has been sponsored
and is currently known as the

Carling Cup. Throughout its
history, sides have declined to
take part or fielded understrength
teams in the early stages, but
the competition now awards a
UEFA Cup place to the winners
and is a major prize for clubs
not chasing a Champions
League spot.

Number of wins
7 – Liverpool
5 – Aston Villa
4 – Nottingham Forest
3 – Chelsea, Leicester City,
Tottenham Hotspur
2 – Arsenal, Manchester City,
Norwich City, Wolverhampton
Wanderers
1 – Birmingham City, Blackburn
Rovers, Leeds United, Luton
Town, Manchester United,
Middlesbrough, Oxford United,
Queens Park Rangers, Sheffield
Wednesday, Stoke City, Swindon
Town, West Bromwich Albion

ON THE CONTINENT

For over four decades, British
teams have had plenty of
success in Europe. Below is
a list of the clubs that have
made the final of a major
European cup competition.

2005 Liverpool, Champions
League, winners
2003 Celtic, UEFA Cup,
runners-up
2001 Liverpool, UEFA Cup,
winners
2000 Arsenal, UEFA Cup,
runners-up
1999 Manchester United,
Champions League,
winners
1995 Arsenal, Cup-Winners'
Cup, runners-up
1994 Arsenal, Cup-Winners'
Cup, winners
1991 Manchester United, Cup-
Winners' Cup, winners
1987 Dundee United, UEFA
Cup, runners-up
1985 Everton, Cup-Winners'
Cup, winners
1985 Liverpool, European Cup,
runners-up
1984 Liverpool, European Cup,
winners

1984 Tottenham Hotspur,
UEFA Cup, winners
1983 Aberdeen, Cup-Winners'
Cup, winners
1982 Aston Villa, European
Cup, winners
1981 Liverpool, European Cup,
winners
1981 Ipswich Town, UEFA Cup,
winners
1980 Nottingham Forest,
European Cup, winners
1980 Arsenal, Cup-Winners'
Cup, runners-up
1979 Nottingham Forest,
European Cup, winners
1978 Liverpool, European Cup,
winners
1977 Liverpool, European Cup,
winners
1976 Liverpool, UEFA Cup,
winners
1976 West Ham United, Cup-
Winners' Cup, runners-up
1975 Leeds United, European
Cup, runners-up
1974 Tottenham Hotspur,
UEFA Cup, runners-up
1973 Liverpool, UEFA Cup,
winners
1973 Leeds United, Cup-
Winners' Cup, runners-up
1972 Tottenham Hotspur,
UEFA Cup, winners
1972 Rangers, Cup-Winners'
Cup, winners
1972 Wolverhampton
Wanderers, UEFA Cup,
runners-up
1971 Leeds United, UEFA Cup,
winners
1971 Chelsea, Cup-Winners'
Cup, winners
1970 Manchester City, Cup-
Winners' Cup, winners
1970 Arsenal, Inter-Cities Fairs
Cup, winners
1970 Celtic, European Cup,
runners-up
1969 Newcastle United, Inter-
Cities Fairs Cup, winners
1968 Manchester United,
European Cup, winners
1968 Leeds United, Inter-Cities
Fairs Cup, winners
1967 Celtic, European Cup,
winners
1967 Rangers, Cup-Winners'
Cup, runners-up
1967 Leeds United, Inter-Cities
Fairs Cup, runners-up

1966 Liverpool, Cup-Winners' Cup, runners-up

1965 West Ham United, Cup-Winners' Cup, winners

1963 Tottenham Hotspur, Cup-Winners' Cup, winners

1961 Rangers, Cup-Winners' Cup, runners-up

1961 Birmingham City, Inter-Cities Fairs Cup, runners-up

1960 Birmingham City, Inter-Cities Fairs Cup, runners-up

APPEARANCE RECORDS

Most league appearances
1005 – Peter Shilton (1966–97)

Most league appearances at one club
770 – John Trollope, Swindon Town (1960–80)

Most appearances in consecutive games
401 – Harold Bell, Tranmere Rovers (1946–55)

Most international caps
England
125 Peter Shilton (1970–90)
108 Bobby Moore (1962–73)
106 Bobby Charlton (1958–70)
105 Billy Wright (1946–59)
90 Bryan Robson (1980–91)

Scotland
102 Kenny Dalglish (1972–87)
91 Jim Leighton (1983–99)
77 Alex McLeish (1980–93)
76 Paul McStay (1984–97)
72 Tommy Boyd (1991–2001)

Wales
92 Neville Southall (1982–98)
85 Michael Hughes (1990–2004)
75 Dean Saunders (1986–2001)
73 Peter Nicholas (1979–1992)
73 Ian Rush (1980–96)

Northern Ireland
119 Pat Jennings (1964–86)
91 Mal Donaghy (1980–94)
88 Sammy McIlroy (1972–87)
73 Jimmy Nicholl (1976–86)
71 Michael Hughes (1992–2004)

Youngest international cap
England – Wayne Rooney (17 years, 111 days)

Scotland – Denis Law (18 years, 235 days)
Wales – Ryan Green (17 years, 226 days)
Northern Ireland – Norman Whiteside (17 years, 41 days)

GOALS

Most goals in a career
550 – Jimmy McGrory (Celtic, Clydebank and Scotland)
464 – Arthur Rowley (West Bromwich Albion, Fulham, Leicester City, Shrewsbury Town)

Most Premiership goals
250 – Alan Shearer (1992–2005)

Most goals in a season
60 – Dixie Dean, Everton (1927–28)

Most goals in a game
13 – John Petrie for Arbroath v Bon Accord, 1885

LEADING INTERNATIONAL GOALSCORERS

England
49 Bobby Charlton (1958–70)
48 Gary Lineker (1984–92)
44 Jimmy Greaves (1959–67)
32 Michael Owen (1998–2005)
30 Tom Finney (1946–58)
30 Nat Lofthouse (1950–58)
30 Alan Shearer (1991–2000)

Scotland
30 Kenny Dalglish (1972–87)
30 Denis Law (1959–74)
23 Hugh Gallacher (1924–35)
22 Lawrie Reilly (1949–57)
19 Ally McCoist (1986–98)

Wales
28 Ian Rush (1980–96)
23 Ivor Allchurch (1951–66)
23 Trevor Ford (1947–57)
22 Dean Saunders (1986–2001)
16 Mark Hughes (1984–99)

Northern Ireland
16 David Healy (2000–05)
13 Colin Clarke (1986–93)
12 Gerry Armstrong (1977–86)
12 Joe Bambrick (1929–38)
12 Iain Dowie (1990–2000)

HIT THE NET

www.thefa.com
The webpages of the English Football Association, with information on the England national team, clubs and league tables, plus a section on the FA Cup.

www.premierleague.com
The official website of the English Premier League.

www.football–league.premiumtv.co.uk
Home of the English football league on the net, with club profiles and the latest news and results.

www.scottishfa.co.uk/index.cfm
The website of the Scottish Football Association, with links to its museum of football, as well as match reports and results at all levels of the game.

www.scottishfootballrecords.com
An incredibly thorough collection of results, records and standings in Scottish football, at club and international level.

www.faw.org.uk
The website of the Welsh FA, with details on competitions in Wales, as well as details on its international squads.

www.irishfa.com
The homepage of Northern Ireland's FA, with news and details of their international men's, women's and youth teams.

www.givemefootball.com
The website of the Professional Footballers Association (PFA), with features on the top players of the past and present, the latest football news and interviews with players and managers.

www.rsssf.com/engpaul/FLA/league.html
The complete tables for every season of the English league from 1888–89.

www.footballnetwork.org/dev/communityfootball/index.asp
A great selection of webpages examining FIFA's Fairplay initiatives and also how football violence is tackled in the UK.

www.pyramidpassion.co.uk
A celebration of football grounds and the culture of football below the professional leagues in Britain.

www.footballeconomy.com/world.htm
A fascinating website looking at the economics of football, with attendance figures and finances of the leading clubs.

www.clivegifford.co.uk
The author's website, which features regularly updated football tips and links to other football webpages.

GLOSSARY

Advantage rule A rule that allows the referee to let play continue after a foul if it is to the advantage of the team that has been fouled against.

AFC The Asian Football Confederation, responsible for running football in Asia.

Agent A person who represents footballers and negotiates contracts and transfer moves.

Anchor A midfielder positioned just in front of, and who protects, the defence. An anchor player may allow other midfielders to push further forwards.

Assist A pass that releases a player to score a goal. An assist can be a pass on the ground, a flick or a cross from which a headed goal is scored.

Away goals rule A rule used in some cup competitions. If the scores are equal over two legs, the team that has scored more goals away from home wins.

Backpass rule A law stating that a deliberate pass backwards by a player to his or her goalkeeper cannot be handled by the keeper.

CAF The *Confédération Africaine de Football*, which runs football in Africa.

Cap Recognition given to a player for each appearance in an international game for his or her country.

Catenaccio A defensive tactical system in which a sweeper plays behind a solid defence.

Caution Another word for a yellow card (a warning from the referee to a player for a foul or infringement). A player who receives two yellow cards in a match is automatically shown a red card and sent off.

Central defender The defender who plays in the middle of the last line of defence.

Chip A pass lofted into the air from a player to a team-mate or as a shot on goal.

CONCACAF The Confederation of North, Central American and Caribbean Association Football, which runs football in North and Central America.

CONMEBOL The *Confederación Sudamericana de Fútbol*, which runs football in South America.

Counter attack A quick attack by a team after it regains possession of the ball.

Cross To send the ball from a wide position towards the centre of the pitch, often into the opposition penalty area.

Cushioning Using a part of the body to slow down a ball in order to bring it under control.

Derby A match between two rival sides, often located in the same town or city.

Direct free kick A kick awarded to a team because of a serious foul committed by an opponent. A goal may be scored directly from the kick.

Dissent When a player uses words or actions to disagree with the referee's decision.

Distribution The way the ball is released by a goalkeeper or is moved around the pitch by a team.

Dribbling Moving the ball under close control with a series of short kicks or taps.

Drop ball A way of restarting play in which the referee releases the ball for a player from each team to compete over once it has touched the ground.

Extra time A way of deciding a drawn match. It involves two periods of additional play, usually lasting 15 minutes each.

FA (Football Association) The national football federation of England.

Feinting Using fake moves of the head, shoulders and legs to deceive an opponent and put him or her off balance.

FIFA The *Fédération Internationale de Football Association*, the international governing body of soccer.

Formation The way in which a team lines up on the pitch in terms of the numbers of defenders, midfielders and forwards.

Fourth official An additional match official responsible for displaying added-on time, checking substitutions and aiding the referee and his or her two assistants.

Futsal A type of five-a-side football, supported and promoted by FIFA.

Golden Boot An award given to the player who scores the most goals at a World Cup. It is also an annual award given to the top goalscorer in European club football.

Golden goal A system used to decide a drawn knockout game in extra time. The first goal scored wins the game.

Handball The illegal use of the hand or arm by a player.

Hat-trick Three goals scored by a player in a single match.

Hooligan An unruly and violent fan.

Indirect free kick A kick awarded to a team because of a minor foul committed by an opponent. A goal cannot be scored from the kick unless the ball is first touched by a player other than the kicker.

Instep The part of a player's foot where his or her bootlaces lie.

Interception When a player gains possession of the ball by latching onto a pass made by the opposition.

Jockeying A defensive technique of delaying an attacker who has the ball.

Laws of the game The 17 main rules of football, established and updated by FIFA.

Libero *See* sweeper.

Man-to-man marking A system of marking in which a defender stays close to and goalside of a single opposition player.

Marking Guarding a player to prevent him or her from advancing the ball towards the goal, making an easy pass or receiving the ball from a team-mate.

MLS Major League Soccer, the American professional male league.

Narrowing the angle A technique in which a goalkeeper moves towards an attacker who has the ball in order to cut down the amount of goal the attacker can aim a shot at.

Obstruction When a player, instead of trying to win the ball, uses his or her body to prevent an opponent from playing it.

OFC The Oceania Football Confederation, which runs football in Oceania.

Offside A player is offside if he or she is closer to the other team's goal than both the ball and the second-to-last opponent at the moment that the ball is played forwards.

Offside trap A defensive tactic used to trick opposition attackers by leaving them offside. Defenders who play the offside trap usually move upfield together, in a straight line, when the ball is played towards their goal.

Overlap To run outside and beyond a team-mate down the side of the pitch in order to create space and a possible passing opportunity.

Overload When an attacking team has more players in the opposition's half or penalty area than the defending side. An overload often leads to a scoring chance.

Penalty shootout A method of deciding a drawn match by a series of penalties, all taken at one end of the pitch.

Playmaker A skilful midfielder or deep-lying attacker who co-ordinates the attacking movement of a team.

Play-off A match, pair or series of matches used to decide a final placing. In the World Cup, the two losing semi-finalists contest a single play-off game for third place. In many leagues, play-off matches are used to decide relegation and promotion issues.

Professional foul A foul committed intentionally by a defender to stop an opponent who has a clear run on goal.

Referee's assistant An official who assists the referee during the game by signalling for fouls, infringements and offsides.

Reserve team A team made up of players who are not in the first team at a club or national side.

Scout A person employed by a football club who attends games and training sessions to look for up-and-coming players.

Set piece A planned play or move that a team uses when a game is restarted with a free kick, penalty kick, corner kick, goal kick, throw-in or kick-off.

Shielding A technique used by the player with the ball to protect it from a defender who is closely marking them. The player in possession keeps his or her body between the ball and the defender.

Silver goal A system, used at Euro 2004, to decide a drawn knockout game. If a goal is scored in the first 15 minutes of extra time, it wins the game. If no goal is scored, a second period of extra time is played.

Simulation Pretending to be fouled or feigning injury in order to fool the referee. A player found guilty of simulation by the referee receives a yellow card.

Stoppage time Time added to the end of any period of a game to make up for time lost during a major halt in play – to treat an injured player, for example. Also known as added time or injury time.

Substitution Changing the team line-up on the pitch by replacing one player with another from the substitutes' bench.

Sweeper A defender who can play closest to his or her goal, behind the rest of the defenders, or in a more attacking role with responsibility for bringing the ball forwards.

Tactics Methods of play used in an attempt to outwit and beat an opposition team.

Target man A tall striker, usually the player furthest upfield, at whom team-mates aim their forward passes.

Through ball or pass A pass to a team-mate that puts him or her beyond the opposition's defence and through on goal.

Total football A style of football in which players switch positions all over the pitch. It was made famous by the Dutch national side and Dutch clubs such as Ajax.

UEFA The Union of European Football Associations, which organizes football in Europe.

Volley Any ball kicked by a player when it is off the ground.

Wall pass A quick, short pair of passes between two players that sends the ball past a defender. Also known as a one-two pass.

Wing-back A defender on the sides of the pitch who, when the opportunity occurs, makes wide runs forwards in attack.

WUSA The world's first professional football league for women, based in the USA.

Zonal marking A defensive system in which defenders mark opponents who enter their area of the pitch.

INDEX

Note: references to main entries are in **bold**.

ACKNOWLEDGEMENTS

The publisher would like to thank the following for permission to reproduce their material. Every care has been taken to trace copyright holders. However, if there have been unintentional omissions or failure to trace copyright holders, we apologize and will, if informed, endeavour to make corrections in any future edition.

Top = t, bottom = b, centre = c, left = l, right = r

All images supplied by Empics with the exception of: pages 4–5 Getty/Manchester United 2005/Matthew Peters; 8tr with the kind permission of Acme Whistles Limited, UK; 8l Getty/AFP; 9t Getty/Hulton/J.A. Hampton; 11br Getty/Hulton/Reinhold Thiele; 16tr Corbis/Sygma; 19br Getty/AFP/Patrick Lin; 21cl Corbis/Reuters; 23cr Getty/Stuart Franklin; 24c Getty/AFP/Stan Honda; 24br Getty/AFP/Vincenzo Pinto; 27bl Getty/AFP/Christophe Simon; 27br Getty/Clive Brunskill; 28c Getty/Manchester United 2005/John Peters; 29br Getty/AFP/Patrick Herzog; 30–31t Corbis/Reuters/Eric Galliard; 30br Corbis/Reuters; 31br Corbis/Reuters; 48t Getty/AFP/Paolo Cocco;

49tr Getty/Ben Radford; 63cl Corbis/Reuters/Jose Manuel Ribeiro; 67bl Corbis/Reuters/Ian Hodgson; 72tl Getty/Ben Radford; 79tl Corbis/Reuters; 80r Corbis/Reuters/Petr Josek; 82bl Corbis/Reuters/Andres Stapff; 83tr Getty/AFP/Chi Jae-Ku; 84tl Corbis/Reuters/Bruno Dominges; 88tl Corbis/Reuters/Mohamed Hammi; 90bl Corbis/Reuters; 92–93 Corbis/Sygma/Jacques Langevin; 94bl Getty/AFP/Oliver Lang; 95tr Getty/Tom Shaw; 96cr Getty/Shaun Botterill; 96br Getty/Ross Kinnaird; 98b Getty/Ross Kinnaird; 100c Getty/AFP/Mladen Antonov; 102 Getty/AFP/Goh Chai Hin; 103tr Getty/AFP/Xavier Soriano; 104br Corbis/Sygma/Sunday Times/Joe Sefale; 105tl Getty/Laurence Griffiths; 105c Getty/Pascal Rondeau; 109bl Getty/AFP; 113bl Corbis/Bettmann; 114t Getty/AFP; 114b Getty/Simon Bruty; 115b Corbis/Reuters; 117tl Getty/Robert Cianfone; 123cl Corbis/Reuters/Radhu Sigheti; 124tc Corbis/Reuters; 124bl Corbis/Reuters/Andrew Wong; 125tr Getty Images; 125bl Corbis/Reuters; 126br Getty/AFP/Jiji Press; 127br Corbis/Reuters/Marcos Brindicci; 128bc Corbis/Reuters/Victor Fraile; 129bc Corbis/Reuters; 130c Getty/AFP/Rabih Mograbi; 130–131b Getty/AFP/Luis Acosta; 132tr Corbis/Reuters/Gleb Garanich